L7
BSS
A
13.40

W9-BZL-570

20.351

QH
368
W3

GN 743. W33 1976

Waechter
Man before
history

DATE DUE

MR 8 84			
NO 21 89			
DE 8 89			

Man before history
QH368.W3   20351

Waechter, John
VRJC/WRIGHT LIBRARY

Man before History

The Making of the Past

Man before History

by John Waechter

ELGIN REGIONAL
JUNIOR COLLEGE LIBRARY

ELSEVIER · PHAIDON

Advisory Board for The Making of the Past

John Boardman
Reader in Classical Archaeology, University of Oxford

Basil Gray
Former Keeper of Oriental Antiquities, British Museum

David Oates
Professor of Western Asiatic Archaeology,
Institute of Archaeology, University of London

Series Editor   Courtlandt Canby
Managing Editor   Giles Lewis
Editor for this Volume   Margaret Histed
Picture Editor   Andrew Lawson
Design   Edward Gould
Index   Griselda Taylor
Visual Aids   Roger Gorringe, Maurice Wilson

Frontispiece: Adam and Eve. An engraving by Albrecht Dürer (1471–1528)

ISBN 0 7290 0018 4

Elsevier Phaidon, an imprint of Phaidon Press Ltd.
Published in the United States by E.P. Dutton & Co. Inc., 201, Park Avenue South, New York, N.Y. 10003

Elsevier-Phaidon, an imprint of Phaidon Press Ltd,
Littlegate House, St Ebbe's Street, Oxford

Planned and produced by Elsevier International Projects Ltd, Oxford, © 1976 Elsevier Publishing Projects SA, Lausanne. All rights reserved. No part of this publication may be reproduced, stored in a retrieval system, or transmitted, in any form or by any means, electronic, mechanical, photocopying, recording or otherwise, without the prior permission of the Publishers.

Origination by Art Color Offset, Rome, Italy
Filmset by Keyspools Limited, Golborne, Lancs.
Printed in Belgium

Contents

Introduction 7

Chronological Table 8

1 In Search of Early Man 9

Visual story: The Evolution of Man 20

2 Tools of a Trade 25

3 The Making of Man 45

Visual story: Swanscombe:
a Prehistoric Site in England 66

4 The Beginnings of Culture 73

Visual story: Primitive Man Today 93

5 The Spread of Man 101

Visual story: The Art of Early Man 117

6 Man the Artist 125

Further Reading 137

Acknowledgments 138

Glossary 139

Index 149

Maps

The sites of the early discoveries 10
The extent of the Pleistocene glaciation 26
The main sites of prehistoric finds in Europe 27
The main sites of discoveries in Africa 48
The location of Olduvai Gorge 75
The main sites of discoveries in Asia 91
The main sites of discoveries in the Middle East 105
The main cave sites of France and northern Spain 127

Preface to the series

This book is a volume in the Making of the Past, a series describing the early history of the world as revealed by archaeology and related disciplines. The series is written by experts under the guidance of a distinguished panel of advisers and is designed for the layman, for young people, the student, the armchair traveler and the tourist. Its subject is a new history – the making of a new past, uncovered and reconstructed in recent years by skilled specialists. Since many of the authors of these volumes are themselves practicing archaeologists, leaders in a rapidly changing field, the series is completely authoritative and up-to-date. Each volume covers a specific period and region of the world and combines a detailed survey of the modern archaeology and sites of the area with an account of the early explorers, travelers, and archaeologists concerned with it. Later chapters of each book are devoted to a reconstruction in text and pictures of the newly revealed cultures and civilizations that make up the new history of the area.

Titles already published in the series

The Egyptian Kingdoms   **Biblical Lands**
The Aegean Civilizations   **The New World**

Titles to appear in 1976

The Spread of Islam   **Man before History**
The Emergence of Greece   **The Greek World**
Barbarian Europe   **The Rise of Civilization**

The First Empires   **The Kingdoms of Africa**
The Roman World   **Rome and Byzantium**
Ancient Japan   **Prehistoric Europe**
The Persian Revival   **India and Southeast Asia**
Ancient China   **Archaeology Today**

Introduction

The moving finger writes; and, having writ,

Moves on, nor all your Piety nor wit

Shall lure it back to cancel half a Line,

Nor all your Tears wash out a word of it.

Omar Khayyam

We may be powerless to alter what has gone, but man will always be fascinated by the drama of the past and believe he can apply its lessons to his present predicaments.

A glance over one's shoulder encounters no visible boundary – we look back to our parents who are the product of their parents; the 20th century is the product of the 19th; New York is descended from ancient Athens which is in turn descended from Abraham's tents or a prehistoric cave in France. We are our past. Man has no end and, strictly speaking, no clear beginning. From the half-man grubbing for food to the highly sophisticated Wall Street tycoon is an unbroken chain. The chipped pebble has made good: an atomic laboratory is used to date it.

This volume concerns itself not only with the foundations on which man's culture is based, but also with the creation of man himself. The wealth of beautiful objects one associates with ancient civilizations are largely lacking from these pages; the struggle for existence over nearly four million years by a creature with few weapons other than his developing brain allowed little time for activities not immediately concerned with survival.

Are his artifacts dull and his life prosaic? Perhaps at first sight this appears to be the case, but we are watching the first steps in the creation of the most complex creature nature has ever produced – the puny animal which rules the world and the only one now capable of achieving its complete destruction. Can we not imagine ourselves with the tribe carefully easing a herd of elephant into a marsh in Spain over half a million years ago, when a false move could cause one's death; or in almost total darkness in a cave deep in the Pyrenees, cold and terribly afraid, watching the elder disguised in mask and skins paint a mammoth on the wall?

The evidence prehistorians can provide is often tantalizingly incomplete, leaving much of the story to be filled in by the reader's imagination. His views are often as good as anyone else's, and among the maze of false relationships, cultural as well as human, and evolutionary dead ends, often confused rather than clarified by new evidence, the nonspecialist can give rein to his fancies.

The vast jigsaw which makes up the story of early man consists of pieces from many sciences, geology, botany, zoology and physics all playing a part. In his bag the prehistorian has many resources on which to draw, and this book is an attempt to give not only an outline of the story, but also some indication of the methods used in piecing it together.

Chronological Table

GEOLOGICAL TIME SCALE			
		Recent 10,000 years	
	Quaternary	*Pleistocene* 5–4 million years	Age of Man
Cenozoic	**Tertiary**	*Pliocene* 14 million years *Miocene* 35 million years *Oligocene* 45 million years *Eocene* 70 million years	Age of Mammals
Mesozoic	**Secondary**	*Cretaceous* 135 million years *Jurassic* 190 million years *Triassic* 225 million years	Age of Reptiles
Paleozoic	**Primary**	*Permian* 280 million years *Devonian* 395 million years *Silurian* 440 million years *Ordovician* 500 million years *Cambrian* 570 million years	Age of Invertebrates
		Precambrian 4,500 million years+	

1. In Search of Early Man

No peoples are completely indifferent to their history, and the tribal traditions of even the simplest communities are testimony to this. But it is only relatively recently that man has actively sought to trace his beginnings by means other than the study of oral tradition.

The search for early man has proceeded along two lines, tracing both the development of culture and the actual mechanics of human evolution. The theories we hold today about man's origins and development and the enormous timescales to which we are now accustomed would have been quite unacceptable as recently as the beginning of the last century.

The first finds, the first theories. Both the Romans and the Renaissance nobility collected works of art from earlier periods – the Romans from the Greeks and the Italians from the Romans. However, this embellishment of their villas and castles did not contribute much towards increasing knowledge of the past, and to archaeologists such "collecting" is often considered a euphemism for looting.

While the Renaissance magnates made little direct contribution to archaeological research, their encouragement of the study of classical authors sowed seeds which were to bear fruit in the 17th and 18th centuries. Knowledge of the classics became the foundation of the schooling of every man who had any pretensions to education, and it was largely from this source that most people obtained their ideas of their past, aided by a lifelong acquaintance with the Old Testament. This enthusiasm

Above: William Blake's interpretation of the creation of man.

led to speculation about, and later excavation of, ancient monuments, particularly in England, and produced a body of antiquarians who were to lay the foundations of modern archaeology.

While this reading and excavation led to an understanding of some sequences of events and produced a great deal of material in the form of pottery and tools, the early antiquarians did not give much thought to the question of time, nor did they consider this a serious problem, since it appeared to have been solved already. In the 17th century Archbishop Ussher had provided a date for the creation (4004 BC) based on adding up the generations listed in the Bible, and this date was later made more precise by Bishop Lightfoot, who pinpointed it at 9 am on 23 October. This modest timescale contented most people throughout the 18th century, since it appeared long enough to contain all known events and had the further advantage of the support of holy writ.

This comfortable state of affairs might have continued for much longer had it not been for the advent of the new science of geology, whose exponents were thinking of a creation, at least of the world, far in excess of Ussher's chronology. One of geology's major revelations was that the older the strata in the rock sequence, the less complex its fossil remains, and it was soon apparent that an age of marine creatures had been followed by reptiles and finally mammals. These ideas implied that not only was the

Archbishop's date for the creation far too recent but, Genesis notwithstanding, if the animal kingdom was created in the fourth and fifth days there must be a serious discrepancy between divine time and our own.

The question of the evolution of man did not become a serious issue until comparatively late. The concern in the 17th and 18th centuries was the antiquity of man who, as he was still considered to be the result of special creation, had not yet become a pawn in the evolutionary game, though it was through archaeology rather than geology that his true age was revealed.

Many of the pre-Roman antiquities in Britain were already arousing interest in the 16th century, and most major standing monuments, such as Stonehenge, had been surveyed by the end of the 17th century. The information gained from this activity was augmented by excavations carried out during the following century, particularly in the burial mounds scattered over the chalk downs of southern England. Such sites covered a range of periods from Neolithic through Bronze Age and Iron Age to Roman and Saxon – cultural divisions not always appreciated by the early excavators. The muddle induced by enthusiastic amateur diggers among the local gentry was due to the fact that they were less concerned with what they actually found than with what they were looking for.

The sites of the early discoveries.

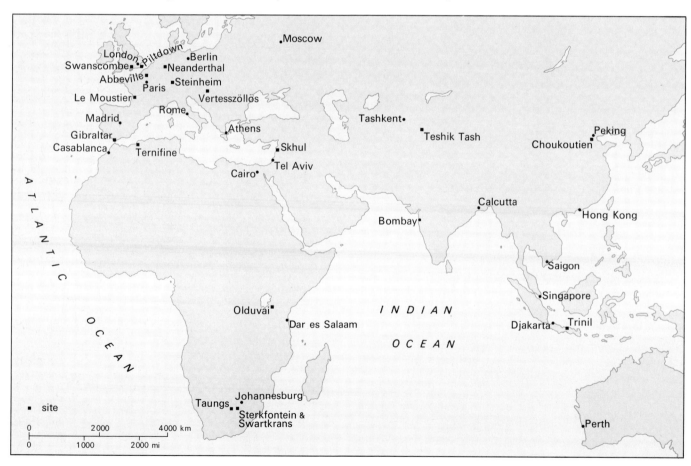

An early 18th century concept of an "ancient Briton" by Stukeley. The Druid is standing under an ancient oak.

Latin texts referring to Britain described the indigenous inhabitants as well as providing much information about Gauls and Germans. Particularly appealing to 18th-

Below: an early view of Stonehenge with Druid figures. For a long time Stonehenge and similar monuments were attributed to the Druids.

century antiquarians were references to the Druids, who became the personification of ancient Britain.

None of this work in any way altered the current ideas of chronology as laid down by Ussher. The human remains found buried in the mounds were clearly human and the animal bones were all of modern species. The fact that the culture thus revealed was inferior to that of the Romans was clear enough, but in terms of creation these early men were certainly respectable.

Evidence of man's association with extinct mammals, implying a far greater antiquity than Ussher's chronology, dates back to the end of the 17th century, when what are now accepted as stone implements were found together with mammoth bones by a man named Conyers in Gray's Inn Lane, London. This find led to a predictable reaction, with the Latin authors providing the solution: the mammoth became one of Claudius's elephants and the tools were ignored. Late in the following century John Frere found similar implements at Hoxne in Suffolk associated with extinct animals. In this case Frere made the correct deduction, describing them as belonging to "a very remote period indeed; even beyond that of the

Above: the original illustration of one of Frere's hand axes from Hoxne, England, late 18th century – the first time these early stone implements were recognized as being of human origin.

present world." Frere's foresight passed unnoticed; such a concept of man's antiquity was indeed premature.

By the beginning of the 19th century the incidences of finds of human artifacts associated with extinct animals increased, demanding new patterns of thought on the part of the antiquarians, who were becoming torn between their loyalty to the biblical narrative and the mounting body of evidence apparently contradicting it. Three possible courses seemed open to them: to ignore the whole

A "catastrophe" painted by the Victorian artist John Martin.

archaeological evidence and remain in the ranks of the fundamentalists; to accept the evidence and discredit the biblical account; or, by a slight reinterpretation of the creation story, weld the apparently irreconcilable concepts into an acceptable whole.

The third solution, which was in fact an attempt to sidestep the issue, took the form of what has been called the Catastrophic Theory. This envisaged a series of catastrophies of which the biblical flood was the last. Each episode wiped the slate clean as far as living creatures were concerned, and the whole process of creation started afresh, the final creation leading to man and all existing animals. While this required a slight adjustment of doctrine, it seemed to explain the association of man with extinct animals, the older forms having been washed into later deposits. It also gave rise to two rather attractive terms, ante- and postdiluvian.

The manner in which such theories could be made to explain the increasing evidence is illustrated by the exploration of the cave of Paviland in Wales by William Buckland in 1823. Buckland was in a somewhat equivocal position – he was the first Reader of Geology at Oxford, and was later to become Dean of Westminster. As might be expected he was a keen supporter of the Catastrophic Theory.

During his excavations at Paviland, Buckland found a human skeleton associated with stone tools and extinct animals including mammoth and woolly rhinoceros. As the human bones were stained with red ocher the name "Red Lady" was given to the find, though they subsequently turned out to be male. Buckland, wearing his fundamentalist mantle, claimed that the lady was "clearly not coeval with the antediluvian bones of the extinct species." As there was a Roman camp nearby, the poor woman was relegated to the position of camp follower – a true scarlet woman!

A French customs officer, Boucher de Perthes, probably made the most important contribution to the understanding of man's place in the ancient world. Abbeville is a town on the river Somme, which runs northwards into the English Channel. Bordering this river, as with many others, is an ascending succession of old terraces recording the early history of the river. These terraces are mainly composed of sand and gravel from the bed of earlier rivers which flowed at these heights.

As these deposits had a commercial value, they were being dug over a wide area, producing deep sections of considerable geological importance. Boucher de Perthes spent much of his leisure time watching these commercial excavations, and amassed a vast collection of bones of the many animals who had lived on the banks of the early Somme, including elephant, rhinoceros, cave bear and lion.

These discoveries alone would not have changed the

climate of opinion to any great extent as similar remains had been found many times before, but also found were implements recognized as human artifacts – identical to those found by John Frere. The argument that the associated animal bones were antediluvian forms washed into the gravels was beginning to wear a little thin. In many parts of the river the same association was being demonstrated, and the idea of the chance association of the two was becoming less easy to sustain. Whatever the age of the fossil bones, the Somme gravels, which contained both bones and stone implements, had clearly been laid down far earlier than most people were at that time prepared to consider.

Boucher de Perthes, like John Frere, claimed that the tools were of the same age as the gravel deposits in which they were found, thereby implying that not only was man living at the same time as the elephant and rhinoceros, but he was probably hunting them. Frere's remarks had been ignored, but Boucher de Perthes' publication of 1847 was received with derision, and it was not until several years later that some eminent geologists went out to examine the Somme sections for themselves and lent their support to his views.

The Somme gravels were not the only site producing evidence for the antiquity of man. During the first 60 years of the 19th century many excavation projects had been undertaken. In Britain caves in Devon were confirming the evidence found by Buckland at Paviland, but this time the excavators were coming to the right conclusions, though these were not receiving much support.

Buckland, dressed for a geological expedition. Dean of Westminster and lecturer on geology at Oxford, he was one of the pioneers of British prehistory.

Boucher de Perthes, who found many early tools among the gravels of the Somme River.

One of the strongest pieces of evidence for the association of man with extinct animals came from the cave of La Madeleine in southwest France, where Edouard Lartet and Henri Christy found a piece of mammoth tusk with a fine engraving of a mammoth on it, drawn by an artist who was obviously very familiar with his subject. Enthusiasm for the excavation of earlier archaeological deposits increased throughout the 19th century, and by its close much of the broad framework of western European prehistory had been sketched out and the antiquity of man pushed back some half million years.

Running parallel to the development of prehistoric archaeology were certain ideas of evolution being considered by the end of the 18th century, coinciding to a large extent with the birth of geology. Rock finds were beginning to show clearly that during the earth's history there was a succession of stages in the development of living creatures, each new stage being more advanced than the previous. As more information came to light the Catastrophic Theory became less and less easy to support. It was too farfetched to suppose that after each destruction a new creation should start exactly where the previous one

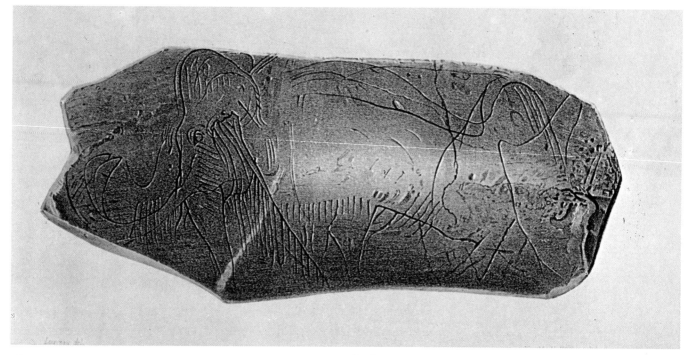

Above: a mammoth engraved on a piece of mammoth tusk, from the cave of La Madeleine in southwest France.

Below: a portrait of Charles Darwin at the time of the voyage of the *Beagle*, during which he formulated his ideas on evolution.

had stopped; besides, no such catastrophies could be shown to exist in the geological record.

Darwin and the theory of evolution. Charles Darwin is generally credited with the theories of evolution which are now widely accepted, but during the first half of the 19th century accumulating fossil evidence led many naturalists to speculate along evolutionary lines, including Darwin's own grandfather. If man himself had not been swept into the evolutionary net such ideas would have caused less excitement than they did, and much of the excitement would have been centered on the mechanics of evolution rather than the principle of evolution itself.

Many of the older scientists objected to early ideas of evolution on the grounds that this naturally implied the mutability of species, whereas the inability of species to change was one of the cornerstones of the Catastrophic Theory as well as biblical orthodoxy. Further, it is possible that the supporters of older ideas were already beginning to suspect that these newfangled views were bound to lead to the questioning of man's place in nature. Had the early evolutionists harbored such views, they prudently kept them to themselves.

The dissension aroused by these conflicting views was muted compared with the explosion which was to follow the publication of Darwin's *On the Origin of Species by means of Natural Selection* in 1859. Prior to this event disagreements took place among scientists and a small educated elite, and although such differences of opinion were often expressed in somewhat acrimonious terms, they were limited to a comparatively small section of the population. The attack on the special creation of man which Darwin's book implied reached into every home in Britain, and it was largely the outraged middle classes, whose fundamentalist approach to the biblical narrative was challenged, who formed the vanguard of the assault on the concept of human evolution.

The theories outlined in Darwin's book were not the result of any particular epoch-making discovery, but were based on data available to everyone. Darwin's contribution was the patience and observation of a brilliant naturalist who not only was able to marshal a mass of facts into an intelligible pattern, but had the courage to publish the inevitable conclusions, though even he was not wholly prepared for the resultant storm. Darwin himself did not invent the theory of evolution, but demonstrated the mechanics by which it could have operated, his theory of natural selection seemingly fitting the known facts.

It was the anatomist Thomas Huxley, Darwin's great champion, rather than Darwin himself who ignited the fuse which set off the great evolutionary explosion. One of Huxley's contentions was that physical differences between some apes and man were smaller than those between apes. This comparison of man and ape was taken by the public to imply that man was descended from the apes – a theory which was never claimed by the evolutionists of the time. This widely held misconception outraged Victorian Britain and provided ample ammunition for the cartoonists of the day. Had we been descended from a more noble animal, society might have been less affronted – a horse or a dog (preferably of sporting breed)

Below, left to right: Thomas Huxley – a cartoon from *Vanity Fair*; Charles Darwin in conversation with one of his relations; Bishop Wilberforce ("Soapy Sam"), the great opponent of the theory of human evolution – from *Vanity Fair*.

possibly, but an ape? Never! One cannot say for certain whether the attack on their religion or their pride hurt the Victorians most.

While Huxley stood champion to Darwin, there was one ready and as suitably equipped to take up the gauntlet on behalf of all good churchmen: Samuel Wilberforce, Bishop of Oxford – an eloquent if somewhat unctuous orator with the nickname "Soapy Sam." The two met to defend their different points of view at the famous Oxford meeting of the British Association in 1860. There can be no doubt that both were perfectly sincere in their convictions, but in the ensuing debate the authority of Genesis proved inadequate against the mass of irrefutable evidence produced by the scientific opposition.

There are still many, particularly in parts of America, to whom the rejection of a special creation of man is anathema, but the battle of the fundamentalists was lost at the British Association meeting which saw the last serious assault on the theory of human evolution.

While evidence was marshaled in support of the general principles of evolution, Huxley was in no better position than Wilberforce when it came to producing proof of the descent of man. Huxley's arguments were largely based on comparative anatomy, which so strongly underlined the similarity between man and the apes, implying that they were in some way related. If one had been subjected to a long process of development there was no good zoological reason for the other to be the only member of an entirely different scheme. One factor which might have weakened the scientific case was that man appeared to have no demonstrable ancestors – simpler and less specialized

THE
LONDON SKETCH BOOK.

PROF. DARWIN.

This is the ape of form.
Love's Labor Lost, act 5, scene 2.
Some four or five descents since.
All's Well that Ends Well, act 3, sc. 7.

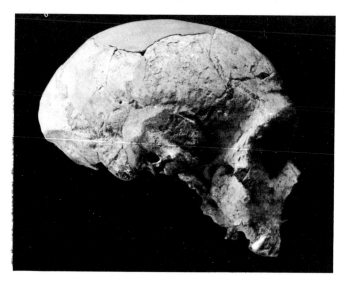

Side view of the original skull from Gibraltar, found in 1848 and "lost" for several years in the local Gibraltar library. It is now in the Natural History Museum, London.

creatures comparable to proto-dogs, proto-horses or proto-cats. Plenty of human remains representing the Ancient Britons were available, all of modern type, but where were the makers of the primitive tools found in the Somme gravels? Where were the hunters of the mammoth? There was no archaeological evidence to show that these early inhabitants of the earth were in any way physically different from the members of Wilberforce's Oxford congregation. The reasonable inference was that man had been created earlier and under different circumstances from the individuals recorded in Genesis, but his apparent antiquity was no reason for denying him his special creation.

If no new evidence of early man had come to light, the controversy might well have remained at stalemate, but it soon came in abundance. The first find was a well-preserved skull unearthed in a quarry in Gibraltar in 1848. It aroused no interest and remained in the Garrison Library, unrecognized, until the end of the century. The next find fared rather better: it came from a quarry at Neanderthal in Germany in 1856, three years before the publication of Darwin's book. The Neanderthal skull was far less complete than that from Gibraltar, consisting only of the skull cap; nevertheless it became the type specimen for the Neanderthals.

Huxley was one of the first to accept this specimen as representing ancestral man, since its clearly primitive characteristics were what he would have expected to find. His opinion was expressed in *Evidence as to Man's Place in Nature*, published in 1863, but played no part in the arguments at Oxford in 1860. Not all of Huxley's colleagues were prepared to support his views, and some considered the primitive features of the skull to be of pathological origin.

As in the case of the association of man with extinct animals, a problem which was eventually resolved by a steady accumulation of solid evidence, Neanderthal Man stood alone for only a very short time. His position was soon strengthened by further finds of a similar type, some from cave deposits associated with archaeological material of which he was clearly the maker.

By 1890 not only had finds of Neanderthal remains increased in number, establishing a creature related to but distinct from modern man, but finds in Java were demonstrating the existence of older and even more primitive humans. By the turn of the century a steady stream of human fossils had been uncovered, together showing an enormously complex ancestral pattern whose details are still being argued about by human paleontologists. This phenomenal progress was not without setbacks, some the result of genuine mistakes and others not.

Errors and forgeries. Boucher de Perthes' long and distinguished career as the great pioneer of prehistory was sadly marred towards the end by his claim to have found a human jaw contemporary with the tools and animal bones from the high terraces of the Somme. The Moulin Quignon jaw, as it was called, aroused a great deal of controversy, partly because it appeared to be very modern and partly because, when sectioned, it was found to contain more animal matter than could reasonably be expected from a bone of its alleged age. Unfortunately, the claim that the jaw was a forgery was also leveled against the stone tools, which were clearly genuine, and these accusations detracted from Boucher de Perthes' deservedly high reputation. The Moulin Quignon jaw, clearly modern and intrusive, has now disappeared into the underworld reserved for archaeological mistakes.

If one considers the conditions under which most of this early material was found, particularly that from gravel workings, it is not surprising that some errors should have occurred and, far from detracting from the value of the greater part of the archaeological evidence, these mistakes have become warnings which modern archaeologists are not too proud to heed.

A good example of the type of problem facing the early investigators is the skeleton found in north Kent. Galley Hill, less than a mile from the famous site of Swanscombe and situated on the same high terrace of the Thames was, like Swanscombe, excavated for gravel and chalk for many years. In 1888 an almost complete skeleton came to light about eight feet below ground. It was found by a workman and reported by him to a local antiquarian who, not unreasonably, claimed it as being a human contemporary with the early deposit in which it was found and, by implication, the maker of the associated stone tools which were of the same type as those from the Somme and from John Frere's site at Hoxne.

In anatomical terms the Galley Hill skeleton was clearly of modern type and, since the deposit in which it was found was generally accepted to be earlier than those associated with the much more primitive Neanderthals, the find was suspect from the start. Recent analysis of the bone has shown clearly that the remains, though fairly old, were in fact intrusive.

Mistakes of the same type were made in other gravel sites, but bearing in mind how many bodies must have been buried near the surface of these gravels, and the fact that most of the finds were not made under controlled excavation conditions, with trained personnel on the spot, one can hardly be surprised that they should have occurred. Techniques developed over the last 30 years for assessing the relative ages of fossil bones will make such errors less likely in future.

These examples of human frailty are easy to understand and are inevitable in an infant science. The other setbacks were the result not of human error but of human greed. Forgery – that is, the falsification of evidence with intent to deceive – is common enough in the art world but fortunately rare in archaeology, though the sale of faked antiquities is not. Motives for archaeological forgeries are varied – sometimes a wish for personal gain, mainly in terms of prestige; sometimes to discomfort a colleague; most often for money.

In the early days of archaeological enthusiasm forgeries for monetary gain seem either to have been rare or to have remained undetected, though many a young man brought back some very dubious objects from the Grand Tour. It was not until late in the course of archaeological studies that enough knowledge was available to make the

Taken in 1869, this is the only known portrait of Flint Jack, the renowned forger of stone tools, sitting poised for the camera with a hammer in one hand and a piece of stone in the other. The early days of archaeological studies witnessed a vogue for the collection of stone tools, bringing with it a boom in the buying and selling of forged implements.

reproduction of stone tools a practicable proposition.

During the latter part of the 19th century the collecting urge of the amateur prehistorian was so strong as to make attempts at forgery by shadier members of the public almost inevitable. The name of only one of these characters has come down to us. Whether **Flint Jack** should be described as a reproducer of stone tools or a forger hangs on the question of intent. Many prehistorians before and since have experimented in stoneworking techniques in the interests of science, and many such implements attributed to Flint Jack are preserved in museums, but it is not clear whether these were originally sold as reproductions or as genuine tools.

The opening of many gravel pits, particularly in the lower Thames Valley, led to the finding of a vast number of stone tools, with the result that enthusiastic and keenly competitive collectors roamed gravel workings offering to buy tools from the workmen. This had two predictable results. First the less prolific pits augmented their finds by importations from richer areas, bought from fellow workmen at "trade" prices and sold to collectors at a considerable profit. So steady was this trade that in some areas stone implements took on the role of currency. Many of the hand axes now enshrined in our national museums were exchanged for liquor in pubs around Stoke Newington in London, and in one case stone tools were offered and accepted as surety for unpaid rent! This manipulation of archaeological evidence caused a great deal of confusion. Material was attributed to deposits from which it did not come, with the result that many of the older collections are of very little scientific value.

A second result of the collectors' enthusiasm was that as their demand for tools increased, so did the number of forgeries. They were unwittingly contributing to their own deception by lending specimens to workmen and explaining the salient points of genuine implements. Needless to say, it was not long before the required implements turned up! By the close of the century this rather sordid episode came to an end as the fashion for collecting stone tools died out.

Another aspect of forgery is the fabrication of archaeological evidence to discredit a colleague or to obtain renown for oneself, as in the case of the Neolithic site in eastern France excavated during this century. One of the workmen, jealous of the publicity given to prehistoric finds in western France, set out to enhance the status of the site on which he was employed. His method was to produce a script written on potsherds, which he inserted into the sections of areas due to be excavated the following day. His claim for the invention of writing at so early a date naturally aroused the interest he had hoped for. Had he not made the mistake of becoming more proficient in his work as the excavation proceeded, so that the earlier the material was the more sophisticated it became, the deception might have been hard to detect, but the culprit finally confessed.

Piltdown and after. The cause célèbre in prehistoric forgeries was perpetrated at the side of a road in the small village of Piltdown in Sussex in 1912. The finder of this controversial material, Charles Dawson, was a lawyer with longstanding antiquarian interests. His attempts to trace the origin of some unusual roadmending material led him to a shallow gravel working near Piltdown. The deposits had never been dated with much certainty, and a determination of their age depended on their content – not a very satisfactory situation. Dawson's first visit produced nothing but on the second, according to an early account, he was handed part of a skull by one of the workmen. This was the first of a series of objects, comprising further parts of the skull, half of a "human" lower jaw and many animal bones. The animal remains were broken bone pieces from an early form of elephant, and teeth of hippopotamus and beaver, and from the surface of the next field a horse tooth and a piece of red deer antler in the same fossilized state as the pieces found in the gravel.

The Piltdown finds posed two problems: first, did the animal remains date the deposit? and second, what was the status of the human remains in terms of evolution? As far as the date of the deposit was concerned, the animal bones seemed to contradict each other: the elephant remains suggested a period much earlier than did the teeth of the

Excavating the Piltdown gravels in 1911, with Dawson (right) and Smith Woodward (center).

hippo and beaver, with the combined fauna representing the two opposite ends of the Pleistocene period. In terms of dating at that time, this meant a difference of about 500,000 years. The obvious implication to be drawn from this mixed fauna was that the earlier species had been washed into the deposit before the hippo and beaver, but this did not show to which end of the timescale the human remains belonged, and some anatomists implied that they were contemporary with the earlier bones.

The real controversy centered on the relationship between the jaw and skull fragments, but before discussing this it is necessary to see the position at which theories of human evolution stood in 1912. The general principles had been accepted, but there was still a shortage of evidence as to the stages involved. The original member of the Neanderthal race found in 1856 had been joined by further examples, and by this time Neanderthal man had been established as a precursor of modern man. Two further hominids appeared to take evolution back further: one was the skull fragment found by Dubois in Java, and the other was the lower jaw from the sand pit at Mauer in Germany. Both these specimens were more primitive than

A painting made soon after the Piltdown finds. Standing on the right of the group are Smith Woodward (bearded) of the London Natural History Museum and Charles Dawson, the discoverer of the remains.

Neanderthal man, and their geological age was greater. The word "primitive" was used to imply that the further one went back along the human ancestral tree the more apelike man became, so that the idea of a missing link, half man/half ape, was readily acceptable. This dual character appeared to be present in the Piltdown remains. The skull fragments, though very thick, tended towards the human end of the scale and bore an even greater resemblance to modern man than the Neanderthals, but the jaw was extremely apelike. From this evidence two possible conclusions could be drawn: either jaw and skull did not belong together, or they represented a proto-hominid nearer to the human/ape junction than anything yet found. The latter implied that the human remains were contemporary with the earlier animal remains.

The anatomists who examined this material had problems: the points where jaw and skull fit together were missing, the face was absent and the skull was in several pieces. The major cause for disagreement was how the skull was to be reassembled – some anatomists made it look more human than others, and each criticized the attempts of his colleagues.

As more human material came to light in other parts of the world – the skulls from China and, more particularly, the earlier specimens from South Africa – Piltdown man or Eoanthropus (Dawn Man), as he was now called, became more and more of an anomaly. Even if the jaw did not belong, the skull itself became a less convincing contender for the role of "missing link," for it had no primitive traits such as brow ridges, and its cubic capacity was much nearer modern man than that of China or Java, whose ancestor it was supposed to be.

The testing of the bones for their fluorine content (a new method of relative dating) not only exposed the chaotic situation of the Piltdown deposits, but proved beyond doubt that the whole setup was a forgery. If the bones were all of the same age their fluorine content would be much the same, and all would have high percentages if they were as old as was claimed. The result was that the bones showed a wide range of fluorine and clearly could not have belonged together; moreover the least fluorine came from the human skull and jaw, and even these contained different amounts.

These fluorine tests were not alone in making the skull and jaw suspect – further X rays showed that the ancient canine tooth not only exhibited artificial wear, but had had a hole neatly stopped! Other tests showed that the heavy staining present on all the bones, which was taken as an indication of their age, was also artificial. In fact, the whole assemblage was faked. The skull was certainly that of modern man, though possibly an old one, the jaw was that of an ape, the early animal bones were traced to a site in North Africa, and the hippo tooth may have come from anywhere.

The identity of the Piltdown forger is something that will probably never be known. The blame naturally fell on Charles Dawson who, in terms of notoriety, certainly had the most to gain, but it is doubtful whether he had the knowledge to initiate the fraud or the sangfroid to carry it through. In the background of the affair was a young man of great intellectual stature and with considerable paleontological experience, who fits the picture better than Dawson. Did he play a practical joke on a rather pompous provincial, which gathered momentum before he could stop it? His subsequent career fully atoned for any embarrassment he may have caused. Other possible contenders were members of the Natural History Museum's technical staff, whose chief, Smith Woodward, had made predictions that such a creature must have existed. Perhaps the staff obliged him with a little instant evolution as a hoax, which was so successful that retreat became impossible. Most of the actors in the drama are now dead, but the identity of the perpetrators is less important than the lessons to be learned from the hoax. Forgeries on such a scale are not likely to have equal success in the future – prehistorians have had ample warning and the tests which are now routine should make such faking almost impossible.

The study of early man's physical and cultural development has never had the same appeal as the later periods in man's history. The interest aroused by Schliemann's finds at Troy or the enthusiastic reception of the Egyptian antiquities brought back by Napoleon's savants, which were to have such an influence on French Empire design, have no counterpart in the study of early prehistory. Apart from some interest in prehistoric art and curiosity regarding the antiquity of man, the man in the street can raise little enthusiasm for the bones and stone among which the prehistorian works.

VERNON REGIONAL
JUNIOR COLLEGE LIBRARY

The Evolution of Man

The Order Primate to which man belongs includes a wide range of creatures. Some, like the ape, are clearly close relatives, but in the case of the smaller primates such as bush babies and lemurs the relationship is not so easy to establish. This is because the latter branched off the line of development leading to man at an early stage, followed by the Old and New World monkeys, who resemble man more closely. The final major branching of the stem was the divergence of man and ape which may have occurred about 30 million years ago. The similarity of the gorilla (top skull below) to man is very marked, but this creature has reached the end of its line of specialization whereas man, as the lower skulls show, progressed through several further stages to reach his present state. Tracing man and the Great Apes back to their common ancestor – a creature with characteristics of both – has produced a fascinating jigsaw puzzle with fossil remains from all over the world covering a period of more than 30 million years.

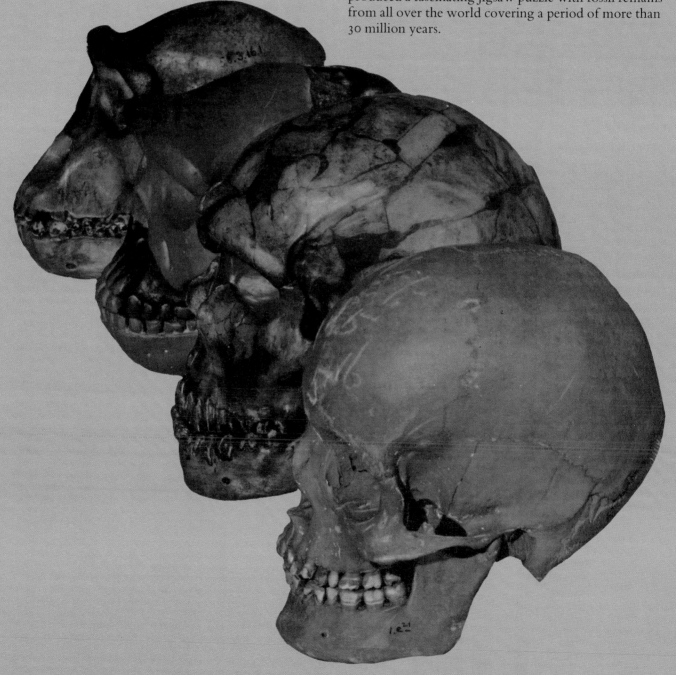

Left: changes in skull shape resulting from mental development. Reading from top to bottom: the gorilla is characterized by heavy brow ridges, a low vaulted skull and a protruding face; Java and Neanderthal man show the skull becoming progressively more rounded with a fuller frontal area, the brow ridges less prominent and the face more vertical; modern man, from about 30,000 BC, shows all the characteristics of existing races, resulting from upright stance and the extensive development of the brain.

Right: one of the many possible interpretations of the human/ape relationship, based on the evidence of existing fossils. The left hand side of the chart covers the four Great Apes – gibbon, orangutan, chimpanzee and gorilla, and the right hand side the possible ancestors of man. At the very bottom of the chart is a creature from Egypt, which appears to have already diverged from the monkeys. The next major development is the separation of ape and man between 35 and 15 million years ago. It is difficult to place finds from this period correctly on the family tree. By 14 million years the ape line seems clearly established with very little change in the form of its members, while the human branch is complicated by much South and East African material appearing in the period between 2 million and 500,000 years. Some of the recent finds from Lake Rudolf and Ethiopia probably belong on the main human stem rather than on a side branch. By 100,000 there are two major human groups, Neanderthal man and ourselves (*Homo sapiens*), and here the relationship is probably closer than the chart suggests.

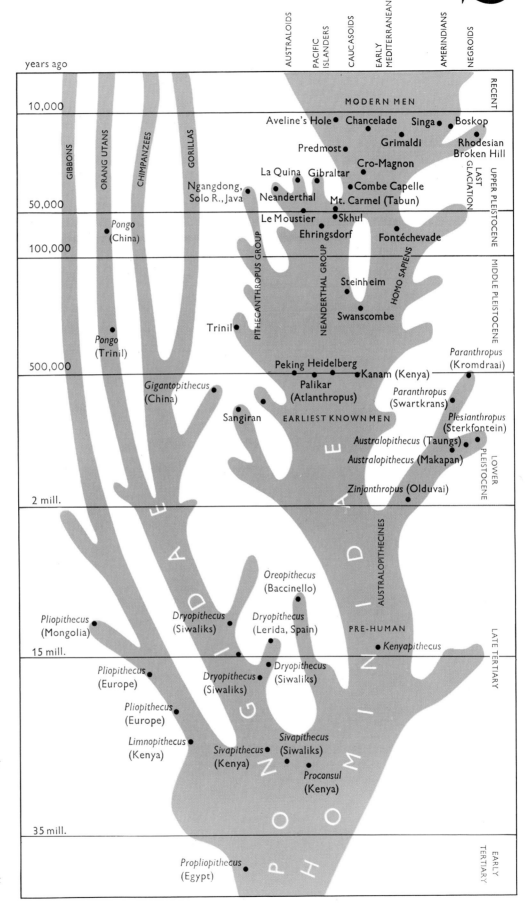

macaque

capuchin

Howler monkey

baboon

Spider monkey

marmoset

The Anthropoidea, showing their range of form and main lines of evolutionary development, blue to platyrrhine monkeys, red to catarrhine monkeys and to apes and man.

Fossil platyrrhine monkeys

lemurs

tarsioid

primitive lemuroid

omomyid

mangabey

langur

guenon

colobus

gibbon

gorilla

mesopithecus

apes

ramapithecus

australopithecus

man

M.Wilson

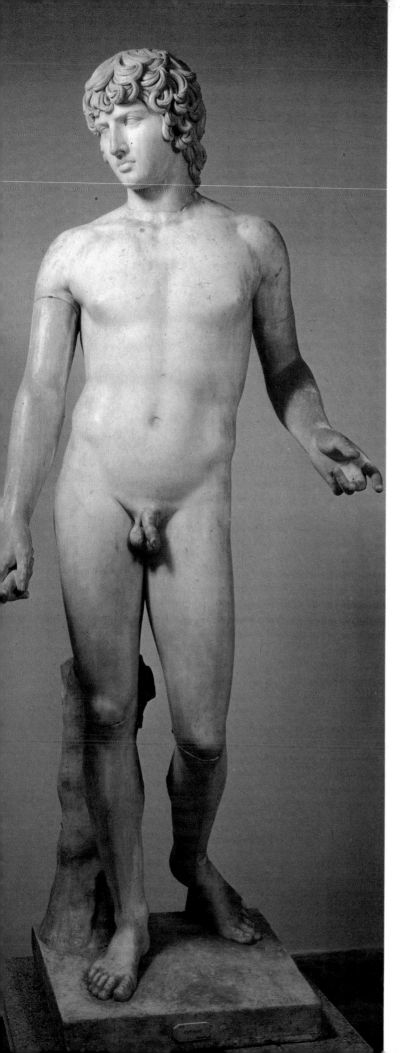

MAN·IS·BVT·A·WORM·

Above: this 19th century cartoon from *Punch* pokes fun at the idea of human evolution. The process starts with an earthworm, which gradually acquires a head and loses its tail. The head becomes first more monkey-like and then more human, and the creature develops via the ancient Briton to become a Victorian man-about-town. Such an idea is totally unacceptable to present-day scientists, as it was of course to Darwin himself (seated centrally), whose claim that man and the Great Apes had a common ancestor was quite different from saying that man developed from the apes, which is what the cartoon implies. The significance of the relationship of all the primates may be understood by considering a family tree extending over several generations. The founder of the family is common ancestor to the individuals following him through the centuries. Thus all members are related to some degree by virtue of their common ancestor, but this relationship becomes more difficult to establish as time goes by. If one reckons that the common ancestor of all the primates lived some 70 million years ago, then the present members of the Order, having developed many distinct life-styles, have become very different not only from the founder of the family but from each other. The line of specialization which the human stem pursued included the acquisition of an upright stance, the growth of manual dexterity leading to toolmaking and the development of the brain. Which of these had priority is difficult to determine, but as the illustration shows, the skull shapes of man and the apes reveal the most striking contrasts.

Left: a Roman statue of Antinous, a contemporary of the Emperor Hadrian. Like the Greek statues on which it is based, this work shows the human body in an idealized form – the peak of human evolution.

While the controversies regarding human evolution were being argued about, archaeological excavation was accumulating an increasing body of evidence for early cultural change and development, bringing into being what was virtually a new subject – prehistoric archaeology.

The division of prehistory into Stone, Bronze and Iron Ages by the Danes was soon to prove an oversimplification, and the history of prehistoric archaeology has been one of continual subdivision, made necessary as new areas are explored and the timescale steadily extended.

Before considering man's cultural or evolutionary development, which will be dealt with in later chapters, it is necessary to examine the tools of the prehistorian's trade, for evidence is drawn from many different subjects.

Geology, zoology, botany. As it was largely by means of geological evidence that man's antiquity was established, it is not surprising that geology remains essential to the study of prehistory. It provides the main basis for relative dating, and stratigraphical methods for establishing archaeological sequences are derived from geological practice. In addition to geology, prehistorians have drawn on the natural and physical sciences for information

essential to the forming of a complete picture of man's past.

It is obvious that the enormous range of geological time must be subdivided. The initial four major divisions, Primary, Secondary, Tertiary and Quaternary, are further subdivided, each subdivision being characterized by special faunas or special formations.

If we accept that the principle of evolution applies to man as well as to other creatures it is possible, at least in theory, to trace all living things back to simple, unicellular organisms, almost at the beginning of geological time. As we are dealing with man's immediate ancestry, we need only concern ourselves with the last two major geological divisions – the Tertiary and the Quaternary or Pleistocene. During the former man's physical development begins to take definite shape, and during the latter his cultural development begins.

The exact duration of the Pleistocene is still uncertain, but we know from carbon 14 dating (a technique described later in this chapter) that it ended somewhere around 10,000 years ago. For a long time geologists estimated its duration as being about 600,000 years, but recent evidence suggests something nearer 2.5 million.

In northern Europe and North America the Pleistocene

Previous page: a prehistoric rhinoceros skull in the process of excavation, from Swanscombe, Kent.

The extent of the Pleistocene glaciation, centered on Scandinavia and with regional ice centers such as the Pyrenees and the Alps.

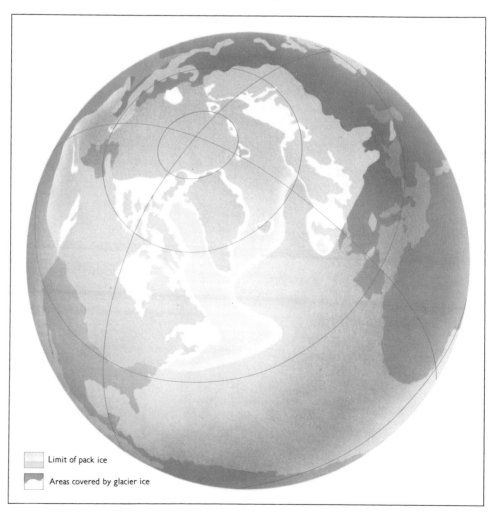

Limit of pack ice

Areas covered by glacier ice

is conveniently divided by major climatic changes. These consist of cold phases or Ice Ages, referred to as Glacials, alternating with temperate periods or Interglacials. There are also smaller climatic oscillations within the Glacials called Interstadials. Thus the Pleistocene can be divided into relatively small units. As these climatic changes have left indelible traces in the geological record, they are invaluable as a tool for relative dating.

Evidence for these geological changes can best be seen in areas which have been directly affected by the advance and retreat of the ice sheets – the product of the glacial periods. As far as Europe is concerned these were centered on Scandinavia. Similar evidence for major climatic changes can be seen in mountain regions such as the Alps and Pyrenees, where local glaciers advance and retreat in step with the major ice movements. In Britain much evidence for ice coverage is clearly visible, particularly in

Right: the main sites of prehistoric finds in Europe.

Below: the Jungfrau glacier in Switzerland, showing the river of ice pushing down the main and subsidiary valleys.

East Anglia, the Midlands and the North, and there is similar evidence in northern Europe and across parts of the North American continent.

The advance of an ice sheet produces much the same effect as that of a mountain glacier, though on the flat instead of on a slope and, of course, on a much larger scale. The abrasive effect of the advancing ice grinds the surface of rocks, pulling up and transporting material over which it passes. As the climate improves and the ice melts this material is left behind in the form of structureless boulder clays, some several hundred feet thick, often filling valleys and blotting out small hills.

Areas covered by ice often show traces of more than one ice advance, and it is sometimes possible to distinguish different boulder clays and hence separate lines of advance by examining the rock material contained in the clay. In many cases it is possible to see clear interglacial deposits lying between two boulder clays, or the surface of the first boulder clay may have been subject to weathering during an Interglacial, and this band of weathering is visible at the point where the later boulder clay overlies the earlier.

Top: a rock surface ground smooth by ice action, indicating that the area was once covered by ice.

Left: tough gray boulder clay of glacial origin resting on interglacial sands and gravels from a warmer period (Hertfordshire, England).

In addition to this sort of direct evidence, an advancing ice sheet has many side effects which often extend much further than the limits of the boulder clays and can thus be used as climatic indicators in areas where there was no ice coverage. Layers of surface soil, distorted by continual expansion and contraction while freezing and thawing, often appear in a section as disturbed and structureless deposits, and where there is a slope this layer often slides down in the form of a sludge during the summer melt. These sludge deposits or solifluctions and frost-disturbed soils are recognizable in areas far removed from the boundaries of ice sheets, though they are naturally more extensive as one gets closer to the regions covered by ice.

Another deposit associated with glacial conditions is *loess*, a fine, windblown dust which is scattered from the edge of an ice sheet. It is made up of minute particles of rock ground and shattered by the freezing and thawing process. As it is an airborne deposit, it is often carried a considerable distance from the edge of the ice. The famous Yellow Earth of China is made up of this fine yellow dust.

During more temperate conditions the deposition of loess is halted and its upper layers become subject to weathering. In northern France there are sequences of loess with weathering zones between indicating a succession of Stadials and Interstadials of the Last Glaciation as well as at least two phases of the previous Glaciation. As archaeological material is frequently found associated with these loesses, they can be extremely useful for relative dating. They can also be found in Belgium, Germany, Austria and further east.

In coastal areas and river valleys over the whole world valuable dating evidence has been provided by the rise and fall of the sea level, which has occurred many times during the Pleistocene. These variations in sea level are directly connected with glacial and interglacial conditions. Vast amounts of water are locked up as ice during a glacial period, thus interrupting the cycle of evaporation–precipitation. This immobilization of water results in a

Raised beaches showing clearly above the modern beach line.

Fragments of chalk scooped up and transported in gray boulder clay (East Yorkshire, England).

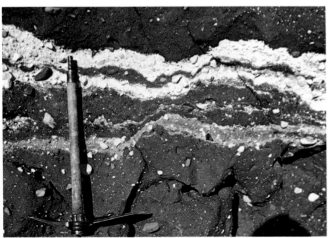

sharp drop in sea level. During Interglacials the ice melts and the normal cycle is restored, thus raising the general sea level. At the coldest stage of the Last Glaciation the drop in sea level is estimated to have been about 100 meters.

Naturally, evidence for high sea levels is easier to observe than that for low, as these signs are of course now submerged. Traces of old high sea levels can be seen far above the tideline on rocky coasts in many parts of the world, in the form of patches of typical beach shingle, often with shells, wave-cut notches and wave-cut platforms, as well as holes bored in the rock by molluscs which live about two feet below low water, and which can sometimes be seen, like miners' shot holes, a considerable height above present sea level.

Fortunately, throughout the Pleistocene there was a steady drop in the ocean floors, so that the high sea levels are found in their correct order, the oldest being the highest and reaching up to 600ft. The use of these levels as a dating tool is not quite as easy as it seems. Their identification depends on their height, but the dating of an archaeological site associated with a particular fossil beach can, in some circumstances, go badly wrong. In many

A diver measuring the extent of undercut, Gibraltar. Such undercuts are found several hundred feet above present sea level.

areas, particularly the south Mediterranean, much earth movement has taken place with the result that some sites on a fossil beach are no longer at their correct height above present sea level. However, many fossil beaches have seashells peculiar to themselves, and are therefore identifiable irrespective of their present height.

A more local problem occurs in areas closer to the center of the ice cap. The weight of the ice causes a depression in the earth's crust, so the land sinks and, with a seesaw effect, rises on the other end of the axis of the movement. The rise and fall of sea level is known as *eustatic change* and that of weight adjustment as *isostatic change*.

These changes of sea level obviously affected the behavior of rivers, whose profiles are of course controlled by the sea as well as by changes in climate and earth movement. The mechanism of these changes of profile is as follows: a rise in sea level raises the profile of the rivers running into it, and this has two effects, one dependent on the other. First, the rate of water flow is reduced, so that the river begins to build up its bed by dropping much of its load. Thus, as the sea and the river profile continue to rise, so too does the river bed. Second, as the sea level drops in response to the onset of cold conditions, so also does the river profile, and the process of aggrading is reversed into one of degrading. As the riverbed is worn down, the edges of the old bed are left suspended on the sides of the valley in the form of terraces which, like the fossil beaches, are in descending order, the oldest being at the top.

Aggradation may result from other factors than changes of sea level. In the upper reaches of a river, intensely cold conditions can overload the water with debris in the form of solifluction slipping down the valley sides. Sometimes there is sufficient summer melt water to clear this material, but often some of it is not swept away, but left as a terrace remnant. These *climatic terraces* are of course formed under cold conditions and not temperate as in the case of eustatic terraces. Frequently in the middle reaches of a river the climatic and eustatic terraces are so intermingled that it is almost impossible to separate them, though each has a different appearance, the eustatic deposits being well washed and sorted and the climatic unwashed and unsorted. Because the river terraces and the sea levels to which they belong can be equated with the glacial and interglacial cycles, many occupation sites found in river valleys in association with terraces or on the seashore can be correctly placed in the geological sequence. These phenomena serve as very valuable dating tools.

In areas outside the range of either direct or indirect effects of Glacials other evidence must be found to establish the chronological position of events. In Africa periods of increased rainfall, Pluvials, alternate with dry periods, Interpluvials. These changes occur throughout the Pleistocene, and there are approximately the same number of Pluvials as there are glaciations. Whether the two are synchronous is still uncertain, though there is some climatological evidence that a marked decrease in temperature in the north would set up climatic responses elsewhere.

The evidence furnished by geological factors as outlined above not only helps the prehistorian to place events in their correct order and indicate their approximate age, but also gives, in broad terms, some idea of the varying conditions under which early man lived. This climatic or environmental information is of considerable importance, as environmental conditions had a profound effect on early man's way of life. This is perhaps difficult to appreciate today as we become increasingly independent of our own environments – insulated buildings, air conditioning and the movement of food and raw materials make it possible to live in the middle of a totally hostile environment, which would have been impossible for early man.

If one claims that the prehistorian's function is total reconstruction of early man's life pattern, then understanding the sequence of events and the changing cultural patterns provided by archaeological evidence is of little value if we have no knowledge of the local conditions under which man lived and no information about the natural resources available to him, either economic or industrial.

Probably the greatest advance made in such studies since World War II has been in the field of what is sometimes referred to as environmental archaeology. As the name implies, this area of study seeks to establish local conditions, climate range, seasonal change, vegetation and available food supplies, and also to provide very much more sensitive chronological indicators than those provided by geological evidence alone.

Early attempts to reconstruct prehistoric environments were based largely on faunal evidence. This consisted of the animal remains found associated with stone tools on prehistoric sites, in most cases representing food debris, but it also included smaller creatures such as rodents and land and water molluscs.

Evidence obtainable from larger animals tends to be rather restricted, as some are more sensitive to climatic change than others. It is thus necessary to consider the fauna from any one site as a whole to get a reasonably accurate picture of local conditions. For animals which are not yet extinct, such as reindeer, red deer and wild horse, we can make a fairly precise assessment of preferred habitat – steppe or tundra, temperate forest or open parkland.

We have less direct evidence of the requirements of extinct animals such as fossil elephant, woolly rhinoceros, cave bear and cave lion, though quite a lot can be inferred from animals with which they associated and about which we have more information. The cold elephant of Europe, the mammoth and its companion the woolly rhinoceros are generally associated with reindeer, arctic fox, variable hare and similar cold-tolerant animals. Sometimes the environmentalist receives unexpected bonuses. In the case of a mammoth found in frozen soil in Siberia, not only was it in good enough condition to be eaten, but its stomach contents were intact, showing that it had been eating buttercups! Such preservation is of course extremely rare, but there is a similar case from Poland where, from a mixed salt and oil deposit, an extremely well-preserved rhinoceros was unearthed, as well as many insects. The study of prehistoric fauna has recently given more attention to insects, as many, particularly beetles, are so well preserved. To this list can be added birds, fish and many microscopic creatures such as ostracods, which are often associated with sites close to water. As well as their use as climatic indicators, faunas also have chronological significance, as will be discussed when dealing with the subdivisions of the Pleistocene.

The most sensitive climatic indicator available to prehistorians is pollen analysis, a technique pioneered before World War II and greatly developed since. Many pollen grains, particularly those from trees and grasses, are almost indestructible and give a very clear and sensitive picture of local conditions. Initially it was only possible to extract pollen from acid or neutral soils, so that much of the earlier evidence came from bog sites in Britain, Scandinavia, northern Germany and (more recently) Poland. From these areas we now have very complete pollen sequences covering the last 12,000 years, divided into zones many of which now have radiometric dates. Recently techniques have been developed for extracting pollen from calcareous soils. The process is long and complicated, but it makes it possible to obtain pollen from limestone cave deposits, which was previously not feasible.

Left: digging out a mammoth tusk from frozen ground in Siberia. The ivory is in sufficiently good condition to be usable.

Below: skeleton of a mammoth reconstructed from bones found in various caves in France.

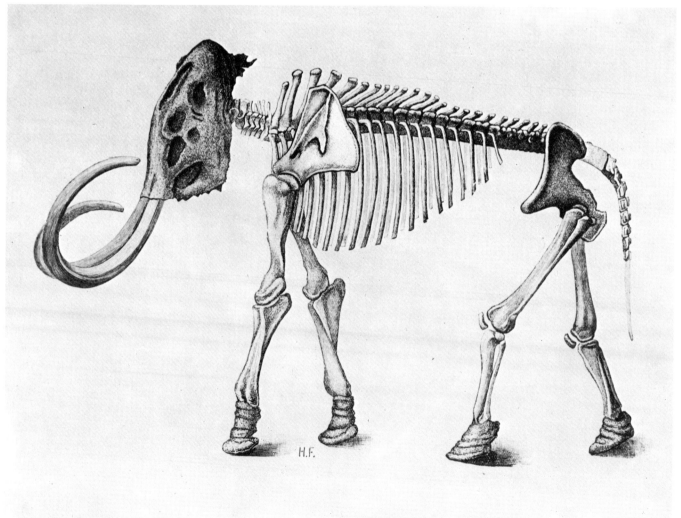

Relative and absolute dating. The techniques discussed above – geological, zoological and botanical – have two basic purposes in the archaeological context: one environmental and the other the provision of dating evidence. As far as the latter is concerned, evidence drawn from the various sciences provides what is referred to as relative dating. For example, two sites associated with the same geological event, ie the second stage of the Last Glaciation, are of the same relative age. How close they are in actual time depends on the duration of the geological event which links them. In broader terms, two sites have faunas typical of an early stage of the Pleistocene and are thus contemporary within the timespan of the Early Pleistocene, which in this case can cover a considerable period. The Early Pleistocene faunas containing the Southern Elephant and the Etruscan Rhinoceros lasted several thousand years before the change to the Straight-Tusked Elephant and Merk's rhinoceros. In later periods, those covered by pollen sequences, time relationships are much closer as the various pollen zones cover only two or three thousand years or sometimes less. While these methods of relative dating give the prehistorian very rough guides as to time, they are by no means precise, and the search for absolute rather than relative dating continues.

The first attempts to establish a more precise timescale were mathematical and astronomical, based on the variation of solar radiation. The best known of these calculations was drawn up by Milankovitch, who produced a curve showing the variations of solar radiation during the Pleistocene. The peaks and troughs of his curve closely matched the glacial/interglacial pattern established on geological grounds, including the smaller units or Interstadials. It was claimed that the variations shown in the curve could be dated mathematically, thus providing not only a timescale for the Pleistocene as a whole but also dates for the individual climatic phenomena within it. Milankovitch arrived at a figure of some 600,000 years for the beginning of the Pleistocene and 25,000 years for the end of the Last Glaciation. Subsequent systems of absolute dating have reduced the end of the Last Glaciation to nearer 10,000 years, and increased the duration of the Pleistocene by about four times. These later modifications are due to the stretching of the Pleistocene by adding to the beginning what was originally classed as Late Pliocene, rather than any basic error in the original calculations. Certainly the figure of 600,000 years was a great advance on the 60,000 years estimated for the same period by early geologists.

The next major advance in the search for absolute chronology came from the field of atomic physics and was pioneered in America. The various techniques generally known as radiometric dating depend on the known rates of decay of a radioactive isotope, or the replacement of one isotope by another, also at a known rate. The first of these techniques to be applied to archaeology is generally referred to as *carbon 14*. In principle all living organisms absorb the radioactive carbon 14 isotope from the atmosphere during their life. When the organism dies, the C^{14} isotope is no longer absorbed, and that already inside the organism begins to decay. As we know the rate of decay, the date of death of the organism can be calculated on the basis of the amount of the isotope remaining. Obviously the longer the time involved the less there is to measure, so that a point is reached where there is either too little to measure or nothing at all.

Recently enrichment techniques have been developed which give reasonable results for quantities originally too small to calculate, thus extending the timescale. So far, dates of about 40–50,000 are possible. There is, however, a margin of error which increases as the date gets older – a variable factor of about 200 years is not very serious in a date of about 20,000 years, but would make a medieval date pretty useless.

Only a limited number of materials from archaeological sites are suitable for C^{14} dating – charcoal from hearths, bone, antler and shell, the last being the least suitable as a considerable quantity of material is required to give an acceptable result.

A factor which affected the credibility of the method in its early stages was that of sample contamination. There are many conditions under which a sample can acquire additional C^{14} from its surroundings, seriously affecting test results. Modern tree roots, percolating water, and even the material of the packing in which the sample has been wrapped for transport to the laboratory can affect the result. Acquisition of additional C^{14} in this way naturally led to much incorrect dating in early days, making many dates too young, but the gradual elimination of these errors and the consistent pattern of dates for specific archaeological episodes have confirmed this as a very satisfactory dating tool.

Taken in relation to the full range of archaeological time, the upper limit of the C^{14} method covers less than 10% of the timespan, so other methods for dating earlier periods were essential.

The most widely used method for obtaining dates earlier than those from C^{14} analysis is potassium–argon or K/Ar analysis. Rocks from volcanic eruptions contain small amounts of the isotope potassium 40, which decays into argon 40 at a known rate. The half-life of this process is far greater than that of carbon 14, so that the technique is useful for much earlier dates. Unfortunately, while carbon 14 has an upper limit of about 70,000–50,000 years, the K/Ar method has a lower limit of about 600,000 years. This gap of some 500,000 years between the two methods covers a most significant period in man's physical and cultural development. To fill this gap other isotope methods are being developed based on the same principle, eg thorium/uranium and prolactinium/thorium. These new methods seem likely to fill the gap as their half-lives are much more suitable for this timerange than K/Ar.

An interesting new technique is the analysis of deep sea cores. The skeletons of minute creatures form much of the seabed sediments, and as these creatures are very sensitive to temperature changes, the species represented in a core sample give a clear indication of the range of temperature at the time of their deposition.

Although the climatic curves obtained from the above techniques belong to relative rather than absolute dating, the climatic curve obtained from deep sea cores closely resembles that of the glacial and interglacial curve, and as the cores can be dated in absolute terms this should, if the two curves are complementary, date the Glacials and Interglacials also.

Two other methods of absolute dating, both developed before World War II, are varve analysis and tree-ring dating or dendrochronology. While both have only local applications, they have proved very useful.

Varve analysis works as follows: the retreating Scandinavian ice sheet deposited fine sediments or varves in the glacial lakes into which the annual melt water flowed. Each layer of sediment represents a year's deposition, and thus analysis of a section through an old lake bed will give a very accurate timescale which, if linked along the length of the retreat line, will express in years the length of time

Extraction of a core of deep sea sediments by an oil prospecting team. Such cores can provide evidence of climatic change over long periods.

during which the ice retreated, up to the point at which it finally melted. The thickness of each varve depends on the amount of melt water each year, and so a succession of, say, ten or twenty varves has its own characteristic pattern and can thus be matched with varve deposits from other lakes.

Tree-ring analysis is based on much the same principle, with the counting of annual growth rings. Each year a tree adds a ring to its girth so that, when the trunk is sectioned, these rings show the complete history of the tree's life. Not only is its age recorded, but the variations in thickness of the rings show the changes of micro-climate during the tree's existence. These outside influences affect all trees of the same species in the same area in the same way, and two trees of the same age will show an identical ring pattern. If the patterns of young trees are added to those of older trees where the appropriate rings overlap, it is possible to establish a sequence of dated rings over a very long period, especially with trees like oak.

Many of the timber-framed structures of pre-Columbian America have been dated by tree-ring analysis, and in Britain dated plots go back as far as Roman times. Medieval records in Europe are often available as a cross-check for the dates of buildings whose timbers have been thus dated. There are many cases where timbers have been reused but, as few new buildings are made entirely from old timber, this fact can usually be recognized.

As the wood dated by this method is also a suitable material for carbon 14 dating, tree-ring dates can be used as a cross-check for C^{14}. This has given a very accurate range of values for carbon 14, allowing a correction table to be applied to dates as far back as about 4,000 years BC, the present limit of the tree-ring method.

The various new techniques which have recently become available might suggest that all the problems of chronology have now been solved, but this is far from being the case. The processing of samples is a long and complicated business, and too few laboratories are equipped for the work. Further, each technique requires a long period of testing before it gains full acceptance among prehistorians. The number of dates for the Pleistocene is increasing, but it is still necessary to depend largely on relative dating for correlations.

In comparatively restricted areas, for example Scandinavia, Britain, northern Germany or areas of similar size, it is possible to relate sites to each other fairly closely in terms of relative dating, as the small subdivisions of the Pleistocene are generally well defined. In wider correlations, for example between events in China and Africa, it is only possible to relate in terms of much larger time units.

To express these larger time units the Pleistocene has been divided into three parts – Lower Pleistocene (or Villafranchian), Middle and Upper. These three subdivisions are largely based on fauna. Throughout this period the major areas of the world had their own faunas,

Lower Pleistocene (Villafranchian)	Middle Pleistocene					Upper Pleistocene		Post Glacial
Several early cold episodes	Glacial	Interglacial	Glacial	Interglacial	Glacial	Interglacial	Glacial	
	Gunz	Gunz/Mindel	Mindel	Mindel/Riss	Riss	Riss/Würm	Würm	
	1 2		1 2		1 2 3		1 2 3 4	
Time scale	1,000,000		500,000 250,000	200,000		150,000	80,000	10,000 years ago

Subdivisions of the Pleistocene (dates are approximate).

so that it is rarely possible to compare one area with another species by species. For example some of the early elephants died out in Europe before they did in Africa, and forms which would be very early in one place continue much longer in another. Comparison is therefore based on change rather than on the existence of individual animals. In Asia, Africa and Europe there is a change of fauna in which many of the forms still surviving from the Pliocene die out. This loss of archaic fauna occurs at approximately the same time in all three areas and represents the transition from the Lower to the Middle Pleistocene. Two early hominids, from Asia and from Africa, belong to a period of faunal change and thus date from roughly the same age, ie early Middle Pleistocene. The few dates so far available for the Early and Middle Pleistocene from Asia and Africa seem to confirm this broad correlation.

In Europe similar faunal changes mark the triple division of the Pleistocene, though there is not full agreement as to where demarcation lines should be drawn in terms of glacial and interglacial sequences. To establish some measure of consistency we have throughout this book adopted the boundaries used by the Finnish paleontologist, Kurten. We will also continue to use the old names of the four European glaciations – Gunz, Mindel, Riss and Würm – names adopted from river valleys in southern Germany, where evidence for the four glaciations was first established. Many European geologists have taken to describing local glacial phenomena by local names, but as these can be equated with the old terminology, it is less confusing to retain the classic terms.

Archaeology: methods and definitions. Data drawn from the natural and physical sciences provide the chronological framework and environmental background to the history of early man, but this information plays only a supporting role in the prehistorian's main concern, which is the study of man himself. It may seem strange that this aspect of archaeology needs to be stressed, but there is a tendency while pursuing the scientific aspects of the subject to lose sight of its main purpose. It has been said that archaeology is in fact paleo-anthropology, and while the methods used by the anthropologist are radically different from those used by the archaeologist, the end product of the two disciplines is the same – the total reconstruction of the cultural, spiritual and intellectual life of a particular people. However, it is obvious that much evidence available to anthropologists is denied their archaeological colleagues – the amount of information gleaned by the latter is pitifully small compared with that obtainable from fieldwork among living communities.

It is necessary at this point to define certain terms which have become current as the subject of archaeology has developed over the years. Originally the term "prehistoric" was coined to cover the preliterate groups who came before the classical or biblical peoples, and "protohistoric" covered the peoples who, while not themselves literate, were referred to by the classical authors. Good examples of the latter are the German tribes described by Tacitus – we have a great deal of information from him, but none is supplied by the Germans themselves. These two definitions, though clear when first created, have become increasingly blurred over the years and are nowadays disregarded by the prehistorian.

If one accepts that all preliterate societies come under the aegis of the prehistorian, the subject would, in the light of our present knowledge, become impossibly complex, and for this reason it has been divided into two parts.

The original subdivisions of time based on raw materials (stone, bronze and iron) suggested one possible method of division, but in fact prehistorians now divide on the basis of economy rather than on considerations of material.

Throughout the greater part of man's existence he has depended for his food on hunting and food gathering, the

A group of hunters in Kenya, still gathering food in the same manner as prehistoric man.

Middle East. Within Europe the early prehistorians found that the three stages of Lower, Middle and Upper Paleolithic followed on from each other very consistently, and thus these terms tend to be used in a chronological sense. As archaeological research opened up other areas these terms became less well defined. Although prehistorians still say that this or that assemblage is of Lower Paleolithic type, this no longer implies a chronological position, as the various stages occurred over widely different periods in various parts of the world.

Something should perhaps be said now about archaeological methods. Excavation is of course the basis of all archaeological research, whether in the realm of early history or prehistory. Some information can be gleaned from material found on the surface of the earth or exposed in natural sections cut by erosion, but the value of this type of information depends on the solid evidence provided by systematic excavation.

Prehistoric sites fall mainly into two groups – open and enclosed. The first are campsites without natural cover, generally found near water and where possible with some protection from the elements (eg in the lee of hills or folds in the ground). How elaborate the sites are depends on the residents' standard of culture and length of occupation and, to some extent, the climate, since in very cold conditions some form of structure – tent or hut – would be essential. The absence of caves in eastern Europe means that open sites are common. Elaborate huts, sometimes made of the larger bones of mammoth, are well known, particularly in Czechoslovakia and the south Russian plains. It seems that these mammoth bone huts were occupied for long periods during the year and may even have been used as permanent dwellings.

The amount of information obtainable from such a site depends on its age, the length of time it was occupied and any damage it has suffered. If fully excavated, open sites can provide very detailed information regarding settlement patterns, and some of the examples dating from the Last Glaciation display a variety of equipment and art objects. Unfortunately these eastern European sites have produced little organic material, such as wood, and one has the feeling that one is seeing less than half of the occupants' possessions and activities. Many open sites lack solid structures like those provided by the mammoth bone, and were probably no more than tented camps. However strong winds made it necessary to dig the tent poles into the ground, and these postholes, the position of the hearth and the area covered by manufacturing debris often give a very clear idea of the shape of the dwelling.

In more temperate conditions structures tend to be absent or at most consist of a simple windbreak with stone foundations. The main evidence for a camp is the scatter of imperishable material – usually stone tools, the wastage from their manufacture and food debris.

While these open sites often provide a wealth of valuable information, they tend to be isolated in terms of

latter including scavenging, and has made no attempt to augment his food supply by agriculture or stock-keeping. In certain favored areas in the Middle East, India, China and America this early subsistence pattern gradually gave way to one of greater independence. Pigs, oxen, sheep and goats became domesticated and cereals, originally gathered wild, were cultivated and stored for future use. This independence and the flexibility it afforded changed living habits, making possible a more static existence leading to the founding of permanent settlements. While this changeover was not of course as clear-cut as the above suggests, it provides a point at which the immensely long prehistoric period can be divided up.

Thus one group of prehistorians is concerned with the long period of man's existence as hunter-gatherer and the other, following the change in economy, with pastoralism and agriculture, the latter leading to the village and later to city communities.

The original subdivision reflects this economic change – Paleolithic or Old Stone Age and Neolithic or New Stone Age, the latter followed by the Bronze and Iron ages. The Paleolithic was further divided into Lower, Middle and Upper, the last finishing at the end of the Last Glaciation. Later it became necessary to create the term Mesolithic to cover the time gap between the end of the Last Glaciation and the arrival in Europe of the early farmers from the cultural sequence and, unless one or more occupations are superimposed, it is not always possible to put a number of sites with varying equipment in their correct chronological order.

The second group of sites comprises caves and natural rock shelters. Although one frequently hears early man referred to as caveman, this is not strictly true. There are many cave sites but a larger number, particularly in France, are rock-shelters – mere overhangs providing some shelter from wind and rain. And of course there are more open sites than either caves or rock-shelters. In spite of this caves and shelters have, over the years, provided by far the most important evidence for at least the later stages of cultural development, and the long occupational sequences of many of these sites have provided the basic framework for much of the study of the subject.

It is obvious that in any climate (but particularly a cold one) these natural shelters were in great demand, and this fact has proved of much value to prehistorians. What was suitable for one family was suitable for a whole succession of families over thousands of years, each leaving behind layers of rubbish resting on that of their predecessors and to be covered later by that of their successors. These layers of debris not only show the cultural pattern of successive occupants but also put the occupational evidence in its correct sequence. Cultural sequences established in caves are also the means of dating isolated material from open sites.

For many years it was assumed that the inhabitants put up with whatever amenities the cave or shelter provided, but more recently it has become apparent that modifications were made. Some caves have dry stone walls, and the presence of postholes suggests that tents or another form of draught excluder were erected inside. In the shallow caves or shelters light was no problem, but in deeper ones only the front area could be used as living

The interior of Gorham's cave during the course of excavation, showing a mixture of dark layers of rubbish and clean windblown sand from the beach outside.

Gorham's cave in Gibraltar, sculpted out of the cliffside by the sea, and occupied by prehistoric man over a period of 40,000 years.

space as the light diminished rapidly towards the back. Later inhabitants had a form of artificial lighting, but the entrances and the terrace outside were still the main living areas.

Excavating a single occupation horizon in a cave gives much the same information as that available from an open site, with the additional advantage that deposits have often been better protected. Many of the caves in France and northern Spain are of limestone, which results in very good preservation of bone and antler – evidence often lost in open sites in acid soils. The ages of the animals killed for food give a clue to the seasons during which the site was occupied, and show that many were in use all the year round. Doubtless this long-term use made elaborate adjustments worthwhile, and the inhabitants were probably very comfortably settled and would have been as well protected from the elements as modern people living under very cold conditions and with a similar economy. Many of the later peoples, those associated with the end of the Pleistocene, seem to have occupied some sites only seasonally – for example small bands were living in Gibraltar during the autumn, as evidenced by the nutshells and mussel shells they left behind. The inhabitants of Swanscombe in Kent were in residence when the fallow deer were in antler, from September to March. As no traces of young animals or males without antlers have been uncovered, the hunters must have been living elsewhere during the late spring and summer.

Evidence like the above, while suggesting some seasonal movement, does not necessarily imply that the hunter-gatherers moved over great distances, and it is more likely that they circulated around a fairly small territory. However there are signs pointing to long journeys – for example sites well inland have produced seashells, and some raw materials are known to have been carried over considerable distances. Modern anthropological evidence shows that bands were prepared to raid several hundred miles from the home territory to obtain a scarce commodity.

We have referred briefly to terminology, but this is a subject which requires more consideration. In addition to the enormous number of scientific and technical terms derived from the natural sciences with which the prehistorian needs to be familiar, he has created almost as many of his own. These strictly archaeological labels describe the various facets of human culture, chronological or regional, and the wide variety of tools made from different materials which man has created over more than two million years.

As mentioned above the terms Lower, Middle and Upper Paleolithic and Mesolithic lack precision. Under each of these headings are a number of facets sufficiently different to warrant special names. Archaeological assemblages from particular sites or levels within a site, if demonstrably new, are generally given a name derived from the site where they were first recognized. If the site name has already been used, then either a district or parish name is employed. For example, the site of La Micoque in France produced two levels, both with new material – one was called Micoquian after the site and the other Tayacian after Tayac, the commune or parish in which the site stood. This custom of using site names has naturally produced a long list of terms in a wide variety of languages which, to the student coming to the subject for the first time, appear somewhat daunting. As more sites were dug and excavation techniques refined, small differences in assemblages became apparent, with the result that tools which had originally been grouped under one heading became subdivided, either into numbered stages (if the differences were chronological) or by the allocation of separate names.

A simple hut of branches and leaves made by pygmies living in the forests of northern Zaire.

Excavation: the interpretation of finds. In the process of physical and mental development, man has passed through many evolutionary stages since becoming a toolmaker, and it is not surprising that his technical skills and living standards should also show signs of change. However, it must not be forgotten that environmental pressures can have as much influence on material equipment as increased mental ability and the accumulation of inherited knowledge.

Man living under very simple conditions generally seems disinclined to develop his skills further than his immediate needs require. This means that a particular assemblage does not always give an accurate reflection of a group's mental potential. A good example of how environmental factors affect material culture can be seen in a comparison of the Eskimo living within the Arctic circle and the Ituri pygmy of the Congo forests. The environment of the former demands a highly-developed technology for survival, with an extensive toolkit to cover the needs of hunting, travel and the manufacture of shelters and clothing. By contrast the Ituri pygmy can get by with the absolute minimum, living on the abundant local vegetation and practicing simple hunting techniques, meat being a luxury rather than a necessity. In spite of these marked cultural differences between the two races there is no difference in their mental potential.

The terminology required to cover the various assemblages is simple compared to that needed to cover individual tools, of which several hundred forms are recognized, made from a wide variety of raw materials.

The basis for the classification of tools is that of assumed function, and here the word "assumed" is important. Classifying tools is, at best, a rather subjective pursuit and different prehistorians have tended to analyze assemblages along different lines. There has also been much dispute over the definition of particular tools, which inevitably led to a great deal of confusion and made it extremely difficult to compare material from various sites even if one understood the system a particular worker was using. Since World War II the development of statistical methods has made uniformity imperative and, as a result of international conferences, an increasing measure of agreement is becoming possible. It was at one time hoped that there would be a universal system of classification, but it is now clear that this is unrealistic and it is necessary for each region to have its special tool list. A further problem arises from the vagaries of the toolmakers and their lack of sympathy with our attempts to systematize their efforts!

Tool assemblages, or industries as they are generally called, show variety not only in types or typology but also in manufacturing techniques. The same tool can be made in more than one way, and these technical differences are often important as they can indicate separate traditions in industries with similar types.

Basically there are two methods of making stone tools – either by shaping implements from blocks of stone or, the

An Eskimo man and woman outside their summer tent, on the fringe of the Arctic Circle.

reverse, using flakes taken from the blocks. The first method is to take a lump of raw material and, by chipping with a hammer-stone, obtain the desired shape as a sculptor does with his marble. With this process the tool is fashioned out of the block and the chips, or flakes, are the waste product. By the second method, the flakes from the block become the blanks for tools and the block or core becomes the waste.

The choice of a suitable stone is important. Since the stone is worked in all directions in flaking, the material must have no cleavage planes and must be what masons call a freestone. Laminated rocks such as slate are of very limited use since they can only be worked in one direction. Further, the material must be tough enough for the work in hand, and the flakes should come off with naturally sharp edges. The siliceous rocks such as flint, jasper, chalcedony, quartz and quartzite are the most suitable for toolmaking as they fracture with a very sharp cutting edge similar to glass. By far the best material, though rather limited in distribution, is volcanic glass or obsidian. In some areas suitable materials were not always available, and prehistoric man was forced to make use of some strange raw materials such as fossil wood, but he was capable of making traditional tools out of almost any stone.

Tools made from the blocks, or core tools as they are called, are the heavy-duty implements such as choppers and cleavers. Smaller tools are generally made from the flakes and often used without modification as they are admirable cutting tools. To make formal tools further chipping of the flakes is required. This secondary work, or retouching of the primary flakes, forms the implements

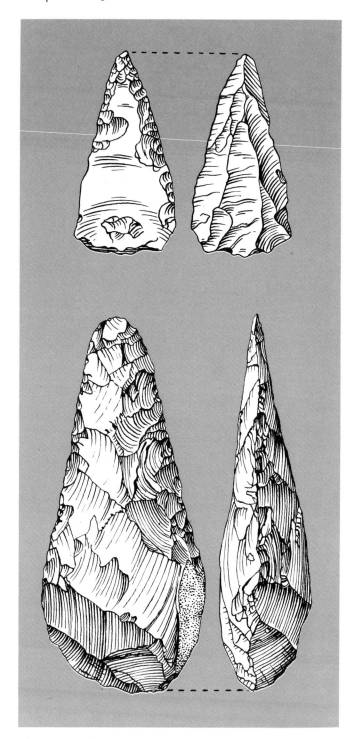

Above: a typical hand ax (half natural size), made by chipping a block of flint into the required shape. *Below:* a flint flake (two-thirds natural size) converted into a spear point by delicate chipping around the edge.

which are classified into functional tool types: scrapers, blades, projectile points, engraving tools, etc.

No industry consists exclusively of core tools. The early ones in which core tools predominate also used some flakes since these were readily available as waste. Some of the later industries used only flakes, and later still long flakes called blades were in vogue, made from specially prepared cores. Many industries share the same basic toolkit, but are distinguishable either because of differences in manufacturing technique or because the tools occur in different proportions.

Most of the techniques for making stone tools were understood from very early times and developed not so much by the invention of new techniques as by the increasing complexity of the toolkit, with more specialized forms coming into use in later periods in response to a greater diversity of activities.

In discussing early man's tools, emphasis has been placed on the stone tools as these are often all that remains of a particular group's activities, but man was, from the advent of toolmaking, capable of utilizing a wide variety of raw materials. It is, however, very rare for organic material to survive. There are a few exceptions – part of a pointed piece of yew wood, possibly a spear, was found at a site on the Essex coast and dates at least as far back as 200,000 years. Similar finds of worked wood have been made in Africa, dating from about 60,000 years.

One material which has survived well, especially in caves, is bone and its related material antler. In some of the later periods of Europe when the climate was intensely cold and wood probably rather scarce, bone and antler were used for a wide variety of purposes, either carved or ground into the required shape. In some of the earlier periods bone from the larger animals such as elephant was treated as if it were stone and chipped into shape. Bog sites have produced a wealth of material from periods following the Last Glaciation in Europe in the shape of wooden objects, including bows and arrows and dugout canoes and their paddles. Dating from later still in the Bronze and Iron Age, complete bodies tanned by acid soil conditions have been found, with their clothing and even the stomach content, a thin gruel, intact. In view of the state of preservation of the mammoth already mentioned, there is still hope for a bonus in the form of a frozen human at least as old. One such has already been claimed!

In addition to the purely utilitarian objects there is abundant evidence, particularly from later periods, of personal ornament: beads of carved bone, pierced seashells and animal teeth for necklaces, and pendants of various materials. Burials have been found with beads adhering to the corpse's skull and scattered among the bones of the thorax, suggesting that they had been sewn onto caps and tunics like the beads on a Red Indian's skin clothing. Coloring matter derived from natural earth pigments is known from very early times. This was of course the material used in cave paintings, but it was probably also employed as a cosmetic and for ritual body painting (as for example in Australian aboriginal initiation ceremonies today).

Our increased understanding of the complexities of early cultural development is largely due to the use of more refined excavation techniques, a field in which the

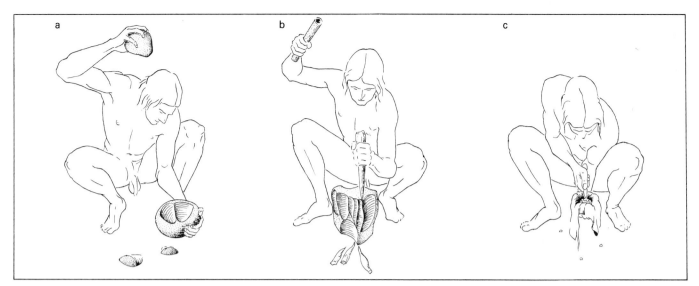

Methods of working stone: a) knocking flakes off the core with a hammerstone; b) delicate chipping of a flake edge by means of a hammer and bone chisel; c) forming the shape of a tool by pressing small flakes off the edge.

French have made the main contribution. In excavations of the last century the excavators, though fully aware of the significance of various layers visible in a sequence, were inclined to separate these on lines which were too broad. If a layer of, say, a meter thick, appeared to contain material belonging to the same culture from top to bottom, then it was treated as one cultural unit and the material from the whole layer was lumped together. While there is no constant time factor for depth of deposit, a meter of occupational debris takes a long time to accumulate and

Left: a group of bone spear points and awls from the cave of Cro-Magnon, southwest France.

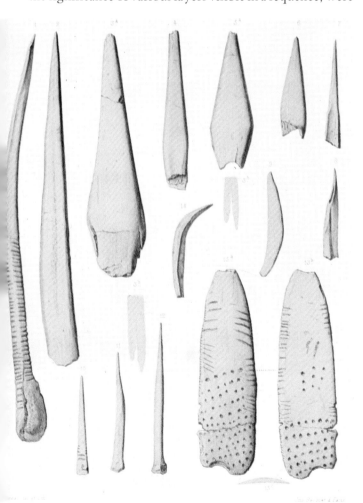

Tollund man, found preserved in a bog in Sweden.

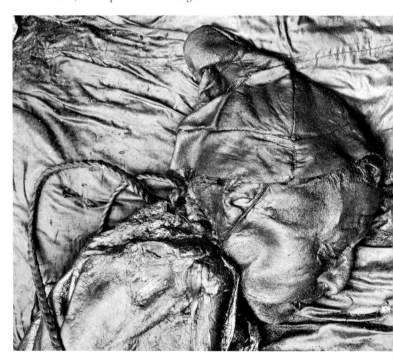

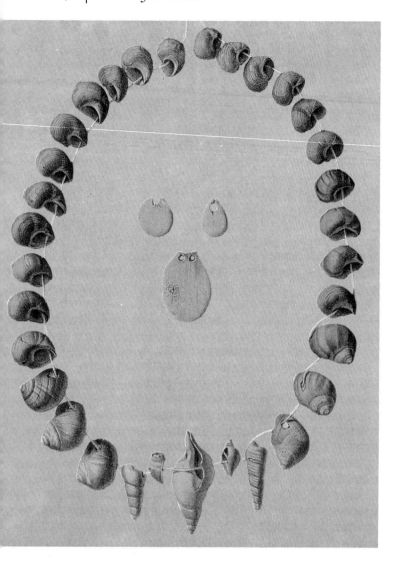

development. There is, however, one further subject to be considered – anthropology.

Early man: modern parallels. As we mentioned earlier, the aims of archaeology and anthropology are basically the same. The outlook of the Victorian anthropologists was somewhat narrower than would be accepted today, since they were principally concerned with the study of what, for want of a better word, were called primitive peoples. The object of these studies was the gathering of information covering every aspect of a group – its physical characteristics, its material culture, and its spiritual and intellectual attainments.

The information derived from such studies has interested prehistorians from the very beginning, and it appeared that modern peoples living on a hunting and food gathering economy under various environmental conditions might be an obvious source of information regarding prehistoric peoples practicing the same economy and living in broadly similar environmental conditions.

This borrowing of anthropological data by prehistorians led not only to direct comparisons of living patterns and the function of particular tools, but also to comparisons of modern patterns of behavior and thought with those of prehistoric man. This last seemed parti-

Left: reconstruction of a shell necklace from the cave of Cro-Magnon, with three bone pendants.

the excavators were combining materials covering a very long period. Sometimes, if the deposit was particularly thick, some rough subdivision would be made, but this was still not enough to reveal the finer nuances of change. In modern excavation every slight change of color or texture in the deposit is treated separately, so that it is possible to see a number of changes in tool types and proportions during the occupation of one ethnic group – changes which would have been masked by older digging techniques. In addition to the refinement of excavation methods, the modern excavator has a clearer understanding of the conditions under which cave deposits were formed. The occupants' rubbish forms only part of the content of a cave, and much of the deposit is made up of material blown in from outside during dry conditions, clayey layers laid down when the climate was more humid, and layers of limestone from the walls and ceiling broken off by frost in periods of intense cold.

Information drawn from either the natural sciences or the prehistorians' own observations has produced a mass of data covering chronology, environment and cultural

Right: North American Indians disguised in wolfskins, stalking buffalo, by the 19th century American artist, George Catlin. There are indications in prehistoric art that early man used similar hunting techniques.

cularly valid for interpreting the motives for prehistoric art, as modern ritual practices seemed to provide suitable explanations.

In view of the extremely cold conditions in Europe during the Last Glaciation, a comparison with the Eskimo communities of the Arctic Circle seemed appropriate. While there was no archaeological evidence of anything similar to the maritime economy of the coastal Eskimos, the inland groups or Caribou Eskimos seemed a reasonable comparison. The caribou, a subspecies of the European reindeer, formed the staple diet of the French cave dwellers, suggesting not only that the climate of prehistoric Europe was similar to that of the Arctic Circle, but also that there may have been identical hunting methods and similar patterns of living. Both groups seemed to have a certain amount in common – for example like the Eskimo the last of the inhabitants of Glacial Europe certainly had skin clothing, as prehistoric art shows; both groups used fish spears and fish seems to have been a source of food to prehistoric man as it is to the Eskimo; and both used a version of the spear-thrower.

The inland Eskimos' economy is based almost entirely on the caribou, without which survival would be impossible. Pressure from the forest Indians in the south and the coastal Eskimos to the north kept the inland tribes sandwiched between the two on the very inhospitable tundra. This terrain is almost devoid of vegetation, and has an animal population totally inadequate for supporting life throughout the year (and certainly not during the extremely long winter). Subsistence was possible owing to the fact that the caribou are migratory, moving northwards in the spring to the summer pastures on the tundra and returning, fat and with pelts in beautiful condition, to the shelter of the forests during the autumn. The Eskimo intercepted the caribou returning to their winter quarters, ambushing the herds either in narrow, rocky defiles or at water crossings. The meat thus obtained and frozen was sufficient to last through the winter and could, to some extent, be augmented from the deer returning in the spring. During the late spring and summer fishing, setting snares for small game such as arctic hare, netting birds and collecting wild fruits provided a varied diet for the three summer months.

To the early prehistorians such a subsistence pattern seemed to mirror that of the inhabitants of Glacial Europe, but even the information at their disposal showed several differences. Certainly the Magdalenians, the late glacial occupants of the French caves, relied heavily on the reindeer, but in Europe at this time there were two species of reindeer, one migratory and the other the forest form, and thus their supply of meat did not depend entirely on annual migration. Also there were other large animals

available – herds of wild horses, the European bison and wild ox, as well as bears, lions and other carnivores who were probably only hunted for their skins.

The main areas of occupation in France at this time were on the slopes of the Massif Central and the northern slopes of the Pyrenees, the valleys of which must have been sheltered enough to provide trees. Pollen from conifers is certainly present in many caves in this area. This tree cover must have been a boon to the prehistoric women whose Eskimo counterparts spend long hours collecting scrub for fires. The prehistoric inhabitants of the southern steppes of Europe seem also to have had a fuel problem, as they burned a considerable quantity of bone.

Like the Eskimo, prehistoric man used most of the raw material which his game provided. The bone and antler of the reindeer provided raw material for many tools – spear-throwers, bone awls, and possibly projectile points and the barbed heads of fishing spears. Skins were most likely used for making summer tents as well as clothing, and many of the stone tools were probably used for preparing them. Some skins, like that of the arctic fox, were possibly prized then as now for their beauty – they certainly make a very effective edging to the hood of a parka.

The comparison of ancient and modern peoples, while requiring some caution, nevertheless has a value for the prehistorian in that it shows the range of possibilities available for overcoming specific environmental problems, and the possible range of techniques available for hunting and trapping. We have modern examples of driving, ambush, stalking, trapping with either snares or fall-traps, digging pits for larger animals, and driving game into swamps, these last two probably being the methods employed by the prehistoric Europeans to catch the mammoth and woolly rhinoceros.

Recent studies of modern hunting groups show that the warmer the climate, the less part meat plays in the diet. Food for thought regarding "man the hunter" is provided by a modern account of an Australian walkabout. The arrangements for supplies to cover the journey were nil, and the party started with practically no food, on the assumption that what would be required could be picked up on the way. This proved to be the case. Apart from gathering vegetable foods, almost anything in the meat line seems to have been acceptable. Lizards, snakes, frogs and grubs were gathered en route, and the only "hunting" was when the men of the party chased a kangaroo, as much for fun as anything else. It is interesting to observe that the occupants of intensely cold regions seem to have a more predictable food supply, and one has the feeling that the late inhabitants of Glacial Europe probably lived better than their cousins in more temperate regions.

The vogue for direct anthropological comparison fell

Man the hunter – an Australian aborigine returning from a successful expedition. The bag consists of snakes, lizards, wallabies and a scaly anteater.

into disrepute between the two World Wars, but has recently been reconsidered, though with a more cautious approach. It is now believed that for an area with a known food potential, a calculation can be made of the estimated population it will support. The size of the campsite gives some idea of the number of occupants. Recently, the contents of abandoned modern campsites belonging to seminomadic hunting groups have been analyzed, and the material left behind gives some indication of the length of occupation of similar prehistoric sites.

The results of such studies are never likely to be conclusive, but they form the basis for reasonable suppositions and, perhaps even more important, keep alive in prehistorians' minds the fact that they are dealing with human beings battling with very human problems.

Before dealing with the evidence collected from archaeological sites and discussing its interpretations, we must first consider the most fundamental aspect of the whole subject – the physical and mental development of man himself.

3. The Making of Man

While the 19th century saw the acceptance of the theory of the evolution of man, the 20th century drew aside the curtain a little to reveal not only the various stages involved but also a timescale far in excess of anything dreamed of by the early pioneers.

Man's family tree. The acceptance of man as part of the animal kingdom, subject to the same evolutionary laws, necessitated his scientific classification with other animals in the system originally conceived by Linnaeus in the 18th century. Within this classification man clearly belongs in the group containing the great apes and the monkeys of both the Old and New World. Among these are a group of creatures whose relationship to the others is not very apparent. This large group is the order Primate, in which are included the prosimians, lemurs, pottos, bush babies and the like, the Old and New World monkeys, and the apes (family Pongidae) and man (family Hominidae). The obvious similarity between man and the great apes led the early evolutionists to examine in particular the relationship between these two, but evidence obtained over the last hundred years has provided a great deal of information regarding the development of the order Primate as a whole.

As with all living creatures the genealogical tree of man resembles a family pedigree, with a line stretching from the first discernible ancestor of the group to the present representatives of the family. Between the two extremes is a structure with many side-branches, whose only connection with each other is via the ancestor on the trunk at the point from which they branched. As a result, the further one goes down the trunk, the more branches a single ancestor is seen to be responsible for. The two branches which led to the anthropoid apes and man thus had their last common ancestor at the point at which they parted company. The problem facing the Human paleontologist is the placing of each piece of fossil evidence in its correct position on the family tree. Does it precede the divergence of man and ape, thus being ancestral to both, or does it come after the divergence, being ancestral only to one?

The real problem is that both modern man and the apes are end products of specialization. The further one goes back towards their common ancestor the more alike they tend to become, and there is some excuse for anatomists often appearing very uncertain as to where a particular fossil should be placed.

The early ancestors of the primates are discernible as far back as the first stage of the Tertiary (the Eocene) some 70 million years ago, and certainly the ancestral forms of the prosimians were in existence at that time, having been

Man's nearest relatives – a gorilla (above) and a chimpanzee (below).

A chimpanzee showing characteristic knuckle-walking.

posture and manual dexterity, are of course closely related. Man's present method of locomotion seems to have developed from the knuckle walking of the great apes. A change of stance to the upright position freed the hands from their walking role and allowed them to become more sensitive and flexible, giving rise to the precision grip as opposed to the power grip only. It also had considerable effect on the skeleton, particularly the pelvis and the position of the skull in relation to the rest of the body.

It is not possible to say how each of the three developments outlined above affected man's evolution, since they are so intertwined, nor do we know for certain whether or not the acquisition of these traits accelerated man's evolution.

Over the last seventy years an increasing number of human fossils have been found, particularly during the last twenty. Not only has this greatly added to our store of material, it has also led to much of the older material being reexamined.

We have already referred to the breakaway of the Old and New World monkeys in the Oligocene. In the succeeding Miocene, beginning about 35 million years ago, there was a group of small primates, lightly built and intermediate in size between a chimpanzee and a gibbon.

A baby gibbon standing on its hind legs. To maintain this attitude for any distance it needs to keep its arms outstretched for balance. Gibbons are the smallest of the four anthropoid apes, which are man's nearest relations. The others are the orangutan, the chimpanzee and the gorilla.

found in both the Old and New Worlds. In the succeeding Oligocene the Old and New World monkeys are distinguishable, and they probably divided out in the early Oligocene. It is not clear whether their common ancestor was a monkey or some form of prosimian.

The next major landmark in the ancestral tree is the point of separation of man and the apes, but before entering this rather confused area of relationship it is necessary to consider the various traits which separate man from his nearest relative.

It would be an oversimplification to say that man differed from the apes in only three characteristics – his brain, his manual dexterity and his upright posture. There are other traits which distinguish him, but it is the exploitation and development of the above three in particular which has given rise to man in his present form.

During Human evolution the brain has developed in overall size and in complexity, and it is particularly the increase in the latter that has given man his present superiority. Perhaps the most productive of man's acquisitions are memory and the ability to communicate.

The need to accommodate areas of the brain containing the higher centers led to alteration of the skull's basic shape and to an enlargement of the particular areas where these accomplishments were developing. For instance as the frontal lobe developed the frontal bone became progressively more upright, resulting in a backward movement of the face, further modified by a decrease in the size of the jaw and teeth as the diet became more varied.

The other two factors distinguishing man, upright

Left: one of the simple primates and a relation of man – a bushbaby from Africa.

To this group the name Dryopithecus has been given, bringing together several forms occurring in Africa, the East and Europe, which had been classified under several different names. The Dryopithecines' relation to man and the apes is not yet clear as they have a number of characteristics which could place them in either branch, although most anatomists suggest that they may be considered as proto-anthropoids rather than proto-hominids.

One group originally classed with the Dryopithecine but now treated separately is Ramapithecus. The original specimen from India was considered to belong to the pongid rather than the hominid line. However, recent reevaluation of the material indicates that Ramapithecus belongs to the human stem and in fact appears to be the first recognizable member of the purely human branch. The Ramapithecus material dates from the latter part of the Miocene and, as Dryopithecine and Ramapithecus seem to have been in part contemporary, it would seem that the Hominid/Anthropoid breakaway took place in either the late Oligocene or the early Miocene. From Kenya came a primate which Louis Leakey originally called Kenyapithecus but which is now classed with the Ramapithecus from India. This African specimen from Fort Ternan apparently used to break open bones with lumps of lava, presumably for the extraction of marrow. Kenyapithecus has a K/Ar date of about 14 million years, and the earliest known gibbon, probably the first of the anthropoids to branch away, is known to be about 23–24 million years old. One can therefore assume that if Ramapithecus belongs to the human stem, the separation of anthropoid and man took place somewhere between these two dates. The succeeding hominid group occurs around 2 to 2.5 million years and includes the Australopithecines and their relatives.

While we know very little about the habits of Ramapithecus, there is little doubt that like the chimpanzees and gorillas he was a ground feeder and probably, like them, a knuckle-walker. There is no reason to think that he was any bigger than the Dryopithecine. The evidence from Fort Ternan suggests that he was at least in part carnivorous, and seems to have been capable of getting more out of the bones than the anthropoids (if these bones were, in fact, broken open by him).

Australopithecus. The name Australopithecus is given to a group of fossil hominids from South Africa, the first of which was found in 1925 at Taungs, a limestone quarry about 80 miles north of Kimberley. The original specimen found at Taungs as a result of quarrying was the almost complete skull of a child, and was given the name of Australopithecus africanus (the Southern Ape) by Raymond Dart, the South African anatomist who first described it.

The skull is unusual in that although only the frontal bone, face and upper and lower jaw are preserved and the

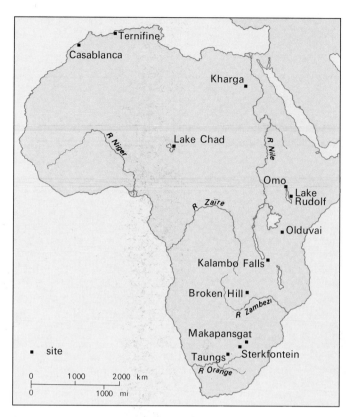

The main sites of discoveries in Africa. Remains of hominids found just south of Olduvai in December 1974 take the date of man's earliest ancestors back as far as 3.75 million years.

greater part of the bones of the vault are missing, there is a complete cast of the brain which, allowing for the thickness of the missing bone, gives the almost complete skull shape. The upper and lower teeth are all present; the majority are milk teeth but the permanent molars are beginning to erupt, indicating an age at death of about six years.

Had the Taungs skull remained the sole representative of the genus Australopithecus, its value would have been rather restricted, as skull morphology changes markedly when the individual reaches maturity and attachments for muscles develop; but finds of further, adult members of the genus have confirmed the original suggestions put forward by Dart. The name Southern Ape bestowed on Taungs by Dart did not in any way imply that he was unaware of its character – in fact Dart was for some time almost alone in stressing its human characteristics and its claim to belong to a position ancestral to man.

The skull is small with a well-rounded vault and a markedly protruding face which shows superficial resemblances to that of a young chimpanzee. Upon closer examination, however, it is in many respects nearer to man than to the great apes, particularly as regards the teeth.

In view of the subsequent finding of adult specimens of the same type, it would be more practical to give a composite picture of the creature now drawn from far

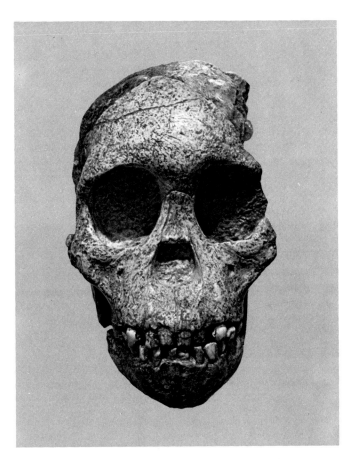

Front view of the child's skull found at Taungs, South Africa, in 1925. For a long time it was considered the earliest human ancestor.

complete pelvis and parts of long bones. The significance of the pelvis is that it allows us to assess posture and gait far more accurately than any other evidence. Further material of the same type came from the site of Makapansgat, and was found by Dart from 1947 to 1962. This site produced another almost complete skull, parts of several jaws and further bits of pelvis.

Originally the material from the three sites was classified under three different names: the Taungs finds as Australopithecus africanus; the Sterkfontein first as Australopithecus transvaalensis and later as Plesianthropus transvaalensis; and the Makapansgat as Australopithecus prometheus, under the mistaken impression that these people used fire.

This complex nomenclature suggested that there were more differences between the individuals from the three sites than in fact there were, and they are now considered to belong to one genus and species – Australopithecus africanus. Taking the material from the three sites together, it is possible to construct a picture of what the individuals must have looked like. They stood about four feet high and were lightly built with a body weight of between 40 and 70 pounds. The pelvic bones suggest that they were fully biped, though they probably did not walk quite as efficiently as modern humans. The arms appear to have been a little longer than our own, and the shoulder

Dr Broom, the South African anatomist, pointing to the skull from Sterkfontein, still embedded in its cave deposit.

more material than was found at Taungs. Not all anatomists agreed with Dart on the position of the Taungs skull in the human ancestral pattern, and a number considered it as being no more than a rather unspecialized ape. However, another South African anatomist, Robert Broom, fully supported Dart's views and himself set about investigating limestone quarries in the Transvaal. In this exercise Broom was extremely successful, and in a few years had accumulated a mass of new material from a number of sites, representing not only further examples of the Taungs type, but also a closely related group.

The conditions under which these fossil hominids were deposited were much the same in all the Transvaal sites. They consist of the fillings of small caves and fissures in the limestone, containing not only human material but also a quantity of animal bone. In most cases the original cave or fissure has been worn away, and all that is left are the cemented remains of the filling. This consolidated filling or breccia, as well as the limestone, has been quarried for lime for many years, and when blasted open the fossil bones were discovered.

Broom's richest site, discovered in 1936, was at Sterkfontein, which he investigated until his death when work was continued by his colleague J. T. Robinson. The importance of Sterkfontein was the finding of a complete adult skull as well as some fragments, plus an almost girdle suggests that they were capable of swinging through the trees, though this was clearly not their normal method of progression but rather a trait retained from an earlier stage of development. The head is small and the skull lacks the strong ridges for muscle attachment which are so characteristic of the gorilla but not so marked in the chimpanzee. The vault is well rounded and much fuller than in the anthropoids. The face is markedly concave with the lower part protruding. The teeth are of considerable interest. The three sites between them have produced teeth from both juveniles and adults, in which tooth patterns are clear and evidence of surface wear and size gives some idea of diet. It seems that these creatures were not exclusively vegetarian, but had a mixed diet of fruit, vegetables and meat.

To sum up, if one considers the total collection of bone available from these sites, general characteristics indicate the human rather than the ape. If the Australopithecines are intermediate between the two there is a clear bias towards the human side. Anything we may deduce as to their social structure and general life pattern must be left

An artist's reconstruction of Australopithecus in a typical African setting. Note the short stature and long arms.

until we have considered the other hominid groups which are more or less contemporary with the Australopithecines. The three sites of Taungs, Sterkfontein and Makapansgat have produced a group of hominids with very uniform characteristics, ranging from juvenile to full adult, though it is not clear whether both sexes of adults were present. Some of the jaws from Sterkfontein and Makapansgat seem too large to belong to the skulls, suggesting that the adult skulls are female. If this is so, then we may expect that the males have skulls which are more robust and with more marked muscle attachments.

The interest engendered by the findings at Sterkfontein and Makapansgat led to investigations of similar limestone quarries. One new site was at Kromdraai, two miles from Sterkfontein, and the other, found by a schoolboy, at Swartkrans in the same area. The original material from these two sites was described by Broom and, after his death, by Robinson. The two sites together have produced skulls (one almost complete), lower jaws and a large number of teeth and, like Sterkfontein, post cranial bones (arm and leg) and part of a pelvis.

If one compares the almost complete skull from Swartkrans with that from Sterkfontein, the differences are at once apparent. Looking at them from the front and side it would be impossible to confuse the two. One's first impression is of the ruggedness of the Swartkrans skull. This is due to the much heavier brow ridges, the large face with heavy cheekbones and the marked crest along the top of the skull. Another feature visible from the front and side is the apparent shallowness of the vault of the skull. In contrast, the skull from Sterkfontein is high and well rounded, with a considerable amount of frontal bone visible from the front above the brow (with Swartkrans the frontal bone is hardly visible from the front and the brain case has the appearance of being tucked behind the upper part of the face). The differences between Swartkrans and Sterkfontein cannot be explained by differences of sex alone. Clearly we are dealing with two distinct creatures, who are nevertheless nearer to each other than appearances might suggest.

Superficially Swartkrans looks more primitive than Sterkfontein, but this is to some extent an illusion. There is some evidence that Swartkrans' diet consisted largely of tough, fibrous vegetable matter which required a great deal of chewing, and this has not only led to the increased size of the teeth, but has also altered the whole setting of the face. An increase in jaw size in turn requires larger muscles to operate it, and gives rise to a need for the crest at the top of the skull for muscle attachment. This has produced a creature whose appearance is largely governed by habit and diet rather than purely evolutionary factors. Swartkrans' teeth, in spite of their size, are as human as Sterkfontein's; the limb bones and pelvis indicate a similar erect posture, but also show that Swartkrans was taller and more robust, and furthermore had a larger brain – about 600 cubic centimeters. This increased brain size may be

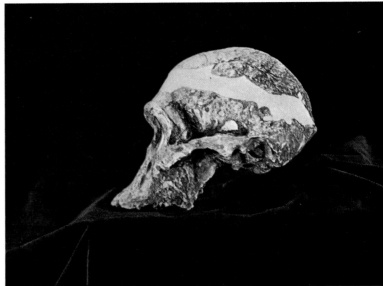

Side views of the skulls from Swartkrans (left) and Sterkfontein, showing the difference in skull shape and facial proportions.

due more to an increase in body bulk than to mental superiority.

Broom gave a different name to this larger group, calling Swartkrans Paranthropus crassidens, and Kromdraai Paranthropus robustus, thus separating them at generic level from the Australopithecus group from Taungs, Sterkfontein and Makapansgat. Human anatomists do not now consider that there is sufficient difference between the two groups to justify so wide a separation, and it is generally agreed that they should all be put into the same genus, Australopithecus, and only separated on the specific level, the lighter form as Australopithecus africanus and the heavier as robustus.

Towards the early hominids. Up to a few years ago the Australopithecus material seemed to fit the intermediate position of a "missing link," had such a creature been acceptable to evolutionists. It was closer to anthropoid forms than any other skull yet found which could be put onto the human branch of the family tree, and it seemed reasonable to see these southern African creatures as the immediate predecessors of the undoubtedly early hominids from China and Java, dated to approximately 5 to 600,000 years.

Unfortunately, neither the deposits in which the southern African material was found nor the associated fauna allowed a very precise date. It was conceded that the africanus material was probably earlier than robustus, but the original dates assigned to both groups were not earlier than Early Middle Pleistocene. This dating of the Australopithecus material posed a problem: if these creatures were to be considered as the form from which the later China and Java hominids developed, then the Lower Middle Pleistocene date seemed too close to that of the

Homo erectus material which they were supposed to have developed into, since this would make the African material and that from the Far East almost contemporary, which seemed impossible in view of the differences between the two groups. This problem could be resolved in one of two ways: either the Australopithecus was a great deal earlier than originally suggested, or the Australopithecus from south Africa was not in fact the immediate ancestor of Homo erectus but the end of a line which had a common ancestor with Homo erectus at a much earlier date.

Up to 1959 it was possible to see the evolution of man in terms of a broad pattern: a divergence of the Hominid/Anthropoid, possibly as early as the Miocene, and the development of modern man through a series of stages – Australopithecus (if old enough), Homo erectus, Homo neanderthalensis, Homo sapiens. Even before 1959 this would have been an oversimplification, but if not very accurate in detail, it gave a general picture which made some sense. So much new material has come to light in the past few years and is still pouring in, that the picture has become, to say the least, somewhat confusing. This new material can only be seen in perspective if we examine the position at the point just before 1959, when the East African material began to appear.

Up to the early 1950s a broad evolutionary picture was generally accepted, with some reservations. Existing material suggested that there were four stages of human evolution – four chapters with a prologue or introduction. The first chapter covered the Australopithecine group, which we have discussed above in detail. The position of their immediate predecessors and their general relationship to the Anthropoids (the prologue of the narrative) was still obscure. The differences between the Australopithecines and the Anthropoids were sufficient to suggest that a considerable amount of time must have elapsed between the Australopithecines and their common ancestor, with the Anthropoids forming the "missing link." None of the material dating from before the Pleistocene seemed entirely suitable for this role, and creatures such as Pliopithecus, Dryopithecus and the related Proconsul from Kenya appeared to have already established themselves on the Anthropoid line rather than the human. Even Ramapithecus was generally put in with the Dryopithecus, at least until 1934 when his change of status was suggested though not generally accepted.

Our understanding of the successors to Australopithecus seemed somewhat clearer. The group forming the second chapter had been known since 1891, when Eugène Dubois found their first representative in the Trinil beds in Java. The initial find consisted of a complete skull cap and a thighbone, the latter found 15 meters upstream but in the same horizon. The Trinil beds are the center of three well-defined deposits in Java, the lowest being the Djetis and the highest the Ngandong. The fauna of the lower beds includes a primitive ox and a saber-toothed cat; from the Trinil beds came an early elephant of the Stegodon type, rhinoceros, deer and antelope; and from the latest deposit, the Ngandong, came axis deer, rhinoceros and a local form of hippopotamus, as well as possible stone artifacts.

The island of Java was to prove a rich area for fossil hominids, and by 1959 further specimens had been found: a skull cap from a tributary of the Solo river from the same Trinil deposit but about 40 miles west of the original site, part of an upper jaw from the same area and the skull of an infant. These last came from the earlier Djetis deposits.

Dubois, borrowing the name Pithecanthropus or apeman from the German biologist Ernst Haeckel, who in 1889 had postulated such an ancestral creature, called his Java find Pithecanthropus erectus implying, largely on the evidence of the thighbone, that he walked upright.

In 1921 the first of a remarkable series of human remains was found in the cave of Choukoutien, 25 miles southwest of Peking. There are a number of caves in this area, but the one which concerns us here, Locality I, is a high cave in a limestone cliff whose roof has collapsed onto the fill of red clay and fallen blocks cemented into hard breccia. Peking man, as he has become, had a somewhat odd introduction to the scientific world. The first indication of hominids from Choukoutien was the finding of two molar teeth by Anderson in a rich fossiliferous deposit. In 1927 Davidson Black, on the basis of the finding of a third molar, created a new genus of fossil man – Sinanthropus pekinensis. This apparently rash action was justified later when more human material was found in the cave. By 1965 fourteen skulls, eleven jaws and a number of isolated teeth had been found. The creation of a separate genus for Peking man again underlines the early tendency to create a special name for each new find. It has recently been shown that the finds from Choukoutien and Java are sufficiently closely related to be grouped under one generic label. It is also generally agreed not only that the two groups should

Excavating in "Dragon Bone" Hill, Choukoutien, the site which produced the remains of Peking Man.

be classified under one heading, but also that their overall characteristics are such that they should be included in the same genus as man. For this reason both Java and Peking man are classified under the name Homo erectus.

In 1964 Chinese archaeologists found further material at Lantian in Shensu province. This consisted of a skull cap in rather poor condition and part of a lower jaw. The relative age of these finds and those from Peking and Java is not very clear, but it has been suggested that since the Lantian skull seems a little more primitive than Peking it is slightly earlier, and may be the same age as the early skulls from the Djetis beds of Java.

There has been some controversy regarding the age of this group. Certainly the Java material belongs to two distinct horizons – the earlier Djetis beds and the later Trinil. Some authorities have placed both beds in the early part of the Middle Pleistocene, others put the Djetis beds at the end of the Villafranchian. Originally the Peking material was considered, on the basis of the fauna, as being roughly contemporary with the Mindel glaciation of Europe, with a possible date of about 500,000 years. Recently a potassium–argon date of 710,000 years has been obtained from the Trinil beds, slightly above the zone which produced the human material. As the Djetis beds are known to be earlier, it seems possible that at least some of the Homo erectus material may date back to nearly 1,000,000.

Taking the East Asian material as a whole, it is possible to get some idea of the appearance of this group, though the kind of bone material found with the Australopithecines, such as limb and pelvic bones, is in short supply. The length of the thighbone indicates an individual about 5ft 4in to 5ft 6in tall, capable of standing fully upright and walking as we do. The thighbone shows signs of disease, with a malformation near the upper end, possibly the result of an injury. This bone is so much more like modern man than the skull parts, that it was for a long time suggested

Full face view of Peking Man, the Homo erectus from Choukoutien (reconstructed), showing the more upright forehead and more human face than those of Australopithecus from South Africa. The original finds of 1921 were lost during World War II.

that the two did not belong to the same group, but fluorine tests have shown that they are of the same age.

Although none of the skulls are complete, there are enough pieces to allow for a reasonable reconstruction. Comparing the reconstructed Peking female skull with that from Sterkfontein, two things are immediately apparent: first, the Peking face is much shorter and its relation to the skull is much closer to the modern human form; second, the skull is much fuller, with the brain correspondingly larger, averaging about 950 cubic centimeters.

The brow ridges are still heavy like Australopithecus robustus, and although there is no longer a crest along the top of the skull, there is still a slight ridge which can be seen when viewing the skull from the front. The teeth are large and the jaw very massive by modern standards. Making a superficial comparison with the Australopithecus material, it is clear that the Homo erectus group is much closer to our concept of a near ancestor. The brain size, although generally small, does overlap in the upper range into the modern range, although the average is below it. Claims for developed speech centers have been made, based on the development of specific areas of the brain, but while these centers are sufficiently developed it is not possible to assess their range of speech with any accuracy.

It is from the content of the caves in the case of Peking Man that we can get an idea of Homo erectus' potential. First, the use of fire is well attested. Ash from fires extends a long way through the section at Choukoutien, indicating not only that the occupation was over a very long period (though probably not continuous), but also that the use of fire was a common practice. How this was learned and for what purpose is, of course, unknown. Second, bones of large animals such as rhinoceros and deer suggest that these people were reasonably efficient at hunting large game. Also found throughout the Choukoutien deposits are recognizable stone tools.

For many years Homo erectus seemed to be confined to the Far East, since only material from Java and China was available. This meant that the Australopithecus and Homo erectus were separated by a considerable distance, making the argument that one was derived from the other difficult to sustain. Leaving aside the material from Europe, the range of Homo erectus was greatly extended by the finding of representatives of this genus in Africa, including areas in which the Australopithecus material had been found. In 1954 and 1955 the French paleontologist Arambourg found three jaws, one almost complete, in a deposit at Ternifine in Algeria. The site also produced stone tools and a great deal of animal remains, giving a fairly accurate date to the deposits.

In 1960 Louis Leakey found at the top of Bed II at Olduvai in Tanzania an almost complete skull cap, lacking only the face. The stratigraphical position of this specimen seems fairly clear, though it had eroded out of a section and was reconstructed from a large number of small

pieces. Although not in direct association, stone tools similar in general concept to those from Ternifine were also found with animal bones, clearly of the same age as the skull.

The third African specimen came from one of the Australopithecus sites in South Africa. In addition to the material representing Australopithecus robustus from Swartkrans, there was a different creature represented by a lower jaw with two teeth in place, part of another jaw and some isolated teeth. Broom and Robinson separated this material from the Australopithecus, giving it the name Telanthropus capensis. Leakey wisely refrained from giving a scientific name to his skull, and it has been referred to as Chellian man, named after the stone industry associated with it. Arambourg created the name Atlanthropus mauritanicus for his Ternifine material. This naming of the two groups suggested that here were two hominids sufficiently different to warrant two different generic names.

Taking the two together it soon became clear that not only were they very close to each other, they also fell within the range of the Homo erectus material from the Far East, eg Java and China.

While it was not possible to relate Homo erectus material directly to the earlier material from South Africa, ie Australopithecus robustus and Australopithecus africanus, nevertheless these could be seen as two possible successive stages in human development. The geographical problems seemed to have been solved with regard to Homo erectus, but there was still the problem of the apparently restricted range of the Australopithecine.

Between 1939 and 1953 von Koenigswald, the Dutch paleontologist, found fragments of jaws in the Djetis beds in Java. Von Koenigswald named them Meganthropus palaeojavanicus and claimed that they represented a form ancestral to Homo erectus. Robinson, Broom's collaborator in South Africa, compared them with Australopithecus robustus, and later Philip Tobias, also from South Africa, suggested that they should be compared to another South African hominid contemporary with the Australopithecine which will be discussed later.

It would thus seem that within the subtropical belt of the Old World, both Australopithecus and his successor (though not necessarily his descendant) Homo erectus were moving freely from one end of the zone to the other.

In 1959 the Leakeys found the first hominid in Olduvai, a site whose richness in fossil hominids was to throw the Australopithecus/Homo erectus relationship once more into the melting pot.

The finds from Olduvai were the first of a series of post-war discoveries in Africa, which not only greatly increased the number of fossil hominids uncovered, but also pushed the human timescale back to an extent which would have

An artist's reconstruction of Peking Man and his family in the cave of Choukoutien.

been undreamed of before World War II. Prior to the finding of the Olduvai material there were a number of unsolved questions regarding the pattern of human evolution. The relationship of Homo erectus to the Australopithecine could not be established and no intermediate forms were known, and although a succession from one to the other seemed possible on anatomical grounds, it could not be proved. A further problem was that the original dates given to the Australopithecine were too close to Homo erectus to allow for the necessary evolutionary change to have taken place. Further, the background to the Australopithecine was extremely obscure. A number of fossils such as the Dryopithecus and Proconsul were clearly older, but their position on the anthropoid-hominid stem was not clear.

Basically, Olduvai can be divided into two parts: Bed I and the lower part of Bed II (the earliest deposits), and the upper part of Bed II together with Beds III and IV. The Leakeys had been working at Olduvai since the early 1930s, and in 1959 found a fossil hominid in Bed I on what was clearly a living floor, with broken bones and a simple industry of stone tools. This hominid, known colloquially as Zinj or Nutcracker man, was given the scientific name of Zinjanthropus boisei by Leakey, the generic name coming from the word Zinj (an early name for part of East Africa), and the specific name from one of Leakey's backers.

When the pieces of Zinj were fitted together they made up an almost complete skull with most of the face and the teeth intact. Two features were immediately apparent – the strongly marked crest across the top of the skull (as in Australopithecus) and extremely large molar and premolar teeth (hence the name "Nutcracker").

Zinj's closest parallels are with the South African Australopithecines, particularly Australopithecus robustus from Swartkrans. Although Leakey's generic name suggested that Zinj was markedly different from the South African material, he is now generally considered a variant of the Australopithecine. Thus three species are now recognized: Australopithecus africanus, Australopithecus robustus and Australopithecus boisei.

As Zinj was found associated with a living floor with unmistakable stone tools and broken animal bones, it was at first assumed that this occupational debris resulted from his activities. This implied toolmaking at a much earlier period and by a much more primitive hominid than Peking man.

The composition of some of the Bed I deposit made it possible to obtain potassium–argon dates of the order of 1.75 million years, far older than would have been considered likely before World War II, and implied that at least some of the Australopithecines are much older than was originally supposed.

The finding of another hominid, also in Bed I but at a slightly lower level than Zinj, led to a different interpretation of the place of the Australopithecine in

Below: the reassembled skull of "Zinj" (Zinjanthropus), from Olduvai Gorge, Africa, with a suggestion of what the missing jaw might have looked like.

Above: the Zinj skull is uncovered.

Below: an artist's reconstruction of "Zinj."

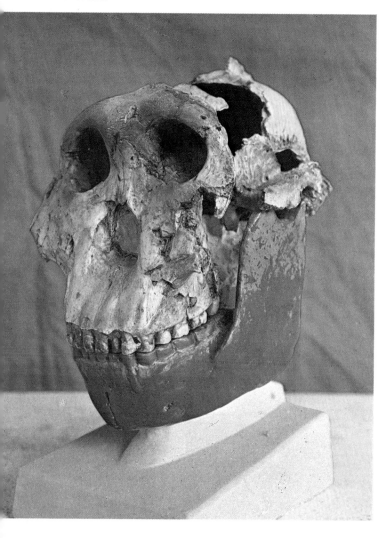

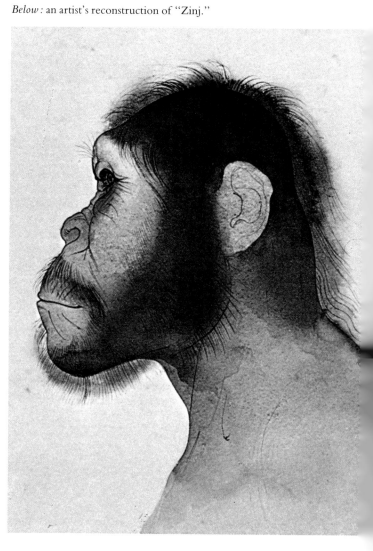

human evolution. The new find consisted of part of a child's skull and the broken lower jaw with nearly all the teeth present. There were also limb bones, including an almost complete foot. Some of these post-cranial bones belonged to an adult. This creature was named Homo habilis by Leakey, and appeared to be slightly more advanced than the three groups of Australopithecines, with a brain capacity of about 600–650 cubic centimeters.

It was to Homo habilis that Leakey gave the credit for the stone tools found throughout Bed I and the lower part of Bed II, and by so doing he relegated Zinj to the position of one of the game animals hunted by Habilis. The placing of this new fossil in the Genus Homo depended on the claim for toolmaking, since the ability to make tools for future use is one of the criteria for separating man from the anthropoids. Leakey further claimed that Homo habilis was in the direct line to Homo erectus, and that the Australopithecenes, though roughly contemporary, were in fact a side branch of the human stem. If this is correct, then Homo habilis would have developed through the lower part of Bed II into Homo erectus or Chellian man in the upper part of Bed II about one million years ago. It has even been suggested that one of the Homo habilis

A view of the Omo river, Ethiopia, where many remains of fossil men have recently been found.

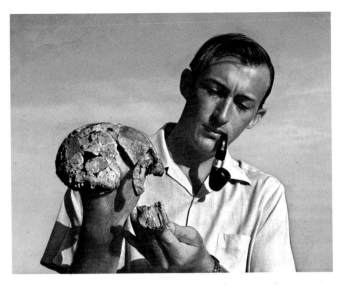

Richard Leakey with skull "1470," a recent find from Lake Rudolf, Kenya. He holds the lower part of the face in his left hand.

individuals from the middle of Bed II is in fact intermediate between the two, and it has also been suggested that Telanthropus from Swartkrans is a proto-Homo erectus.

The finds made over the last few years in Northern Kenya and Ethiopia have not only further modified the evolutionary picture, but also pushed dates back further still.

Richard Leakey, Louis Leakey's son, found further hominid remains near Lake Baringo and later Lake Rudolf, both in Kenya. The Americans and French found similar material on the Omo river, which runs from Ethiopia into the northern end of Rudolf, with dates comparable to those of Leakey's finds

The principal outcome of this recent research has been the finding of male and female Australopithecines, resembling A. boisei from Lake Rudolf, nearly a million years older than the Zinj remains from Bed I at Olduvai. Remains of Australopithecines have also come from Lake Baringo and Omo, not in sufficient quantity to determine the species, but indicating a similar age of about 2.5 million years.

The most spectacular find from this region was that of an almost complete skull from Lake Rudolf. It was found by Richard Leakey in old lake deposits dating back to about 2.6 million years. The surprising thing about this find is the apparent development of the skull. The vault is high and well rounded, with an estimated capacity of 800 cubic centimeters – far greater than the three Australopithecines and even Homo habilis. Richard Leakey very wisely refrained from naming this specimen, and it remains "1470," its field registration number.

The finding of 1470 raises the question of the status of Homo habilis. Louis Leakey had always seen his Homo habilis as being separate from the Australopithecine and, unlike them, in the direct human line leading towards Homo erectus. Clearly the finding of 1470 makes this

The shore of Lake Rudolf, scene of many of Richard Leakey's recent finds. The River Omo, on whose banks American and French archaeologists have made other discoveries, runs into the northern end of the lake.

conclusion very unlikely, since 1470 itself is far more likely to be the ancestor of Homo erectus. Leakey maintained that the human line of ascent was already established as far back as the Pliocene with Kenyapithecus, passing via Homo habilis to Homo erectus, the three species of Australopithecus being side lines which became extinct by the end of the deposition of Bed II at Olduvai.

Recently it has been suggested that Homo habilis is in fact a member of the Australopithecus group, and that 1470 belongs to the human line. This implies that human ancestors are recognizable as far back as 2.6 million years – a date which would have astonished early workers in the field of human evolution. Yet even this astonishingly early date has now been superseded. In December 1974 Mary Leakey discovered jaws and teeth of 11 individuals at Laetolil, about 25 miles south of Olduvai, and these have been firmly dated at between 3.35 and 3.75 million years.

Homo Neanderthalensis. To make the pattern of human evolution a little clearer we will bypass for the moment the immediate successors of Homo erectus and consider the third major group – the Neanderthals.

This group contains by far the largest number of individuals ranging from the very young to the elderly. The reason for the preservation of so many is largely cultural: the Neanderthals had taken to living in caves and rock shelters, and also buried their dead, frequently in the floors of their homes. Burial protected the remains from natural forces and from scavengers, who must have deprived Human paleontologists of many a valuable specimen. This group has a further claim to fame in that they were the first to be considered as ancestors of man.

If we take a rather wide interpretation of the term Neanderthal, their range is considerable, embracing Europe, the Middle East, the Far East and the African continent. Throughout there are considerable variations, though whether these are differences of degree, race or evolution is a matter of some controversy.

The type specimen which gave its name to the group was found in 1856 in the Neanderthal Valley in Germany. This was not the first skull to be found – that honor belongs to the Gibraltar skull found during blasting on the north face at Gibraltar. It was far more complete than that from Neanderthal, but was not described until 1868, thus losing its place as a type fossil.

The original Neanderthal skull, which consisted of the skull cap only without the face, was low in the vault and with a strongly developed brow ridge. If the first skull to

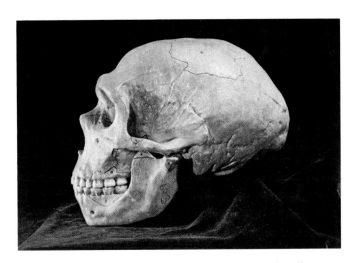

A cast of the reconstructed Neanderthal skull from La Chapelle aux Saints, southwest France. An example of the typical rugged western form of the Neanderthal race.

be recognized as ancestral to man had been a more complete specimen, much early speculation might have taken a different course.

Since 1848 remains of nearly 60 individuals have been found in Europe alone, many of which had been deliberately buried. The best known came from Le Moustier, La Chapelle aux Saints, La Quina and a group of burials from La Ferrassie, all in southwest France. Several early finds came from Spy in Belgium, and there are examples from nearly every European country, but so far none from Britain. The age range of these individuals is considerable, from the elderly at La Chapelle aux Saints, to

Below: the skull of the Neanderthal boy found in Teshik Tash, Uzbekistan, Russia.
Right: a Russian reconstruction of the Teshik Tash child.

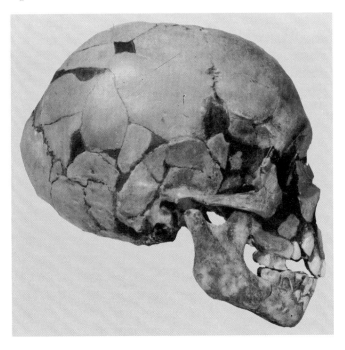

the children aged about 6 to 8 from La Quina in France and another site in Gibraltar, and the slightly older child from Teshik Tash in Russian Uzbekistan. As well as skulls, the burial sites have between them provided all the bones of the skeleton so that it is possible to get an even better idea of the Neanderthals than of the earlier groups.

The adult skulls are large, with a brain capacity as high as 1,600 cubic centimeters, a figure towards the upper end of the modern range. The females, as one would expect from their slighter build, generally have a smaller brain capacity. No known Neanderthal brain is smaller than the human range, though the majority come within the lower end of the scale.

Evidence provided by the long bones indicates that the Neanderthals were generally short, not much over five feet, and thickset with heavy bones. The thigh bone is slightly bowed and the spine lacks the multiple curves of modern man. These two characteristics, together with the slightly forward position of the aperture at the base of the skull where the upper bones of the vertebrae articulate, suggest a distinctly stooped posture, with the head thrust forward. Complete hand and foot bones have also been found. The hand is modern in type with a rather short thumb, but both hand and wrist are fully mobile and certainly had a precision as well as a power grip. The foot bones of a woman from La Ferrassie suggest that she was rather flat-footed and tended to walk on the outer edge of the sole. Prints have been preserved in the clay of some

cave floors, showing a short, broad foot lacking much evidence of a well-developed arch.

If one looks at the skulls of the western Neanderthals several features are immediately apparent. The skull is long and low vaulted, and at the back the occipital bone appears to come to a point, owing to the angle made by the upper and lower planes of the bone. Above the eye-sockets are strongly developed brow ridges forming a continuous bar, a feature which we have already seen in some of the earlier hominids, such as Homo erectus. As this brow ridge suggests, the teeth are large, and the chewing muscles must have been well developed. A very characteristic feature of the western group is the absence of a chin.

The above description covers what have been called the Classic Neanderthals – a very consistent group in western Europe. The bulk of this population lived during the first two stages of the Last or Würm Glaciation, from about 70,000 to 40,000 years ago.

Between the Neanderthals of the Last Glaciation and Homo erectus there is a considerable gap – over 600,000 years if one takes the date of 700,000 for the Java Homo erectus. In Europe human fossils have been found which go some way towards filling this gap.

In 1908, in the Mauer Sands in Germany, the jaw of what is now known as Heidelberg Man was found. Its chronological position, established on geological and faunal grounds, is between the Gunz and Mindel Glaciations, within the timerange of the later Homo

Cast of the jaw from the Mauer Sands, Heidelberg, Germany – a possible example of Homo erectus from Europe.

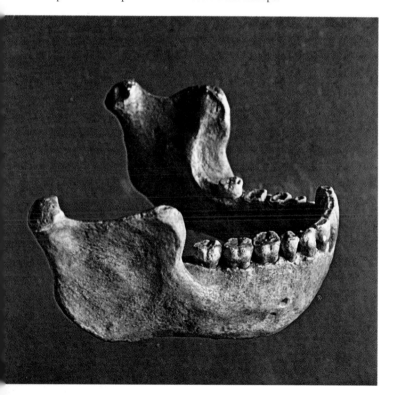

erectus material from Java and China. No trace of artifacts was found with the jaw, and no other human remains. It is practically complete, large and stoutly made with all the teeth present, though some are broken. The size of the jaw and the development of the teeth clearly indicate an adult. From comparison with the Homo erectus material it seems that the Heidelberg jaw has some similarities to Homo erectus, but also some traits suggesting the later Neanderthals.

A recent find in Hungary of a human occipital bone, roughly the same age as the Heidelberg jaw, suggests another comparison with Homo erectus. This find from Vertesszöllös near Budapest came from a living floor associated with an industry of pebble tools similar to the material from the upper part of Bed II at Olduvai, though the greater part of the Vertesszöllös material consists of much smaller tools. Unfortunately one cannot make any useful comparisons on the basis of an occipital bone alone, but it shows a skull fuller and more rounded than those of the typical Homo erectus. Like the jaw from Mauer, it appears to be an intermediate form, as one would expect in view of its age.

Moving on some 150,000 to 200,000 years, to the Interglacial between the Mindel and Riss Glaciations, we are slightly better served with fossil remains, though one of them is tantalizingly incomplete. The first comes from Swanscombe in Kent on the Thames estuary. The site consists of sands and gravels belonging to the 100-foot terrace of the river, which at that time flowed into the high sea level of an Interglacial.

The skull had apparently been washed into the river from a campsite on its bank and the major bones had parted at the sutures and were scattered. The first piece to be found, the occipital, came to light during commercial digging of the gravel in 1935 and was recognized by a keen amateur archaeologist. Nearly a year later a parietal bone was found by the same observer and in 1955, under controlled excavation conditions, the second parietal came to light. The three pieces fit together and form the back and sides of a skull with the frontal bone or forehead missing. In addition to the skull, the deposit produced much fauna and a hand ax industry, the latter of a later type than that found with the Homo erectus at Ternifine in north Africa.

If an evolutionary advance from Homo erectus were claimed for the Heidelberg and Vertesszöllös material, then further advances could be expected from a skull of a considerably later date. This is indeed the case, but before discussing Swanscombe in detail we will deal with the second find of the same age, which includes most of the parts missing from the Swanscombe skull. This second skull came from Steinheim in Germany and although it was not associated with any industry, the related geology and fauna equate it in time with the skull from Swanscombe. Apart from severe crushing of the left side, the skull is almost complete and includes the frontal bone and face, the parts missing in the Swanscombe specimen. Like

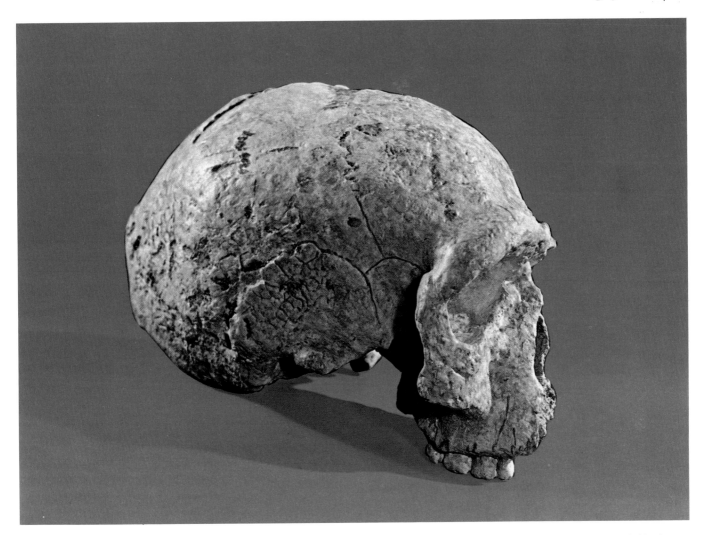

Below: the three separate pieces of the Swanscombe skull from Kent, England, fitted together.

Above: cast of the Steinheim skull from Germany, of probably the same age as the Swanscombe skull, showing what the missing Swanscombe face :nay have looked like.

Swanscombe, the Steinheim skull is that of a young adult, possibly a woman, with a brain capacity variously estimated as from 1,070 to 1,175 cubic centimeters (Swanscombe being estimated at about 1,325 cubic centimeters).

On the basis of the very rounded back of the Swanscombe skull, some anatomists have considered that it is nearer modern man than the succeeding Neanderthals, thus implying an early Homo sapiens already on a different branch from the Neanderthal stock and completely independent of them. If one takes the Swanscombe and the more complete Steinheim together, they qualify better as an early and unspecialized form from which both Neanderthal and modern man could have originated.

Two other hominids have been found in Europe, one possibly and one definitely from the next Interglacial, the Riss-Würm (ie somewhere between 150,000 and 70,000). The first, a jaw, was found in the cave of Montmaurin in southwest France. Unfortunately it was not found under ideal conditions, having come from a fissure. There is

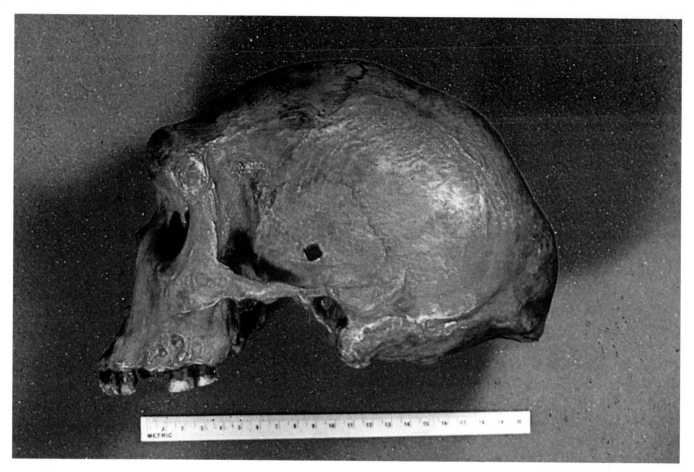

some doubt as to whether it belongs to the Riss-Würm or the preceding Interglacial, making it contemporary with Swanscombe and Steinheim. It has been suggested by some that this jaw fits the Steinheim skull, while others consider it as being predominantly Neanderthal in type, as one would expect if it belonged to the Last Interglacial.

The second hominid came from the site of Fontéche-vade in the department of Charente, western France. It was found under much better conditions, and its age is not in doubt. The cave contained several archaeological levels and the skull came from the lowest. This deposit was laid down under temperate weather conditions, immediately followed by cold – the early stages of the Last Glaciation. Associated with these cold conditions was the stone industry which has been found in conjunction with all the Neanderthal remains in France, North Africa and the Middle East. Two individuals are represented at Fontéche-vade, one of which consists only of a small fragment. The main find comprises both parietal bones and part of the frontal bone of the skull. There is no evidence of brow ridges, which would appear to separate it from the Neanderthals. The apparently modern appearance of the skull has led anatomists who classed the Swanscombe and Steinheim skulls as Praesapiens to include the Fontéche-vade material under the same heading, but there is not enough material available either to put this specimen into a Praesapiens group or to classify it as a pre-Neanderthal.

Above: the Rhodesian skull from the site at Broken Hill, Zambia, showing a strong resemblance to the classical Neanderthals from Europe. *Right:* the "old man" of Cro-Magnon. An early example of modern man from the cave of Cro-Magnon in southwest France. The depression in the forehead is the result of disease.

The Neanderthals are usually discussed in terms of European material. Due to extensive excavations over the last hundred years and an abundance of caves, Europe has produced more specimens than other parts of the world, but there is a great deal of very significant material from other areas.

In North Africa a number of finds comparable with the Neanderthals have been made, and there are also finds which fit into the gap between the Homo erectus of Ternifine and the typical Neanderthals. Two jaw fragments have come from sites in Morocco – one near Casablanca and the other at Rabat. While the exact dating of these jaws is not certain, it would appear that they are roughly contemporary with the third European glaciation, Riss. A third jaw from Temara, near Rabat, is possibly slightly later. All three seem to be nearer in type to the Homo erectus material from Ternifine than to the Neanderthals. Both Casablanca and Temara were associated with hand axes, but of a later type than those from Ternifine.

Moving to the Middle East, two groups of Neander-

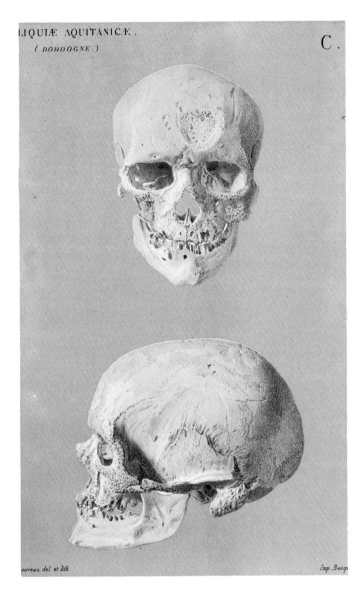

RELIQUIÆ AQUITANICÆ.
(DORDOGNE.)

C.

ouveau del. et lith.

Imp.Becq

from Tabun indicate that the Mount Carmel group is contemporary with finds from Europe, though it has been suggested that the less specialized type from Skhul are slightly later, perhaps 10,000 years. Examples of the Tabun type have been found in other sites in Israel, such as the Galilee skull and those from the cave of Kafseh, also in the Mount Carmel range.

Further east seven skeletons have been found in the cave of Shanidar in northern Iraq, associated with an industry similar to that of Tabun and Skhul, and closer to the former. Some of the individuals appear to have died as the result of a roof fall, but there is also evidence for burials. The top of the layer from which these skeletons came has been dated to about 50,000 years.

Several theories have been put forward to account for the modern appearance of the skulls from Skhul. It has been suggested that they represent an evolutionary position between Neanderthal and modern man, that they are hybrids of Neanderthal with a true Homo sapiens already in existence, and that they represent a variation within the range of Middle East Neanderthals.

In addition to the early intermediate forms already referred to, North Africa has produced a number of hominids which clearly belong to the typical Neanderthals and, like those from Europe and the Middle East, appear to be associated with a similar industry and to be of roughly the same age.

Moving across to the Far East the evidence for a Neanderthal population is more scanty. There is a typical example of a Neanderthal child carefully buried in a cave at Teshik Tash in Russian Uzbekistan. Further east the gap between Homo erectus and modern man contains only one group of hominids – Solo man from Java. This group is represented by eleven skull caps and two tibias. The skull bones are thick, with marked brow ridges and a rather low vault. The brain capacity is put at about 1,000 cubic centimeters, which is within the range of 915–1,225 calculated for Peking Man, the latest of the Homo erectus group. In spite of his apparently small brain, Solo man seems to be a distinct advance on Peking man. The skull is more rounded and the vault higher than in earlier specimens. The dating of this Java material is very uncertain. The Ngandong beds from which the skulls came are the latest of the Javanese Pleistocene sequence, and contained fauna not completely free from extinct forms. Various estimates of age have been put forward for these beds, ranging from 250,000 (roughly contemporary with Swanscombe and Steinheim) to 150,000 (equivalent to the Riss-Würm Interglacial in Europe). Some anatomists have considered Solo a late form of Homo erectus, others an early form of local Neanderthal. Whatever his true position may be, he certainly seems nearer in type to the latter group than the former.

Africa south of the Sahara (a desert of comparatively recent date) has produced two groups of individuals, some with Neanderthal affinities and some early forms of Homo

thals have been found. During the early 1930s three caves were excavated by a joint British and American expedition in a valley in the Mount Carmel range near Haifa. These three caves, Tabun, Skhul and el Wad, were very close together and between them provided a long archaeological sequence.

From Tabun and Skhul, the earlier in the archaeological sequence, came a large quantity of human material – in the case of Skhul some clearly from burials. The fossil human material from both caves was associated with the same stone tools – an industry very similar to that associated with the Neanderthals in Europe and North Africa. However, the people from the two sites were different in appearance. The skull from Tabun is very close in form to the classic Neanderthals of Europe, but those found in the adjacent cave of Skhul have the Neanderthal features much less marked, and a skull much more rounded. This rounding is also present to a lesser degree in the skull from Tabun, and it is clear that both these populations are less specialized than those of western Europe. Carbon 14 dates

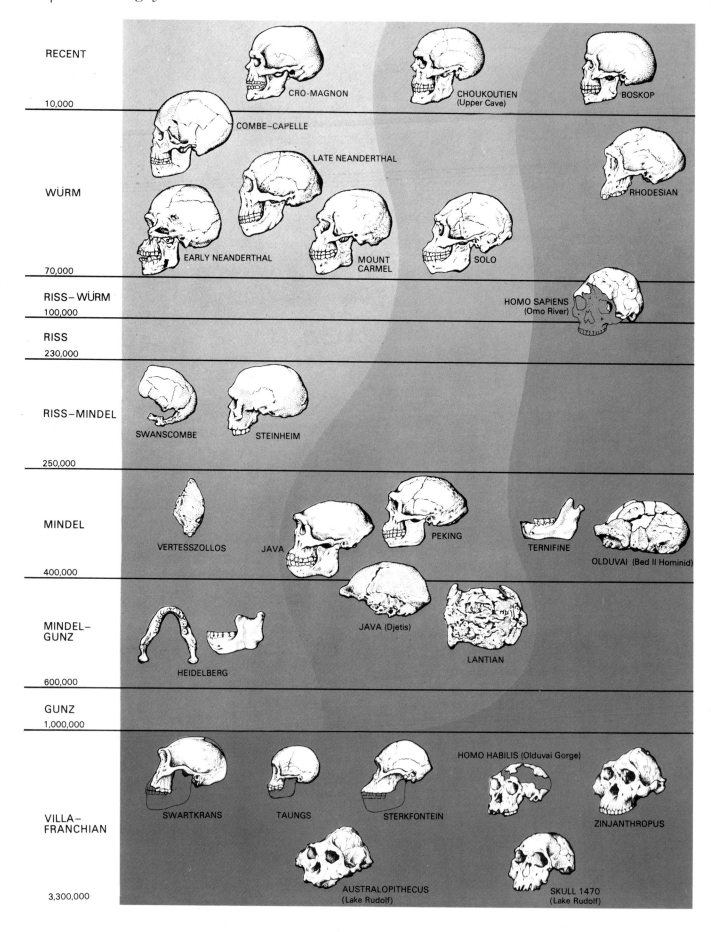

RECENT

10,000

CRO-MAGNON

CHOUKOUTIEN
(Upper Cave)

BOSKOP

WÜRM

COMBE-CAPELLE

LATE NEANDERTHAL

EARLY NEANDERTHAL

MOUNT
CARMEL

SOLO

RHODESIAN

70,000

RISS—WÜRM

100,000

HOMO SAPIENS
(Omo River)

RISS

230,000

RISS—MINDEL

SWANSCOMBE

STEINHEIM

250,000

MINDEL

VERTESSZOLLOS

JAVA

PEKING

TERNIFINE

OLDUVAI (Bed II Hominid)

400,000

MINDEL—
GUNZ

HEIDELBERG

JAVA (Djetis)

LANTIAN

600,000

GUNZ

1,000,000

VILLA—
FRANCHIAN

SWARTKRANS

TAUNGS

STERKFONTEIN

HOMO HABILIS (Olduvai Gorge)

ZINJANTHROPUS

AUSTRALOPITHECUS
(Lake Rudolf)

SKULL 1470
(Lake Rudolf)

3,300,000

A chart showing the chronological position of the later hominids in relation to the glacial and interglacial periods in Europe. Colored bands show, from left to right, Europe, Asia and Africa.

sapiens. One of the most complete skulls ever found in the Neanderthal range came from Broken Hill in Zambia. Generally known as Rhodesian man, it is extremely well preserved, though part of the underside is missing. In addition there are pieces of another skull and several postcranial bones. The latter are fully modern in type and suggest a tall, stoutly built individual, probably taller than the typical Neanderthals further north. The skull is well rounded with an estimated capacity of 1,280 cubic centimeters. The brow ridges are strongly developed, and in this respect Rhodesian man resembles the typical Neanderthals. The Broken Hill finds came from a cave containing a stone industry and fauna. Unfortunately the whole deposit has been quarried away, but chemical analysis has shown that both the human bones and the animal remains belong to the same level.

From further south in Cape Province near Saldanha Bay came parts of a skull associated with stone artifacts. The skull, known as Saldanha, was reconstructed from some 27 pieces, comprising the greater part of a skull cap. In some respects this skull resembles that from Broken Hill, but the anatomical evidence suggests that it is slightly more primitive, though the difference in time is probably not very great. So far no date has been published from the South African site, but a site in Zambia with a similar industry has been given a date of about 58,000 BC. This would put Saldanha in the middle of the Neanderthal range in Europe and the Middle East, and an estimated date for Rhodesian Man of about 45,000 years would seem reasonable. In respect of the limb bones of Rhodesian Man, his likeness to modern Man is more apparent than that of the Northern Neanderthals, and he seems slightly more advanced than his cousins elsewhere.

Homo sapiens. The last of the typical Neanderthals seem to have disappeared about 40,000 years ago, at the beginning of the Würm II/III interstadial. In French sites they appear to have been abruptly replaced by a population indistinguishable from ourselves, the original Homo sapiens. But where did this superior being come from?

The earliest trace of Modern man in Europe (that is to say, man with no discernible Neanderthal traits) is about 35,000 years old. Homo sapiens has been found near the Omo river in Ethiopia, dating from about this time, and examples have come from South Africa and the Far East as well as Europe.

If we retain the old idea of a succession from Homo erectus via Homo neanderthalensis to Homo sapiens, then clearly Homo sapiens is too close in time to have

developed from the latest Neanderthals, even allowing a faster rate of evolution for Modern man.

If one accepts the existence of a group of Praesapiens to which Swanscombe, Steinheim and Fontéchevade belong, this implies a development of Homo sapiens independent of the Neanderthal stage. This idea is further developed in the family tree shown here which, as far as the Europeans and Africans are concerned, bypasses even Homo erectus, a concept which would have gone some way towards mollifying many outraged Victorians.

If, however, one returns to the original concept of Homo erectus – Neanderthal – Homo sapiens, it only required a slight change of ideas to make the picture more logical. Modern taxonomists have questioned the practice of placing Neanderthal and Homo sapiens in separate species, let alone separate genera, as the early paleontologists had done. If one considers the groups included under the name Neanderthal, a wide range of types is apparent – from the extreme form, like that from western Europe, to the so-called progressives of eastern Europe and the Middle East whose similarities to Modern man are too close to have much taxonomic significance.

When we talk of Neanderthal dying out, do we not mean rather that the traits which distinguish him, being functional rather than evolutionary, were bred out since they no longer served a useful purpose?

This idea of the unity of Neanderthal and Modern man has now been underlined by the inclusion of both under the name Homo sapiens, differentiated only at subspecific level. The name Homo sapiens sapiens is used for all modern races, and the others are referred to as Homo sapiens followed by their general name – neanderthal, rhodesian, solo, etc. Modern taxonomists would also include both Swanscombe Man and Steinheim as Homo sapiens, and thus we, as Homo sapiens sapiens, are not as spontaneous as might be supposed, but were already extant as far back as the Second Interglacial, about 250,000 years ago.

The origins of today's pattern of racial dissimilarities are so far completely unknown. Far too few early hominids have been found in far too few localities to show any significant racial differences. There are, however, suggestions that some racial pattern was extant during the Upper Pleistocene, at the time of the emergence of Homo sapiens sapiens. The Upper Pleistocene skull from the Upper Cave at Choukoutien suggests a possible proto-Mongoloid, the Wadjak skull (also Upper Pleistocene) from Java has been likened to the original inhabitants of Australia, and from South Africa there appear to be early forms of Bushman dating from the same period. The early Homo sapiens sapiens in Europe in the Pleistocene are clearly European, with representatives extending to North Africa. It is impossible to go further than this until more areas have been explored.

Swanscombe: a Prehistoric Site in England

Since 1880 Swanscombe, the richest paleolithic site in Britain, has been the source of many finds of prehistoric implements as well as the three pieces of the Swanscombe skull. The gravels form part of the 100 ft terrace of the Thames, and have been dug for almost 100 years. They are divided into two levels representing different periods. The upper part contains hand axes associated with the Swanscombe skull and the lower deposits have produced a flake industry. The hand ax levels have been extensively excavated, particularly in the years 1955–1960. The lower deposits have been largely neglected, but in 1968–1972 excavations produced a considerable number of flake tools and bones of animals such as elephant, rhinoceros, bear and deer.

Above: the prehistoric site at Swanscombe, which is now preserved as an ancient monument. This picture shows the site much as it was left by the gravel-diggers. To the left is the top of the Lower Loam with the Lower Gravels below. To the right is the area from which the human skull fragments were excavated. There are now no more skull gravels remaining on the site, and the upper part of the deposits has been built over.

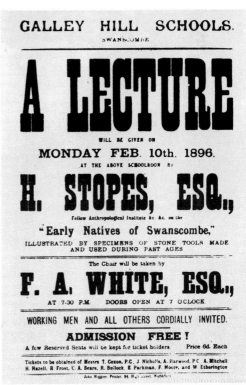

Two of the three pieces of the Swanscombe skull, found in the Middle Gravels. On the right is the occipital bone found by G. Marston in 1935 and on the left the parietal found in 1936. The other parietal was discovered in 1955. The three pieces, spread over an area of about 20 sq yd, fit together and clearly belong to the same individual. The skull had obviously been swept into the river and parted at the seams. Tools in the form of well made hand axes were found in the same deposit. The three pieces of the skull are shown fitted together on p. 61. The Steinheim skull from Germany, shown on the same page, includes most of the parts missing from Swanscombe.

Notice of a lecture given at Galley Hill Schools, Swanscombe, by the anthropologist H. Stopes in 1896, nearly 40 years before the skull was found. Stopes collected material from Swanscombe over the years, buying specimens from the gravel-diggers, which he left to the National Museum of Wales in Cardiff. Such collections are now of little value, as the exact findspot of each specimen is not known.

Left top: a group of flint hand axes from the same deposit as the skull. These tools are characteristic of the upper part of the deposit and were made and used by Swanscombe man. This type, predominantly pointed, was replaced by oval forms at the top of the gravels.

Left center: general view of the recent excavations. Underneath the trees in the background is the site where the skull pieces were found, about 10 ft above the present level of the pits. The huts stand on the surface of the fine, biscuit-colored Lower Loam which, together with the underlying gravel, forms the earliest deposit on the site. The white cover rests on the surface of the Lower Gravel and is protecting bones exposed on the living floor between loam and gravel. The loam itself contained tools and bones found in the positions in which they were left over 250,000 years ago, but those found in the gravel were washed in and therefore not in their original positions.

Below: Barnfield Pit, Swanscombe, 1937. Looking south, this view shows the pit at the time of the finding of the first two skull fragments. The sand and gravel, largely used for building, have been removed over a wide area by this time, as the pits were first dug in the middle of the last century. In the right-hand corner behind the survey pole is the excavation carried out by the Royal Anthropological Institute, following Marston's discovery of the first two skull pieces. Of particular interest is the steam excavator in the right background, filling the trucks. By this time the pits were no longer being dug by hand, with the result that many implements and bones were missed and destroyed in the crushing plants.

Above: an unusual excavation method – cleaning the surface of the Lower Loam by vacuum cleaner operated by a generator. Parts of this surface contained animal footprints filled with sand and pebbles from the overlying Middle Gravels. This proved to be the most satisfactory method for the final cleaning of the footprints.

Right: a view of the complete section through the Lower Loam and Lower Gravels. The rod is divided into 20 cm units. To its left, resting on a gravel pedestal, is part of an elephant skull belonging to the living floor between loam and gravels.

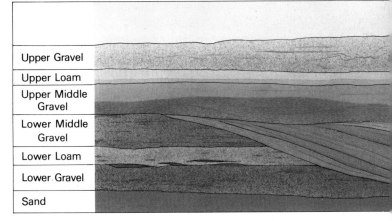

Above: drawing of the deposits exposed at Barnfield Pit. Lower Gravel and Lower Loam form the first cycle of deposition and contain a stone industry of flakes and choppers. The second cycle comprises the Lower and Upper Middle Gravels, containing hand axes and the remains of Swanscombe man. The Upper Gravels were laid down during Glacial conditions.

Above left: surface of the Lower Loams, showing animal footprints being cleaned by a vacuum cleaner fitted with a watering-can nozzle (right), then sprayed with hardener.

Left: taking photographs from above – in this case animal footprints on the surface of the Lower Loam. The hydraulic platform is in fact designed for cleaning street lamps.

Above: a freshwater shell from the junction of the Lower Loam and Lower Gravels. Shells and animal bones give a very good indication of local conditions at the time they were laid down. This particular specimen has a further interest in that its two halves are still attached by the delicate membrane, showing that it has never moved. Flint flakes which fit together demonstrate the same principle.

Below: part of the prehistoric rubbish dump at the junction of the Lower Loam and the Lower Gravels. The various bones and flints are tagged – numbers being used for the flints and letters for the bones. Findspots are recorded by photographs such as this and by a drawing of the whole area, using a squared frame for accuracy. In the center of this picture is a bear's skull (M), part of an antler attached to the skull (O), a piece of shed antler (H) and the top of an ox thighbone (P). This collection suggests rubbish thrown out from the camping area.

Above: cleaning the skull and antlers of a fallow deer found in the middle of the Lower Loam. Both are intact and were probably from an animal butchered on the site. The rest of the carcass would have been taken elsewhere to be eaten. Though complete, the bone and antler are in a very fragile condition. After cleaning, mostly with the aid of dental picks and paintbrushes, they are hardened by the application of special chemicals dripped into the cracks. Next the whole block containing the specimen is hardened in the same way and lifted out in one piece for extraction in the laboratory. Sometimes the specimen is covered in foil and cocooned in expanded polystyrene for protection in transport.

Right: four large flint flakes forming a group. Flints are comparatively scarce in the Lower Loams, but those which have been found are in mint condition. In the case of these four and two similar scatters of smaller flakes many fit together. The very small flake (G) became detached when flake (D) was struck off the core. These flakes represent the remains of a flint-knapping session. The knapper required only the core, and went away taking the core with him and leaving the flakes on the ground.

Above right: the four large flakes fitted together, joining at the corners. The flakes enclose a cavity representing the core from which they were struck. By making a cast of this cavity it was possible to recover the shape of the core. It is interesting to note that although the Clactonian industry is characterized by the production of large flakes, these four specimens were abandoned in favor of the core, from which smaller flakes only could have been produced.

Above: the prehistoric fallow deer was larger than its modern equivalent shown here and frequently had an extra branch of antler. As a source of food the males would have been at their best in the autumn, fat from summer grazing and with their coats in perfect condition. Although deer seem to have been the main source of meat at Swanscombe, the rubbish areas contain remains of elephant, rhinoceros, ox, pig and bear. We do not know how these animals were hunted, but in view of the fact that the site was in the vicinity of a river and the Lower Loam marshy in parts, it seems most likely that the bigger animals were driven into soft ground.

Above left: the skull and antlers of a full-grown fallow deer. So far no deer skulls have been found without antlers, which indicates that the hunters pursued the full-grown males and ignored the females and young. The presence of these skulls with antlers attached gives some idea of the time of year the site was occupied. Fallow deer shed their antlers in the spring, and the new set is not fully grown before the following September. It is therefore reasonable to assume that the site was occupied during the winter months. The inhabitants collected specimens such as these as well as shed antlers. It is not clear why they did so as they do not appear to have made any use of them.

Left: the hoofprint of a fallow deer from the Lower Loam. This is an isolated print, suggesting that the animal was walking on basically dry ground where there was a soft patch. The loam was compact enough for the whole block to be lifted out and hardened.

Right: A prehistoric hand ax made of chert, from the Kharga Oasis in Egypt.

VERNON REGIONAL JUNIOR COLLEGE LIBRARY

4. The Beginnings of Culture

We will probably never be able to fix the exact moment when man became a toolmaker. The transition from using ad hoc tools for an immediate need to making tools in anticipation of a future need is too gradual for this. Further, it is probable that tools were used for a considerable time before they became identifiable as such. It is only when they become stereotyped that they can be attributed with any confidence to human agency.

Tools natural and man-made. The simple techniques used by early man for making stone tools can be, and frequently are, achieved by nature. Many natural forces are capable of detaching flakes from blocks of stone, and once detached their edges are easily chipped, often giving to what is a purely natural object many of the characteristics of man-made tools.

By the end of the 19th century the river gravels and cave deposits of Europe had provided prehistorians with ample evidence for toolmaking – in the case of the river gravels, clearly going back to the beginning of the Pleistocene. If the rather sophisticated tools from these river gravels were dated to the early part of the Pleistocene then it was reasonable to argue that man's earlier efforts must have taken place in the previous geological period. This started the search for Tertiary Man – a controversial issue which divided prehistorians into two fiercely antagonistic camps.

This question needs to be discussed in two parts: first, was it possible in terms of human evolution for man to have reached a toolmaking stage at this period; second, did the "tools" produced in support of the idea of Tertiary Man fulfill the criteria required for their acceptance as artifacts?

There was no clear answer to the first part of the question. The Java skulls dated to the Second Glaciation were clearly Pleistocene, and this left only one possible contender – a skull which had no clear date – Piltdown Man. We have already dealt with Piltdown's place in the history of archaeology and, bearing in mind that so much

of the controversy revolved around the stone tools, we will confine our attention to these.

The first group of tools claimed to date from the Pliocene were the Eoliths or Dawn stones. They came from a number of sites, particularly in Britain and France, and were discovered in deposits which, in geological terms, were not securely dated. The best known series, the Kentish Eoliths, were from plateau gravels around Maidstone in Kent and had been collected over a number of years by a local resident, Benjamin Harrison. There were other British collectors apart from Harrison, and some French.

The deposits which produced these Eoliths were generally considered as being Pliocene, and this apparently early date was the cause of much of the controversy since many prehistorians were not prepared to accept that man could have been a toolmaker so early. As a considerable part of what was then classed as late Pliocene is now classed as Early Pleistocene, and man-made tools have been accepted for dates as old as 2.5 million years, this objection is no longer valid. The other aspect of the controversy revolved around whether the "implements" produced in support of Tertiary Man were in fact of human origin.

Nature has been making pseudo-tools since before the advent of mammals let alone man, and there are many cases where it is extremely difficult to distinguish the man-made from the natural. When dealing with very early material a number of criteria must be considered before accepting specimens as being of human origin:

(i) Does the specimen belong to a repetitive pattern or technique, ie are there a number of similar examples of the same type in the same deposit?

(ii) Are the specimens in any concentration with respect to the rest of the deposit, and are there other objects, such as bones, associated with them in the same restricted area?

(iii) Are the specimens made of a material foreign to the deposit, ie are they made of a rock which does not

Objects once accepted as human implements and now considered to be the result of natural action. *Left to right:* from Kent, England; from early deposits in Suffolk, England; from Kafue Valley, East Africa.

occur naturally in the deposit? (A good example here is the finding of implements in fine water-laid deposits which could only have been brought in by man.)

(iv) If the specimens are all of the same age they will exhibit the same amount of wear and staining or patination, and the patination will tend to be uniform over the specimen.

None of the specimens collected by Harrison and his supporters fulfill all these requirements, and it is interesting to note that the main surfaces of the flakes and those of the scars from the secondary flaking which make them look so plausible show a wide range of patina, as though the flintknapper struck the flake in one geological epoch and completed the tool in another!

The second series of primitive implements came from estuarine and marine deposits in Norfolk and Suffolk underlying the boulder clay of the Mindel or Second Glaciation. These Crag deposits as they are called were originally dated as late Pliocene, but are now classed as Early Pleistocene, except for the earliest which contain no artifacts.

Many of the specimens from below these Crags seem more convincing than the Eoliths from the Kent plateau, and in terms of African dating are well within the range for human toolmaking. So far the criteria laid down have not been completely satisfied and these specimens must remain in doubt until they are found under better conditions.

A number of similar examples have come from various parts of Africa and are called Kafuan, from the gravels of the Kafue river in Uganda. They consist of flat quartz pebbles with one or more flakes removed from one face, either on the side or end. The tool resembles a simple

version of the later pebble tools.

The gravels from which these alleged artifacts came contained a mass of similar quartz pebbles, some with a few flakes removed but the majority unbroken.

The situation of these gravels fails to conform with the third criterion, and it was subsequently observed that similar flaked pebbles were being "produced" in the side gorges of the Zambezi during floods. One observer saw such an "industry" appearing before his eyes!

Olduvai and the pebble tool industries. The earliest artifacts to have universal credit are the Olduvai implements from Olduvai Gorge in Tanzania. The conditions under which they have been found leave no doubt as to their authenticity, and it is probable that the early versions of these implements will remain the first recognizable attempts at toolmaking.

A great deal of this chapter is devoted to Olduvai, owing to the richness of the site and the exceptional conditions under which material has been found. There is a great fascination in seeing primitive man's first steps towards our present way of life – the tiny foundations of our civilization – and few sites can show these early attempts better than Olduvai.

Although it is not the oldest occupation site we know of, Olduvai Gorge has produced more evidence of early

The location of Olduvai Gorge.

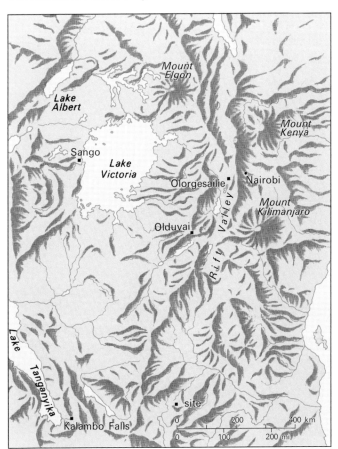

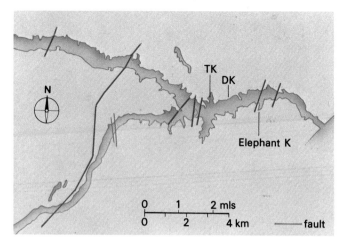

Plan of Olduvai Gorge.

and volcanic dust. There is also a six-mile long side gorge and small side gullies. The filling of the huge depression occupied by the lake gave rise to part of what is now the Serengeti Plain – one of the finest game parks in the world. This wealth of human and archaeological material would have remained concealed for ever had it not been for an accident of nature. Earthquakes tilted the lower end of the Serengeti Plain, altering the drainage pattern, and the erosion of the deep gorge resulted. Erosion continues, exposing new sites annually in addition to the original 60.

The 300-foot depth of the gorge sides has been divided into four major stratigraphical units or beds, the oldest (Bed I) being lowest. Bed I and the lower part of Bed II form one depositional phase and both contain a similar fauna.

In the middle of Bed II there is a major break in the deposition representing a timespan of unknown duration, and above it the fauna changes considerably. The two upper Beds, III and IV, appear to be a continuation of the upper part of Bed II but laid down under slightly different conditions.

man than any other, covering over a million years of human development. It is unique in the number of its living sites, the range of time they date from, their exceptional state of preservation and the unusual circumstances of their discovery.

The main part of the Gorge is over 12 miles long and 300 feet deep with deposits made up of fine lake sediments

View across the Serengeti Plain, Tanzania. Olduvai Gorge, probably the richest prehistoric site in the world, is in the middle of the plain.

Two generations of the Leakey family – Louis, Mary and Philip – excavating in the lower beds at Olduvai Gorge.

As has been mentioned earlier, the lower parts of the section (Bed I and the first part of Bed II) are the deposits from which the original Zinj and Habilis remains came, and the living sites associated with them concern us now. These living areas have been so little disturbed that it is as though a cover has been drawn back and the camps revealed exactly as the inhabitants left them nearly two million years ago.

The occupation sites consist of two main types – living sites and kill or carcass sites. The latter are places where an animal (usually a large one such as an elephant) was dismembered on the spot with the hunters sometimes camping around it until all was eaten or became too putrid even for them. The living sites were generally used for longer periods and were connected with a wider range of activities, so that more artifacts and food debris were left behind.

Like most nomadic hunting groups, the early inhabitants of Olduvai had no need, and probably less inclination, to keep their camps tidy. They were at most only temporary stopping-places to be abandoned at a whim. As a result, the sites give a revealing picture of a way of life and, by their resemblance to camps of modern hunting groups, enable us to feel very close to our early ancestors.

A typical living site is represented by DK at the very base of Bed I. The present area covers about 16 square meters but is not complete owing to the erosion which originally exposed the site. The most important feature of DK, and so far unique at Olduvai, is the foundation of what appears to have been a small circular hut or shelter, the upper part of which was most likely made of branches

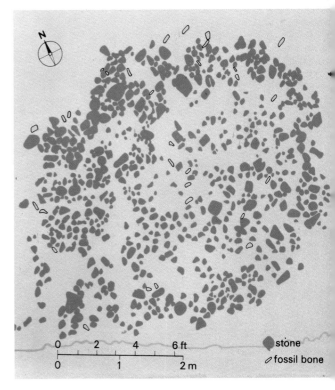

Above: plan of the stone hut from the earliest level at Olduvai Gorge (DK), showing the stone foundations and part of the scatter of stone tools and animal bones. *Left:* a bushman's hut made of branches and grass. In windy weather the base would be secured by large stones in a similar manner to the hut from Olduvai.

and grass. The low stone wall of the foundation has partly collapsed but the outline is clear. This hut is the earliest structure known to date, and surrounding debris indicates that it was the focal point for a variety of activities. In addition to the stones belonging to the hut there were scatterings of similar stones brought in from some distance, which may have belonged to other huts.

Animal bones found among the debris represent Deinotherium (an early form of elephant), various species of antelope (many of them extinct), horse, giraffe, hippopotamus and crocodile. Most of the bones were broken, and the absence of some bones suggests that the animal was dismembered elsewhere – a practice common among modern hunting groups. Many of the bones are broken in such a way as to suggest the extraction of marrow. Others are cut and chipped, implying their use as some kind of implement.

The stone toolkit found at DK consists of simple shapes such as were found in all the sites in Bed I and the lower part of Bed II. The main forms are variants on the pebble chopper, with the working edge either on the end or down one side. The raw material for these implements was quartz or lava, both of which were readily available locally. It is assumed that these small choppers were the main tools used for cutting up game, and the sharp flakes associated with them were either for taking meat off the bone or for cutting bigger pieces into more manageable portions. These flakes would also have been the principal tool for working wood.

There are two good examples of kill sites in other localities – one associated with an elephant and the other with a Deinotherium. The elephant was clearly a youngster, as the ends of the long bones were not completely ossified. The position of the bones shows that the carcass had been dismembered, though the limbs were not widely scattered. The Deinotherium was not dismembered to the same extent as the elephant. An interesting point is that the foot bones were found at a lower level than the rest of the body, suggesting that the animal may have been driven into soft ground before being killed.

Associated with both animals were stone tools. In the case of the elephant these were choppers and rather larger flakes than those generally found on the living sites. Much the same tools were found with the Deinotherium, with the addition of hammer stones suggesting that at least some of the tools were made on the spot.

Throughout Bed I and the lower part of Bed II the living patterns and toolkits remain very uniform, though there are variations in the proportions of tool types from one camp to another. None of the sites have tool forms which are totally absent in others, implying that these tool assemblages represent a broadly similar life-style with much the same resources available.

It was on living floors of this type that both Zinj and Habilis were found, giving rise to controversy over who was responsible for making the tools, who was the feeder

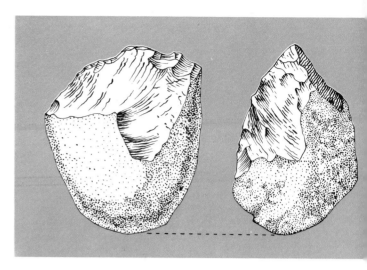

A simple tool made by chipping the end of a lava river pebble. This is the earliest artifact accepted by scholars as man-made.

and who the food. If both belong to the Australopithicene group, as some anatomists have suggested, the artifacts could have belonged to either.

The picture revealed by excavations in the early levels at Olduvai is one of a dozen or so groups, probably small ones, living on the shores of a lake and the small streams running into it. If the game was as plentiful then as it is now in the Serengeti (and there is no reason to think that it was not), their food requirements must have been fairly easy to satisfy. While they clearly had access to meat it is not known if they were hunters or joined the hyenas, jackals and vultures as scavengers. Evidence from the Deinotherium carcass suggests that game was driven into soft ground and either stoned to death or left to die of shock. There were also indications of smaller animals being caught in the same way. Further protein for the hunters' diet was obtained from frogs, snakes, lizards, tortoise, fish and possibly grubs and locusts, and the remainder made up with vegetable foods. While most of their food needs were probably available in a comparatively small area, there is evidence that they wandered as far as eight or ten miles in search of special raw material for some of their tools as some of the rocks found on the sites are not local.

The second time unit at Olduvai, which is represented by the upper part of Bed II and is probably nearly 700,000 years later, shows many typological links with the earlier levels. While there is a general similarity between levels suggesting the continuity of older traditions, there are nevertheless signs of change indicating a possible increase in activities, sufficient to justify the term Developed Olduwan to distinguish this level from the earlier Olduwan.

The occupation sites in the upper part of Bed II follow much the same pattern as those from the earlier horizons, but the major difference between the Olduwan and the Developed Olduwan lies in the tools.

During the occupation of the Developed Olduwan there was some reduction in the size of the lake, probably due to local faulting for which there is plenty of evidence in these upper levels. Owing to the shrinkage of the lake the sites in upper Bed II are adjacent to open grassy plains rather than directly on the shores of the lake, an environment probably very much like the Serengeti today.

It is not clear how much changes in these later industries were due to this change of environment, or whether there was a slight difference in the individuals' activities or even an increase in their standard of living. Although there are no major technical advances in the Developed Olduwan, the industry is more complex with more retouch on the flake tools and a stronger suggestion of specialized tools.

Towards the end of the Developed Olduwan a new tool appears – a simple form of hand ax. This is a core tool, as is the simpler pebble chopper, but the retouch, instead of being confined to the edge or side, is continued all around the edge, the resultant flake scars impinging onto the upper and lower faces. This type of bifacial tool was to have a wide distribution and complicated development during the next evolutionary stage, but apparently independent of these Olduwan examples.

So far, with the exception of an individual of Homo erectus type associated with a separate hand ax industry,

Developed hand axes from the later levels at Olduvai.

no hominids other than Zinj and Habilis have been found in the upper part of Bed II. This suggests that one or other of them was responsible for the Developed Olduwan as well as the earlier Olduwan.

Had Olduvai been the only site available we would have a very restricted view of the timerange of these early creatures, though so far this site has produced by far the most extensive evidence of their culture. The earliest date from the Gorge is 1.75 million, for the basalt at the base of the upper part of Bed I. There is a possible acceptable date of 1.70 million for the upper part of the bed, and probably a fairly short time interval to the top of the lower part of Bed II. We know that both Zinj and Habilis continue over the break in the sequence, so they may well have still been extant about a million years ago or slightly later, when evidence for the emergence of an early form of Homo erectus appears.

Turning to South Africa, where the Australopithecines are particularly abundant, we find that under this general heading there are at least two readily recognizable groups – the light or gracile form represented by Australopithecus africanus and the heavier or robust form, Australopithecus robustus. The relationship between these two groups and their cultural standing is at present unclear. No positive date is available for the South African material, and it has not been proved whether the tools found at one of the sites, Sterkfontein, belong to either group.

The date originally given to the South African Australopithecines was early Middle Pleistocene, but it is now considered that at least some of the material is older, possibly as old as the lower deposits at Olduvai. It is also considered that Australopithecus africanus has an older ancestry than Australopithecus robustus.

The tools from Sterkfontein are, according to Mary Leakey, typical Developed Olduwan with hand axes, an industry identical to that from the upper part of Bed II. Unfortunately the tools and the human remains were not found in direct association.

It was largely the work of the second generation of Leakeys, particularly the second son Richard, that carried the story of man's antiquity many stages further. In addition to this work in Kenya, similar research has been carried out in the Omo river area of Ethiopia.

The age attributed to the toolmaking hominids from Olduvai is startling enough when compared with what was considered acceptable at the beginning of the century. The new work in northern Kenya and Ethiopia has not only greatly increased our knowledge of the duration of man's toolmaking activities, taking typical pebble tools back 2.4 million years, but the finding of 1470 man in particular has thrown the whole subject of the pattern of human development back into the melting pot.

The appearance of 1470 has tended to produce an argument similar to that of Zinj versus Habilis at Olduvai, the morphologically superior creature being credited with the toolmaking. Does the finding of 1470, apparently more advanced than Habilis and clearly earlier, imply that the industry from Bed I belonged to neither Zinj nor Habilis, but to some relative of 1470? This game of evolutionary musical chairs is probably confusing the issue more than it need, and we will most likely find that since the advent of recognizable tools at least 2.4 million years ago, more than one hominid group was producing simple pebble industries.

Early hand ax industries in Africa and Europe. In terms of industrial succession, as far as Africa is concerned, the Olduwan pebble industry is followed by peoples whose toolkit was characterized by the use of hand axes. These tools, generally fairly large and heavy, average six inches in length, ranging from about three inches to the largest specimen known, which is over 14 inches long. They are usually core tools (certainly in the early examples), flaked over both faces and, in their later form, thin in section and very regular in outline. Sometimes the whole edge is carefully retouched, but often this edge retouching is incomplete, one end being left only partly trimmed to facilitate gripping. There is little likelihood of their having been hafted, hence the term hand ax.

The tools may be pear-shaped, ovoid or triangular, and are usually pointed, though some (cleavers) are straight across the end. If one examines a sequence of these tools over their full timerange, it is possible to see

Louis Seymour Bazett Leakey (1903–72) added greatly to the sum of knowledge about the evolution of man through his studies of fossil remains of hominids and other creatures in East Africa. Here he holds a deinotherium tooth in his right hand and a tooth from an early form of elephant in his left hand.

Previous page: an artist's reconstruction showing the men of Lake Rudolf chasing their slightly inferior relations, the Australopithecenes – probably hoping to eat them.

clear developments: not only do preferred shapes alter from one period to the next, but there is a progressive refinement of finish, and in the later stages many of the implements are made on large flakes and are thus not core tools in the strict sense of the term. When one remembers that this tool form persisted for possibly a million years, it seems that man had invented an implement equivalent to the boy scout's knife; it was to prove the all-purpose tool par excellence, suitable for butchering game, grubbing up edible roots and probably many other purposes.

It was a well-made and typical hand ax which a man named Conyers dug up in Gray's Inn Lane in London at the end of the 17th century, and the implements found by John Frere at Hoxne and Boucher de Perthes on the Somme were also hand axes. Though first recognized as tools in Britain, their abundance on the Somme has led to their being named after French sites.

From very early on in the investigation of the Somme terraces, two main stages in the hand ax development were recognized – the earlier called Abbevillian after the town of Abbeville, and the later Acheulian after St Acheul, a suburb of Amiens. The first name has led to some confusion, as the material now known as Abbevillian was originally named Chellian after Chelles-sur-Marne near Paris. A reinvestigation of the gravels at Chelles revealed that they only contained Acheulian tools, and the name

Chellian had to be dropped in favor of Abbevillian, but the original still occurs in older literature.

In addition to the difference of age, the two stages are distinguished by differences in manufacturing technique. The Abbevillian hand axes are made using a stone hammer, which produces thick flakes, and leaves deep scars on the surface of the implement. This means that not only is the overall appearance of the tool very rough, but the working edges are irregular and not very efficient. These hard hammer hand axes are usually thick in section and many are three-sided or trihedral rather than strictly bifacial.

By contrast, the Acheulian hand axes are made with a soft hammer of hard wood, bone or antler. Some of the shock of the blow is absorbed by the hammer so that the flakes removed from the surface are much thinner and the resultant flake scars shallower. This advance in technique results in a much neater finish and edges which are more regular, making the ax more efficient as a cutting and chopping tool.

Though hand axes have played such a dominant part in the prehistory of Europe, particularly in France and Britain, Africa was undoubtedly the place of their origin and the center of their original dispersal. Archaeologically it is not possible to demonstrate the origin of the hand ax industries. It seems clear enough that their genesis was in some form of pebble tool, but so far no sequence has been found which shows the whole process of transition. Theoretically the flaking technique for pebble tools is the same as that for primitive hand axes. It only required the retouch on the pebble tool to be extended around the edge to transform it into a simple hand ax. The encroaching of the flake scars onto the upper and lower surfaces, which makes the hand ax bifacial, is merely a normal development of the process.

Work carried out over many years in Morocco, particularly near Casablanca, suggests a succession from pebble tools to primitive hand axes. In view of this and the evidence from Olduvai, it seems that the early pebble tool industries developed into two separate lines, the Late Developed Olduwan and the early hand ax industries, which met up again in the upper part of Bed II at Olduvai. A similar sequence, though not so well documented, can be seen in the terraces of the Vaal river in South Africa, where the highest terrace has produced Olduwan material, and the chronologically following terrace Abbevillian tools.

In terms of the evolution of early hominids and, by implication, early tools, it has been suggested that both processes took place in the tropical or subtropical zones on either side of the Equator. This is probably true, and it is reasonable to suppose that many areas within this zone were producing early hominids and early tools at much the same time. So far, however, only Africa has produced well-dated early hominids and their tools, suggesting that Africa saw the genesis of toolmaking man. Certainly the evidence accumulated over the last 30 years has not contradicted this view, and it is customary to see Africa as the cradle and center of dispersal of early man.

If the early pebble tool industries are associated with the Australopithecines in the broad sense, then the early hand axes, certainly as far as Africa is concerned, seem to belong to Homo erectus. At Ternifine (or, to give it its old name, Palikao) were found the jaws originally referred to as Atlanthropus mauritanicus but now considered as representing African members of Homo erectus. The deposit from which these jaws came contained several stages of Acheulian, and though it is not clear which was associated with the jaws, it seems likely that the earliest material, which is clearly old Acheulian, belongs to the hominids. Unfortunately the Homo erectus from the upper part of Bed II at Olduvai, Homo 9, was not found directly associated with archaeological material, and as this horizon in other parts of the site has produced both Acheulian and Developed Olduwan, it is not clear which industry belongs to him.

Oddly enough, the Olduwan has a better range of dates than the hand ax industry which succeeds it. This means

An early form of hand ax from Abbeville in France.

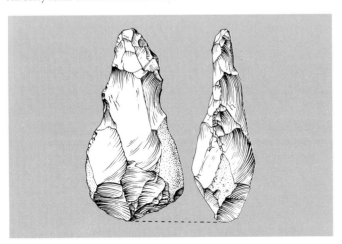

A more sophisticated hand ax from St Acheul, northern France.

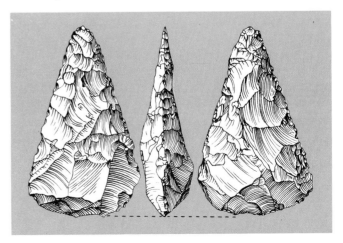

that any dates we give to the beginning of the Abbevillian/Acheulian can only be an estimate. The latest date for the Olduwan of Bed I is 1.7 million years, but we have no dates for the Developed Olduwan of the upper part of Bed II or the contemporary Acheulian. An estimate of 700,000 years for this horizon was based on a very insecure potassium-argon date which, in view of the general probabilities, seems too young. A date of 1,000,000 is more probable for the beginning of *Homo erectus*, though this does not necessarily imply the date for the beginning of the Abbevillian. The date of about 600,000 years for the last of the Far Eastern *Homo erectus* suggests that he may have lasted some 400,000 years.

Late hand ax industries in Africa and Europe.

While the evidence from Ternifine and Olduvai suggests that *Homo erectus* was responsible for the early part of the hand ax industry, he was certainly not the maker of the later stages. In Europe there are much more developed hominids making hand axes, and the latest date of about 58,000 years for the African Acheulian from Kalambo Falls is within the timerange of Neanderthal Man. The skull fragments from Saldanha in South Africa are associated with an industry representing the end of the hand ax industries, and its affinities seem to be with *Homo rhodesiensis*.

The Early Olduwan and Developed Olduwan sites are rare in Africa as are the Abbevillian. Both groups occur in the same areas, namely the deposits at Casablanca and on the Vaal river, the extreme north and south of the continent. On the other hand, the Later Acheulian sites are abundant and frequently very rich, suggesting a possible increase in population.

The conditions which preserved the Olduwan living floors in Beds I and II at Olduvai also preserved the Early Acheulian sites in the upper part of Bed II, though there are only two occupation areas of any size attributed to this industry in this horizon.

At TK, a gully cut into the north side of the main Gorge, five Acheulian occupation horizons have been found in the upper part of Bed II, though only two have produced material in any quantity. Like most of the sites in Olduvai, these living floors were found originally through erosion, so that much of the occupation has probably been lost. Nevertheless, a considerable amount remains.

Two trenches were opened at TK – one about 20 by 25 feet and the other 29 by 15 feet. These trenches were about ten feet apart. The upper level produced 5,180 scattered artifacts. The greater concentration was found on the gully side of the site, suggesting that probably only about half of the original occupation remains. In addition to the artifacts, over 88% of which were waste flakes, there was a scatter of animal bones. This living floor thus closely resembles the sites from Bed I. Both occupations at TK have a mixed fauna and so neither can be considered as a kill site.

Two prehistoric stone balls from Kenya. These may have formed part of a hunting implement similar to the South American *bolas*, where balls wrapped in hide and joined by leather thongs are thrown at a running animal, wrapping themselves round its legs and thereby trapping it.

Pebble tools and hand axes are present in both main living floors and each site has a high percentage of flake tools and utilized flakes. Also found were a number of stone balls which are common in many later African Acheulian industries, particularly those in Bed IV. Various suggestions have been put forward to explain their use. After they were found in groups of three at one east African site, the idea was put forward that they were the components of a *bolas* similar to that used by the Patagonians for hunting. While the majority of the Acheulian examples, being about the size of an orange, would fit this suggestion, many are far too large. Two found in Bed IV weighed 22lb and 56lb. The most likely explanation for these large examples is that they belong to some form of fall trap.

The distribution of the tools and animal bones from TK does not reveal any particular activity areas in either of the main living floors, but this may be in part due to the possible loss of some of the site by erosion.

The two TK sites are particularly rich in light duty tools, made on flakes and showing some deliberate retouching. If one assumes that much of the stone technology was concerned with the processing of animal carcasses, then it seems reasonable to suppose that the heavy duty tools – hand axes, cleavers and large flakes – were made for dismembering, and the light duty tools for detaching meat from the bone. In the latter case, the unmodified flakes are as good as or even better for the purpose than those which have been retouched. What then was the purpose of the wide variety of retouched flakes which are so abundant in many of the Acheulian sites and equally characteristic of the Developed Olduwan and, to a lesser extent, the earlier Olduwan? One clue to the need for this elaborate toolkit is provided by a late Acheulian site in Zambia, southeast of Lake Tanganyika.

Kalambo Falls, a deep gorge associated with a waterfall, has provided an ideal situation for a succession of occupations ranging from the late Acheulian to the Iron Age. In relation to the Acheulian occupation of Olduvai, the Kalambo Falls Acheulian is very late, having a C^{14} date of $57,300 \pm 300$ B.P. (before present).

Although there was no lake associated with the Kalambo river, local ponding produced the same fine sediments as occurred at the lake sites at Olduvai, with a resulting minimum of disturbance to the archaeological material. In addition to the abundant water supply, good raw material for tools occurred locally in the form of quartzite and chert.

Seen as a living floor, there is little difference between Kalambo Falls and other sites of the same type and period. What is unique about this site is the fact that it has remained waterlogged since its first occupation. This extremely unusual situation has led to the preservation of a great deal of organic material, not only plants and fruits but a quantity of wood, some of it worked by man.

These wooden implements consist of what appear to have been clubs, and pointed sticks which could have served a similar purpose as the digging sticks still used by the modern Bushman for digging up roots and opening the burrows of small animals. Also found were sticks with fire-hardened points, which could have made satisfactory spears. There was at least one hearth and a quantity of burned wood, some of which provided material for the carbon 14 determination.

Traces of structures were found in the form of semi-circular groups of stones enclosing an area about six feet in length, the enclosed area being almost free from occupational debris. In addition to this possible shelter, there were two depressions with traces of carbonized grass, which may have been sleeping places.

The presence of worked wood at Kalambo Falls suggests that at least by late Acheulian times this was a

Above: a view of Kalambo Falls, Zambia, at the base of which are prehistoric sites covering a period of nearly 60,000 years.

Left: Kalambo Falls. An archaeologist holds a piece of fossil, probably part of an implement.

much-used raw material, and it is possible that many of the retouched flakes were employed for working it. It was probably the basis of much of the shelter building and the construction of traps and snares.

If one argues that the Acheulian tools were used for butchering and the working of wood, then the presence of retouched flakes in the Olduwan of Bed I suggests that wood was also exploited at this period. It is interesting to speculate whether the early pebble tool industries from Lake Rudolf, dating back to over 2,000,000 years, will be found to have the same possible woodworking equipment.

There are many other Acheulian sites in Africa, though few are completely undisturbed. Those that are show

Two views of a pebble tool from Vertesszöllös in Hungary, showing an implement very similar to those from the earlier deposits at Olduvai.

much the same general pattern but, as one would expect (bearing in mind the long span of time and differences of environment), there are some variations in the composition of the tool assemblages. Some have few hand axes and others have few retouched flakes. These differences can be explained in several ways – differences in seasonal activities, tribal idiosyncracies and, of course, the fact that we are grouping under one cultural heading industries which may well span over half a million years and range over several different human types.

We have given a great deal of space to the early periods in Africa largely because there is so much information available here, principally for the very early stages. This emphasis on one area may well distort the picture, not only of the early toolmakers but also of the general distribution of early man.

Until quite recently there were no industries from Europe which could be dated much earlier than the Middle Pleistocene. There are hand ax industries of Abbevillian type from the Upper Terrace of the Somme and possibly also from the gravels of the River Garonne. The fauna associated with the Somme hand axes dates them probably to the first Interglacial, between the Gunz and Mindel Glaciations, and the height of the terrace in which they were found has been attributed to the high sea level of over 60 meters belonging to this Interglacial.

This chronological position implied that France and possibly Britain were not occupied much before about 700,000 BC, and as no earlier material had come from any part of Europe it suggested that the toolmaking groups of the tropical belt did not begin to expand northwards until after at least 1,500,000 years of development in Africa. Up to 1958 there was no archaeological evidence to refute this opinion unless one was prepared to accept the Harrisonian Eoliths as confirming the existence of early Pleistocene man in Europe.

In 1958 the cave of Vallonet was discovered and was excavated over the next three years. The cave is on the French Mediterranean coast near Cap Martin. The lower deposits are of marine origin laid down during a sea level about 100 meters higher than today. Resting on these are interglacial deposits with a rich fauna of Etruscan Rhinoceros, Southern Elephant and early forms of horse and wild ox. This fauna is typical of Late Villafranchian or Early Pleistocene. Associated with it are pebble tools and flakes. Unfortunately the stone tools are very few in number, but there is nothing to show any major differences between them and their African equivalents.

As well as producing the remains of a possible Homo erectus, the site of Vertesszöllös in Hungary had a rich stone industry of pebble tools and flakes which are typologically very close to those from Africa. An unusual feature of this Hungarian material is the small size of the pebble choppers, which can be held between finger and thumb. The date of Vertesszöllös, based on the fauna, is inter-Mindel or early Middle Pleistocene.

Pebble tools have been recognized in other sites in Europe – in the Balkans, on raised beaches in Portugal and in southwestern France as well as on the highest terrace of the Somme, but so far all this material has been found in a derived condition.

These finds of pebble tool industries suggest that the occupation of Europe had already begun at least as early as the late Villafranchian, and if the Abbevillian hand axes from the Somme are the same age as the tools from Vertesszöllös (as geological and paleontological evidence suggests) there were already two stone tool traditions present by the middle of the second or Mindel Glaciation (about 600,000–500,000).

As far as hominids referable to these early cultures are concerned, Europe has so far produced only two contenders – the occipital bone from Vertesszöllös associated with the pebble tools and the almost complete jaw from the Mauer Sands in Germany, so far with no industrial connection. Though both of these have been compared with the Homo erectus material from Asia and Africa, their exact taxonomic position is still not very clear.

By the second or Mindel/Riss Interglacial, the hand ax industries are abundantly represented in Europe. The axes are now well finished and display a greater variety of shape than in any other period of their development. In the European sites there is more emphasis on flake tools, particularly well-made scrapers, and the straight-edged cleavers made on large flakes (so characteristic of the African Middle Acheulian) are rare, being confined almost solely to Spanish sites.

In northern France and southeast Britain the Acheulian sites are abundant and rich, though few are in situ in the strict sense. Both interglacial fauna and well-made hand axes have come from the 30-meter terrace of the Somme which ran into the Mindel/Riss Interglacial high sea level. Also belonging to this period are numerous sites in the 100-foot terrace of the Thames, particularly Swanscombe in north Kent and the famous site of John Frere at Hoxne in Suffolk.

As in the earlier period, two apparently distinct industrial traditions were present in Europe at this time – the hand axes of the Middle Acheulian already referred to and a second complex based on pebble choppers made on the end of flint nodules and a flake element which, though showing signs of deliberate retouching, is difficult to classify owing to a lack of consistent forms.

The relationship between the hand ax industries and the Clactonian (as the flake industry is called) is far from clear. Both at Swanscombe and on the 30-meter terrace of the Somme the Clactonian precedes the Acheulian at the beginning of the period. The Acheulian occurs towards the end, and the two are separated by an unknown interval.

The simplest explanation for these two groups is that this is merely the continuation of the situation pertaining during the previous Interglacial and the preceding Glaciation, the Mindel. Another suggestion put forward is that the Clactonian is a seasonal variation of the Acheulian, involving activities which did not require hand axes. On balance, the two-tradition theory is to be preferred, as nowhere have the two industries been found interdigitated in a deposit as one would expect if they were basically the same complex.

In spite of the existence of the rich site of Swanscombe and the type site at Clacton-on-Sea, not much is known about the Clactonian. The only sites of any size are in Britain and northern France. Elsewhere in Europe comparable material has been found, but not in good stratigraphical contexts.

The information we have from Swanscombe and Clacton shows that not only were the Clactonians living in very similar environmental conditions to the Acheulians, but they were apparently getting meat from the same animals – elephant, rhinoceros and deer. It is difficult therefore to see why there is so marked a difference between the two toolkits, unless we accept the idea that although the requirements for living were much the same, the traditional approach to problems differed.

So far we have only two hominids dated to the Mindel/Riss Interglacial: the Swanscombe skull without the frontal parts and the more complete skull from Steinheim. There is no doubt that the Swanscombe skull belongs to the Middle Acheulian industry of the Middle Gravels as they have been found in direct association. The archaeological connection of Steinheim is not so clear, though there is a claim for at least one hand ax from the same horizon as the skull. This lack of human material

Chopping tools and flake from the lower cycle at Swanscombe, Kent.

Hand axes from Swanscombe.

means that there is nothing which can be attributed to the Clactonian industry; but it is possible that when such an individual is found he will lie morphologically between a form of Homo erectus and Swanscombe man. How close he would be to either extreme depends on the length of the time gap between the lower part of Swanscombe containing the Clactonian and the later gravels where Swanscombe man was found. The evidence from the hand ax site at Ternifine with its African Homo erectus, and the occipital from the pebble tool industry at Vertesszöllös suggest that some form of Homo erectus was responsible for both traditions at the beginning of the Early Middle Pleistocene. The association of some of these hominids with pebble tool industries is also found in the Far East.

While no precise date is available for either the Clactonian or Acheulian at Swanscombe, an estimate of between 200,000 and 250,000 years for the latter seems reasonable, thus separating the Homo erectus from Ternifine and Swanscombe man by between 600,000 and 700,000 years, sufficient for a considerable amount of evolutionary change.

The European hand axes continue through to the end of the third Interglacial, the Riss/Würm, and the tradition also comes to an end in Africa at about the same time or perhaps a little later. A Late Acheulian from Kalambo Falls is dated to about 60,000 BC, corresponding with the end of the Last Interglacial and the beginning of the Würm Glaciation.

The majority of hand ax sites in Europe are no longer in their original position, but the few that are reveal that sites are very similar in Africa and Europe, and thus patterns of living must have been much the same in both areas. There are, of course, slight differences visible in the toolkits. The African straight-edged cleaver made on a large flake is rare in Europe, and though the Europeans had a similar tool it is made not on a flake but as a straight-edged hand ax. Many of the European sites have a higher percentage of well-made side scrapers, designed for some activity which was less important in Africa, possibly the processing of skins for which such tools are ideally suited.

Of the very limited number of sites found undisturbed, only a few have been excavated sufficiently to give any real idea of the extent of the occupation and the activities of the inhabitants.

A recently excavated site at Terra Amata near Nice has provided occupation evidence similar to that from some of the African sites. At Terra Amata there was clear evidence of huts apparently made of stakes bent over to form a roof, the ridge supported by posts and the base of the stakes supported by heavy stones. Within the area of the hut was a hearth and at least three working areas with large stones, presumably used as seats (though there are some areas clear of debris which suggest that the worker was sitting at least part of the time on the ground). This description covers several huts, all roughly oval in shape, and ranging from 26 by 49 to 13 by 20 feet in area. An unusually personal note is the finding of a human footprint. In some cases (for example in Genista) pollen traces indicate that the sites were occupied in spring or early summer. The archaeological material from Terra Amata is a rather rough Acheulian, possibly a little earlier than that from Swanscombe.

Two butchering sites have recently been excavated in central Spain. One, Torralba, has been known for many years but not extensively excavated, though it has provided several hand axes. The economy of both sites was based mainly on elephant. The animals seem to have been driven into marshy ground to be killed, and the carcasses dismembered on the spot. An interesting technique seen at the second site, Ambrona, is the use of the tusks of larger males as levers to turn the heavy bodies.

Looking at the various hand ax stages in Africa and Europe one is struck by the strong similarity in development in the two continents. Changes in shape and finish are almost synchronous, these strong resemblances having little to do with the wide variety of raw materials employed. It was suggested long ago that the similarity is due to the fact that during cold conditions in Europe the hand ax makers retired to Africa, and reappeared in Europe when conditions improved in the next interglacial, but there is no archaeological proof for this theory. We do know however that the inhabitants of Vertesszöllös were in Europe during the interstadial of the Mindel Glaciation, and that several of the French caves were occupied during most of the stages of the Riss Glaciation. Certainly the inhabitants of Vertesszöllös had fire and those of Terra Amata both fire and shelter. Another possible explanation for the similarities between these hand axes is that variations of shape and increased refinement are merely due to logical development.

Tools in the Middle East, India and the Far East. Still considering Africa as the center of dispersal of the early

Above: cast of a human prehistoric footprint from Terra Amata, southern France.

Above right: suggested reconstruction of an Acheulian hut from Terra Amata.

toolmakers we have so far only examined the north–south axis, from Africa to western Europe, largely because so much information is available in these areas. There is, however, a second line of dispersal, the west–east, through the Middle East to India and the Far East.

The areas to the east of the African continent have produced not only a mass of valuable fossil hominids, as we have already seen, but also a great deal of archaeological information. As one would expect over so vast an area, our knowledge is patchy; owing to difficult terrain and political instability much of the region is still virtually unexplored.

The countries immediately to the east (Israel, Jordan, Lebanon and Syria) have, in spite of much disturbance over the last twenty years, provided a wealth of material from open sites and caves in the limestone, which is the base of much of this region.

The occupation of this area by toolmakers appears to have begun about the same time as that of Europe as far as present evidence goes. The earliest site so far known is Ubeidyieh near Lake Hula in Israel. The finds (which are not in their original position) are very similar to the Developed Olduwan and have similarly been dated to the early Middle Pleistocene. During early excavations part of a skull was found which, it was claimed, belonged to the stone industry, but it has since been considered as intrusive from a much later deposit.

In addition to this late pebble tool industry from Ubeidyieh there are very primitive hand axes from other sites in the Middle East which, on typological grounds, appear to correspond to the Abbevillian of Africa and Europe. It seems probable that all stages of the Acheulian are represented, but it is not yet possible to date them very accurately as correlations between the Middle East and Africa and Europe are not yet based on very secure evidence.

One Acheulian site, also near Lake Hula, has hand axes and typical African cleavers made from rather coarse basalt, and there is a very rich Middle Acheulian settlement at Latamne in Syria. Comparable in time to the Last Interglacial in Europe, there are late Acheulian industries in the base of the sequence in caves near Mount Carmel and around Bethlehem, and similar material from fossil

Acheulian hand axes made of basalt, from Israel.

beaches, particularly in the Lebanon, belonging to the Last Interglacial.

Further east there is clear evidence of Acheulian industries in Turkey, Iraq and Iran, though not much systematic work has been carried out in these countries.

Moving still further east to India and the Far East, the archaeological evidence becomes very patchy. Limited surveys have been made but much of the material, particularly from India, has been collected from the surface or found on river terraces.

The evidence at present available has led prehistorians to divide India and the Far East into two distinct cultural zones – the greater part of India (rich in hand axes obviously derived from the Middle East) and the Far East, Burma, Malaya, China and the islands (represented by industries based on pebble choppers and without any trace of typical hand axes). Our present knowledge suggests that this concept still holds good in general terms, though the lines of geographical division are gradually becoming blurred.

Taking the pebble industries first, there seem to be strong similarities between the Far East and Africa, at least in concept. As one would expect some local differences are due to what raw material was available but, even allowing for this, many of the chopping tools could equally well have come from either Asia or Africa.

The deposits at Choukoutien give a fair example of the pattern of these pebble industries. There are several deposits under the general name Choukoutien. Locality I is the best known, since this site produced the fossil remains representing Peking Man. The stone industry associated with this variant of Homo erectus consists of choppers made either on the end or the side of pebbles, some flaked from one side and others from both. With

these choppers are flakes mostly made of quartzite, often much larger than the by-products of the pebble tool manufacture and very much larger than the flakes from pebble tool industries in Africa. Many of these flakes are detached by what is known as the bipolar technique, resting one end of the core on a large stone anvil and hitting the other, thus producing a flake which, having two points of impact, has two bulbs of percussion. Many of the flakes show retouching though, like the Clactonian of Britain, they are difficult to classify into formal tool classes. (Similar material, though in very small quantities, came from the deposits of Lantien Man.)

Industries of the same general type, known as Anyathian, have been found in terraces on the Irrawaddy River in Burma. The bulk of the tools are made on fossil wood which, though mostly silica, is somewhat intractable, with cleavage planes giving the industry a very distinctive appearance. A pebble tool industry very like that of Choukoutien was found at Kota Tampan in Malaya, and there is further material from Java, though not directly associated with Java Man.

So far none of these tool complexes can be dated earlier than the beginning of the Middle Pleistocene. The deposits of Choukoutien Locality I with Peking Man appear to be roughly the same age as the Homo erectus material from Africa and the industry from Vertesszöllös and slightly later than the pebble tools from Vallonet, though an earlier date must be allowed for Lantien and the lower deposits of Java.

The greater part of the Indian subcontinent belongs to the hand ax zone. It is not clear at what period these hand axes entered India, but they certainly flourished, producing some of the most beautiful implements outside the flint areas of Europe. As yet, nothing has been published discussing work on an undisturbed occupation site, so that we have no information as to whether the activities of the Indian Acheulian were much the same as those from Africa and Europe, though there is no reason to think that there were any major differences.

Parts of West Pakistan appear to belong to the pebble tool province, and a simple industry based on these tools has been found in the vicinity of the Soan river. Attempts have been made to relate the Himalayan glacial phases to those of Europe. Although such correlations are not very secure, it seems probable that the pebble tools from India are no earlier than those from China, ie early Middle Pleistocene.

The pattern of physical and cultural development which has emerged from research over the last thirty years is unusual. Man was originally recognized as a toolmaker only at the Homo erectus stage, Peking being the earliest hominid to have had a recognizable industry, and Australopithecus not being credited with this attribute. Thus toolmaking appeared to be no older than about 700,000 years, beginning at the start of the Mindel Glaciation or just before. It also seemed that Africa, Europe and Asia

Simple tools from Burma made of local fossil wood.

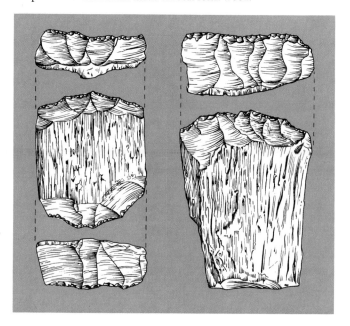

started producing primitive tools at about the same time – Choukoutien, the early terraces of the Somme and the early hand axes from Africa seemed to be roughly contemporaneous, suggesting that if there had been a center of dispersal movement had been very rapid or, alternatively, that the toolmaking idea was generated more or less simultaneously in several places.

Recent finds from East Africa have, of course, greatly modified this pattern. Not only are much earlier and more primitive creatures contending for the position of the first toolmakers, but toolmaking itself has been pushed back to a period 1.5 million years earlier in Africa than anywhere else in the world.

While Africa may justifiably claim to be the cradle of mankind, it does not follow that this is the final answer. What East Africa has produced is a unique series of deposits in an environment suitable for the higher primates to live and develop. Elsewhere within the tropical belt, where similar environmental conditions existed

Above: the main sites of discoveries in Asia.

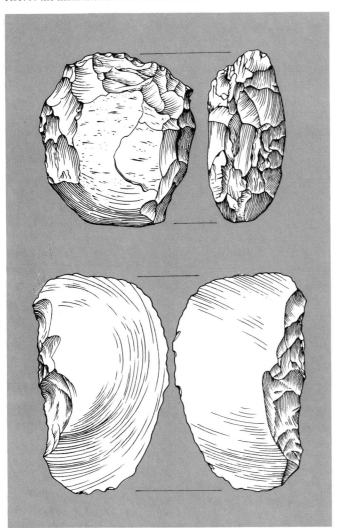

Below, left to right: chopping tool and large flake from the Peking man site at Choukoutien; Acheulian hand axes from India made from quartzite river pebbles.

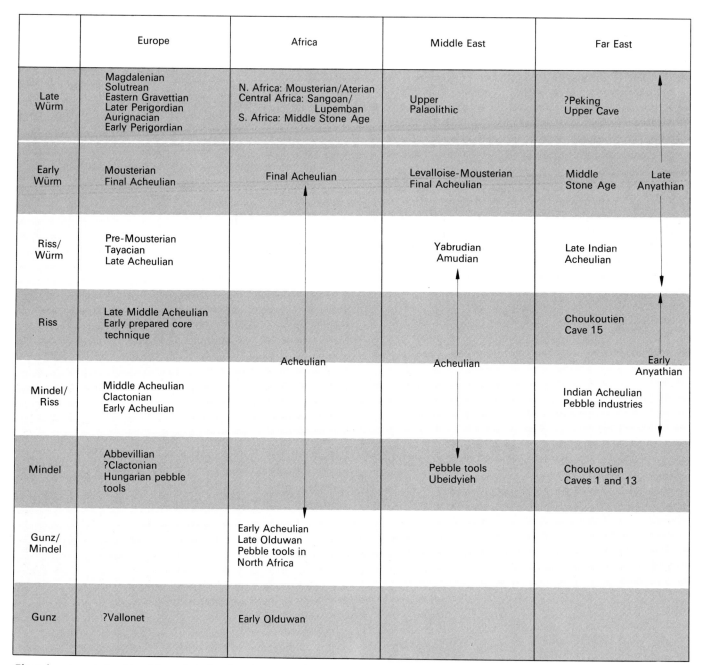

	Europe	Africa	Middle East	Far East
Late Würm	Magdalenian Solutrean Eastern Gravettian Later Perigordian Aurignacian Early Perigordian	N. Africa: Mousterian/Aterian Central Africa: Sangoan/Lupemban S. Africa: Middle Stone Age	Upper Palaeolithic	?Peking Upper Cave
Early Würm	Mousterian Final Acheulian	Final Acheulian	Levalloise-Mousterian Final Acheulian	Middle Stone Age Late Anyathian
Riss/Würm	Pre-Mousterian Tayacian Late Acheulian		Yabrudian Amudian	Late Indian Acheulian
Riss	Late Middle Acheulian Early prepared core technique			Choukoutien Cave 15
Mindel/Riss	Middle Acheulian Clactonian Early Acheulian	Acheulian	Acheulian	Early Anyathian Indian Acheulian Pebble industries
Mindel	Abbevillian ?Clactonian Hungarian pebble tools		Pebble tools Ubeidyieh	Choukoutien Caves 1 and 13
Gunz/Mindel		Early Acheulian Late Olduwan Pebble tools in North Africa		
Gunz	?Vallonet	Early Olduwan		

Chart showing relationship of the early industries of Europe, Africa and Asia.

within the primate range, comparable development is equally possible, and it would be no surprise if Asia produced hominids and tools of similar age.

An extraordinary picture is revealed when we review the enormous range of time from the Lake Rudolf tools of 2.5 million years to the late Acheulian hand axes from the end of the Last Interglacial (c 70,000). Over this vast timespan human progress in cultural terms seems to have remained remarkably static. The living conditions of Homo erectus seem to have differed little from those of the hominids from the base of Bed I at Olduvai. Peking Man may have made use of a wider variety of game, probably obtained by more efficient hunting, and had also mastered fire, but changes in stone technology were minimal. The huts from Terra Amata were larger than the simple shelters from DK at Olduvai and apparently better made – not very surprising if one considers that the climate in southern France was probably much colder.

The change of living pattern over 2.5 million years and the appearance of three hominids (1470, Homo erectus and Swanscombe) is certainly not very impressive. Standards of tool finish improve and there is a general tendency for the toolkit to become more complex, and the use of fire and possibly clothing meant a wider climatic tolerance. These added advantages notwithstanding, the economic pattern of hunting and food gathering remained virtually unchanged, and was to continue well past the advent of modern man.

Primitive Man Today

Previous page: Boscimani from Botswana.

Left: few tribes practicing a purely hunting and gathering economy are free from outside contamination. Some, like the Caribou Eskimo, now use rifles and tinned food but have been well documented. Others, such as the forest dwellers of South America, the Kalahari bushmen and the Australian aborigine continue in their old way of life, though they are unlikely to survive as hunters for much longer. This group of Australian aborigines is cooking a kangaroo in a pit. Its legs can be seen sticking up into the air.

The presence of living tribes still existing solely by hunting and food-gathering has always invited comparison between themselves and prehistoric man. In general such comparisons are legitimate provided they are not carried too far. Certainly the conditions prevailing in Europe during the Last Glaciation presented similar problems to those faced by the Eskimo and Canadian Indians, but as far as the availability of game is concerned, we can safely conclude that prehistoric man was a great deal better off even during the maximum cold. Certain prehistoric tools such as the spearthrower have parallels in Australia and America, and the various modern methods used to catch game were probably known and practiced by our ancestors.

Left: two Australian aborigines in front of a painted rock at Jesse Gap. Only the tribal elders are now able to interpret the paintings, whose meaning is far from self-evident, and at their death much information will be lost. The figure on the left is carrying the basic hunting equipment – throwing stick in his left hand and spear-thrower in his right. As with most hunting groups constantly on the move the minimum of equipment is carried. Apart from the men's possessions, the women will carry wooden troughs and skin bags for the collection and transportation of food.

Right: a family of Tasaday from the Philippines living in a cave. In terms of climate such caves are not strictly necessary, but they are highly desirable as shelter. Cave dwelling is still practiced in parts of North Africa and by shepherds all over the world. Until recently the Vedda of Ceylon lived in caves, and they formed the basis of the American Pueblo dwellings. In Europe such caves would appear to have been essential to prehistoric man during the winter, but the Eastern Europeans survived quite well in mammoth bone huts. The choice of temporary or permanent caves depends largely on available food supply.

Right: Pygmy grass hut from the forests of Zaire. Australian aborigines do not usually make huts, but many hunting groups make similar simple shelters. In cases where wood is scarce the sticks for the frame are carried from place to place. The foundations of such huts have been found in Africa, dating from over a million years ago. Among the Eskimo and North American Indians skin summer tents serve the same purpose.

Above: Tasaday making fire by the most usual method of rubbing two sticks together. The Eskimo use a form of bowdrill. Evidence provided by remains of ashes in caves proves that prehistoric man used fire as early as 500,000 years ago.

Above: Australian aborigines sharpening and hafting stone axes. Some sites bear traces of deep grooves on rock surfaces which were obviously convenient spots for grinding ax edges into shape.

Above: a beautiful picture of South African Hottentots trapping elephant. Sites in Spain provide evidence of extensive hunting of elephant over 250,000 years ago, while in Eastern Europe man was hunting mammoth and making huts from their bones and tusks around 25,000 BC. Alternatively game was driven into swampy ground, and this method seems to have been practiced over a million years ago in East Africa.

Left: Australian aborigines removing bark from a tree to make a shield. The men are carrying a variety of tools – the one on the left has two boomerangs in his belt and is using a stone ax hafted in bent cane and a stone wedge, and his companion carries a throwing-stick-cum-club. The aborigine kit contains many wooden tools, suggesting a similar material for prehistoric man. Wooden clubs are known from Africa about 58,000 BC, and a wooden spear from England dates back to about 250,000 years ago.

Left : Arctic Eskimos hunting seal in Greenland. No other people has developed such an elaborate economy based on the sea. The inhabitants of the Andaman Islands in the Indian Ocean and the people of Tierra del Fuego depended largely on fishing but by no means to the same extent as the Eskimo. Apart from food, the seal provides blubber for fuel and lighting, skin for clothing, bone for tools and gut for the construction of canoes. There is no evidence of a comparable economy in prehistoric Europe. Much of the coastline where this could have been practiced is now under 100 meters of water after the melting of the ice. Prehistoric man in France certainly knew the seal because he drew them, but no site has yielded evidence of seal bones.

Right : a selection of foods eaten by the Tasaday peoples of the Philippines. Apart from fruits and leaves there is meat in the form of two frogs, a crab and three large grubs, all of which were probably obtained at a short distance from the cave. This mixture of vegetables and meat makes a better-balanced diet than that of the Eskimo, for example, which consists largely of meat, supplemented by the stomach contents of the reindeer. The colder the climate, the more meat is required.

Below : a Kalahari Bushman making twine. In this case vegetable fibers are being used and are formed into a length by being rolled on the thigh. Australian aborigines make belts from human hair, bowstrings from sinew and rope from vegetable fibers (for instance strands of creeper) or (the most durable) from strips cut from hide. Prehistoric man probably made use of all these raw materials, his choice depending on what was to hand.

Above left: a Bushman drinking the juice of a wild melon. Like many of the animals, man obtains fluid from vegetable foods, but this alone is not sufficient for his daily requirements. The Bushman uses skin containers or ostrich eggs in a bag for water storage, and many hunters use the stomachs of animals.

Above: Australian aborigine with ritual body-painting. Natural pigments and dyes were probably used for such purposes from very early times, certainly long before any surviving art. Decoration for personal rather than ritual purposes is by tattooing or cutting patterns in the skin.

Left: Australian rock painting covers a variety of subjects, including tribal legend and ritual. Attempts to interpret prehistoric art in terms of Australian or Bushman art are unrealistic, but emphasize the serious intent and importance of art to the modern hunter.

Right: Australian aborigine painting a kangaroo on a piece of eucalyptus bark. Many such paintings and those decorating personal possessions are executed purely for enjoyment. The common conception of man the hunter working desperately during daylight hours just to survive is generally untrue. Hunting and food-gathering often involve long periods of inactivity devoted to talk, dancing and artistic pursuits.

Below: a large abstract rock painting from Emily Gap, Australia. Rock painting is of great importance to the artist. Tribal traditions must be handed down from one generation to the next, spirits must be propitiated and ancestors remembered. While the artist obviously obtains satisfaction from the execution of his painting, this is not its main purpose. Particularly interesting is the use of convention, with signs and symbols representing something totally different from the object drawn, and their significance known to the tribal elders alone.

Below right: Bushman painting from South Africa, bearing little resemblance to Australian art. It displays a mixture of accurately drawn game animals, strange half human/half beast creatures and recording of actual events such as the Bushman driving off Bantu cattle. Elderly Bushmen have interpreted some South African paintings as dance notations, and have danced out the theme portrayed. Other paintings depicting strange beasts record tribal myths and legends.

5. The Spread of Man

The division of a continuous narrative into chapters is a matter of convenience only. Human development is an unbroken process, and the placing of Homo erectus and his predecessors in one chapter and Neanderthal and Modern Man in another is based on expediency alone.

Neanderthal man: the Mousterian in Europe. The Acheulian cultures on the Somme and Seine did not continue beyond the end of the Last Interglacial, and although the deposits continued through the following Glaciation (Würm) it was to the rich cave sequences that 19th century prehistorians turned their attention for an understanding of the later periods.

By the middle of the last century it was clear that the deposits of the caves in southwest France consisted of two readily recognized components. At the base of many caves was an industry made on flakes, with an apparently simple toolkit consisting mainly of thick scraping tools and, more rarely, points (possibly spearheads). By contrast, succeeding industries were much richer in stone tool types whose blanks were principally blades, not flakes. There was also, particularly in the later stages, extensive use of bone and antler, often beautifully decorated.

These typological and technical differences were clear enough but they were further emphasized in human terms. All Neanderthal material found in an industrial context was associated with the simple flake industry, whereas the later, more complex industries were clearly the work of Modern Man.

The site from which Neanderthal Man's industry took its name is Le Moustier, in the department of the Dordogne in southwest France. During the 19th century this area was the center of cave research. Le Moustier was originally investigated by Lartet and Christy in 1863 and consists of two distinct caves, one above the other, on the Banks of the Vézère river. It was the upper cave which gave the name Mousterian to cover the lower part of the French cave sequence. The lower cave, though not excavated until much later, produced the burial of a Neanderthal youth in direct association with Mousterian material, an association which was to be repeated many times in Europe and elsewhere. It was to encompass this Mousterian material that the term Middle Paleolithic was coined, distinguishing it from the earlier hand axes and later blade industries of the Upper Paleolithic.

During the latter part of the 19th and early part of the 20th century the Mousterian was seen as a single unit and prehistorians tended to oversimplify it, considering that the lowly Neanderthals would naturally have a correspondingly crude and simple industry.

Prehistoric dwelling adapted to modern requirements. St Cirq, France.

By the turn of the century the Mousterian was seen to cover nearly all Europe, later to include Greece (which until recently had not produced any material earlier than Neolithic). In no case had Mousterian material been found with a hominid other than Neanderthal, nor Neanderthal Man with any other industry than Mousterian.

The original concept of a single widespread Mousterian was largely the result of unrefined excavation techniques and an oversimplification of the classification of tool assemblages. Early in the present century it became clear that there were at least two recognizable Mousterian industries in France, one with small heart-shaped hand axes and one without. On the basis of these hand axes (which incidentally bear little resemblance to those of the Acheulian) the term "Mousterian of Acheulian Tradition" was created. This term is rather misleading as there is not necessarily a direct connection between this Mousterian variant and the preceding Acheulian.

During World War II and immediately after, detailed studies were made of the Mousterian industries of southwest France. These were made possible by a far greater appreciation of the small stratigraphical differences encountered during excavation. This new approach led to a complete reappraisal of the Mousterian in the caves as well as some of the material from the later levels of the Somme and Seine.

Apart from the presence or absence of hand axes to distinguish Mousterian industries there are also two distinct methods of producing Mousterian flakes. The simpler method is to strike flakes off at random from the core, which naturally becomes smaller as the work proceeds. If the flakes are struck from alternate sides, using the scar of a previous flake as a striking platform for the next, the core eventually becomes biconical like those of the earlier Clactonian. The disadvantage of this method is that the knapper has only limited control over the size and shape of the flakes.

The second method, referred to as the "prepared core" or Levallois technique, though rather wasteful of raw material, allows the knapper to predetermine the size and shape of the flake within the limits of the core. Broadly speaking the core is shaped for the production of one flake and it is necessary to reset it for each subsequent flake. As well as producing large flakes this method makes it possible to obtain reasonably-sized ones from a core too small to be worked by the first method.

The use of these two flaking techniques and the hand ax/non-hand ax distinction of the Mousterian makes for divisions which are both typological and technical. François Bordes and his French colleagues have shown that in the cave sequences of southwest France there are altogether five distinct variants of the Mousterian, and a

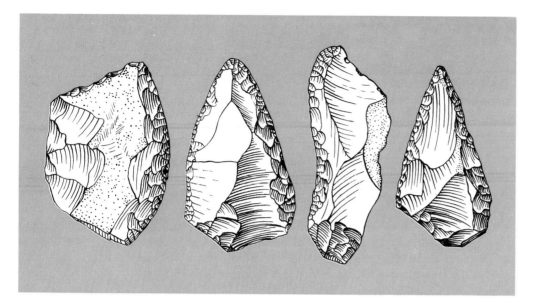

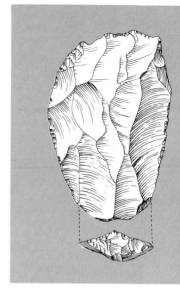

Above, left to right: Mousterian tools used for skin scraping and lance tips (one may possibly be a spokeshave); a large Mousterian flake struck from a prepared core.

Left: a heart-shaped Mousterian hand ax.

Below, left to right: "denticulated" Mousterian tools, possibly early examples of saws; a Mousterian prepared core on the left and a Mousterian disk core on the right.

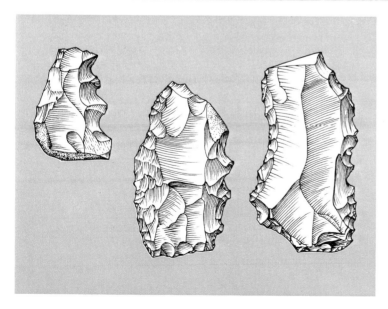

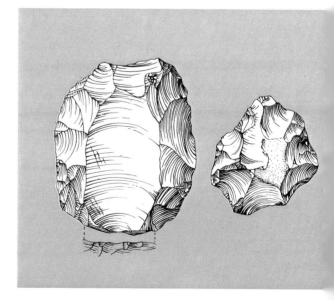

recent statistical breakdown shows their characteristics very clearly.

There are two phases with hand axes, one occurring at the very end of the Mousterian sequence and containing many later elements. The La Quina variant does not use the Levallois technique and has a very high proportion of side-scrapers, including special forms. The La Ferrassie variant has much the same tools but uses the prepared core technique. The two are referred to as Charentian, after the district of Charente where La Quina is situated. There is also a rather peculiar variant in which over 80% of the flakes have serrated edges – the Denticulated Mousterian.

There is some controversy regarding the significance of these Mousterian variants. Are the differences chronological, seasonal, environmental or tribal? Originally it was thought that the variants did not follow any chronological order, but it now seems that chronology may be part of the answer (for example one of the stages of the hand ax Mousterian occurs consistently at the end of the sequence in a number of caves). The excavation of the cave of Combe Grenal by Bordes revealed several consecutive layers with the same industry, covering several periods of climatic change, so it would seem that climate alone could not explain the differences. This leaves us with the possibility that the differences are tribal, with groups based on different traditions and engaged in slightly different activities.

The large number of human remains found with the Mousterian suggests the possibility of recognizable racial differences coinciding with cultural groups. So far no such racial differences can be seen, as nearly all the Neanderthal material has been found with the Charentian in both Europe and North Africa, and in the Mount Carmel caves two apparently different Neanderthals have been found in adjoining sites with the same industry.

Increased material available since the recognition of the Mousterian shows that not only was Neanderthal Man far superior mentally than was originally supposed, but his industries were much more complex, using techniques such as the prepared core which require a considerable amount of forethought and skill.

Evidence from the French caves shows small groups using caves and shelters though also camping in the open, probably during the short summer months. The full range of their activities will probably never be known, but they seem to have been successful in a wide range of climates from the shores of North Africa to full glacial conditions in northern France and Britain. Leaving aside the rather restricted Denticulated variant, the Mousterian toolkit indicates a number of jobs requiring a wide range of specialized tools; for example in the Charentian there are over ten varieties of side-scrapers as well as tools which foreshadow later periods.

Unlike earlier periods many Mousterian sites have provided evidence for burials – a practice which occurs over the whole Mousterian timerange. There can be no doubt that the youth from the lower cave at Le Moustier was deliberately buried, though the excavation was not very well carried out. The body had been placed in a shallow grave dug in the occupation debris of the site – probably in his own home. We cannot tell whether or not the burial party put offerings into the grave, as the bones and tools found with the body could have come from the filling.

Rather better evidence for grave goods comes from La Chapelle aux Saints in the department of Corrèze, where an old man was found in a rectangular grave also dug into the cave floor. Directly above his head were the foot bones of an ox still in articulation, suggesting that the flesh was on the bone when they were put there, possibly as food for the final journey.

La Ferrassie, also in the Dordogne, produced a number of burials in or just outside the shelter, totalling two adults and four children, one a newborn infant. Again the bodies were in shallow graves dug in the occupation levels, and some were partially covered with stone slabs. There is little doubt that the skeletons found at Spy in Belgium in 1886 were burials, though no evidence remains as to the details.

Many more Neanderthal remains have been found in Europe, but in the majority of cases where they were buried the graves have been disturbed in antiquity, and it is possible that some were merely exposed on the floor of the abandoned cave to become incorporated in the occupational debris of later inhabitants. Outside Europe there is evidence for careful burial – in some cases group burial as at La Ferrassie.

This discussion of the Mousterian in European terms is merely a matter of convenience, and does not imply that Europe was the center of its development or dispersal. The reason for this initial concern with French sites is the richness of their remains and the stratigraphical sequences the caves provided.

The detailed breakdown of the Mousterian into several variants, made possible by evidence from France, cannot necessarily be applied to other parts of the world. Taking Europe as a whole, the Mousterian of Charentian type (either with or without prepared cores) seems to be more widely distributed than the Mousterian of Acheulian tradition, which occurs principally in the western part of the continent. In parts of Europe there are local variants outside the five main stages, which in part seem to be conditioned by available raw material. Several Mousterian sites in Italy have an industry called Pontian, based on small pebbles as raw material, and the use of similar material can be seen in Gibraltar.

The Mousterian outside Europe. Using the term Mousterian in a wide sense we find that its distribution is not limited to Europe. Fairly typical material comes from western Africa north of the Sahara, some of it indistinguishable from the Charentian of the French caves. Associated with this African material are typical Neander-

thals, for example at the cave of Djeble Irhoud. Further east, towards the Nile, the industries tend to make more use of the prepared core technique and to have a simpler toolkit.

Moving further east we find a mass of Mousterian material, principally from caves in Israel, the Lebanon and Syria. The most famous sites in this area are the two caves on Mount Carmel (Tabun and Skhul), both of which have also produced valuable human material. The Mousterian from these two caves has been named Levalloiso-Mousterian, a descriptive term for an industry with a strong prepared core element but with typically Mousterian tools.

The hominids associated with this industry in Skhul are referred to as "advanced" or "unspecialized" Neanderthal, and are much nearer to Modern Man than those from western Europe. The woman from the adjoining cave of Tabun is much nearer to the classic Neanderthals, though industries from the two caves are the same.

Tabun also revealed an industry very different in character from the Levalloiso-Mousterian. Clearly contemporary with the late Acheulian, it has been found in a similar position in a cave at Jabrud in Syria and on the Lebanese coast. Originally considered as part of the Acheulian, it was found without hand axes at Jabrud and given the name Jabrudian. Typologically it resembles the French Charentian, without prepared cores and with a high proportion of side-scrapers. Sometimes it has rough hand axes but generally these are absent. So far no hominids have been found associated with this industry. In addition to Tabun and Skhul, Mousterian material has come from many sites including one not far from Mount Carmel, where well-preserved hominids and a rich industry were uncovered. When these finds are fully published, new light should be thrown on Mousterian development in this area. These rich Mousterian industries also occur further east. From the cave of Shanidar in northern Iraq came typical Mousterian finds associated with several hominids, and similar industries are known from Turkey and Iran.

East of Iran the situation becomes rather blurred and it is not clear how far one can stretch the term Mousterian. In India there are industries referred to as Middle Stone Age, based in part on a prepared core technique, which follow the local Acheulian, but so far there is little evidence as to their date.

North of the mountains of Tibet in the southern Russian territories there are industries which are Mousterian by definition, though many of them are very rough compared with the European and Middle Eastern material. One such site is Teshik-Tash in Uzbekistan, where several levels of rather poor Mousterian were uncovered, together with the burial of an eight-year-old child whose grave was surrounded by the horn cores of goats. The industry seemed to be very uniform throughout the various levels, with some use of the prepared core technique and some typical side-scrapers.

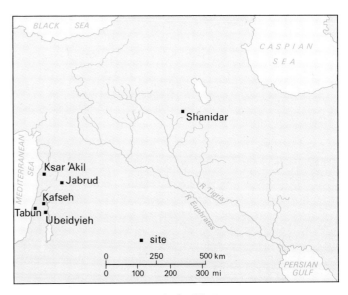

The main sites of discoveries in the Middle East.

Opposite: a reconstruction of a Neanderthal family scene. The skin tent is erected under a rock overhang, and in the foreground a skin is stretched out for curing.

Apart from China the areas east of the Indian subcontinent are difficult to interpret. Evidence at present available shows local industries such as the Anyathian of Burma and the Patjitanian of the islands apparently continuing through the later stages of the Pleistocene, and these areas do not appear to have had a Mousterian complex in the general sense.

The Loess regions of China have produced materials which seem to be related to the general Mousterian complexes in that they are based on a flake technology including the use of the prepared core, but there are no sites with long sequences and not a great deal of material is available. To the north, towards Siberia, there are industries with a mixture of Mousterian and later elements which at present are not well dated.

In Africa south of the Sahara the hand ax industries are not always directly succeeded by industries comparable to those of the north. In the forested areas of central Africa the late Acheulian developed into a complex characterized by heavy pick-like implements. This industry, the Sangoan, is dated at Kalambo Falls to about 40,000 BC, develops into an industry in which the picks become bifacial and turn into lance points, and undergoes further development through to the end of the Pleistocene and beyond.

In east and south Africa the industries following the late Acheulian take a more conventional line, with flake industries based on the prepared core technique. Instead of changing into blade complexes as in Europe and the Middle East these tend to develop locally, retaining the flake technology for a very long time with the tools becoming progressively smaller.

The uniformity of the Mousterian and its wide distribution repeats a situation which we have seen before and

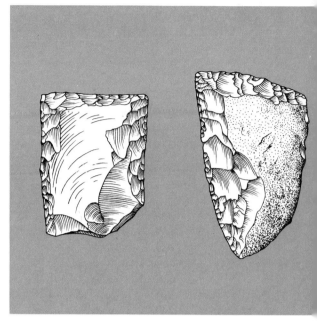

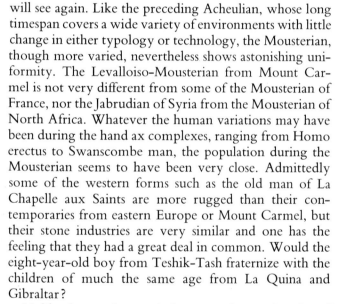

Typical Mousterian tools associated with Neanderthal man, from the cave of Mount Carmel near Haifa, Israel.

Jabrudian side scrapers from Mount Carmel, Israel. This industry is contemporary with the Late Acheulian.

will see again. Like the preceding Acheulian, whose long timespan covers a wide variety of environments with little change in either typology or technology, the Mousterian, though more varied, nevertheless shows astonishing uniformity. The Levalloiso-Mousterian from Mount Carmel is not very different from some of the Mousterian of France, nor the Jabrudian of Syria from the Mousterian of North Africa. Whatever the human variations may have been during the hand ax complexes, ranging from Homo erectus to Swanscombe man, the population during the Mousterian seems to have been very close. Admittedly some of the western forms such as the old man of La Chapelle aux Saints are more rugged than their contemporaries from eastern Europe or Mount Carmel, but their stone industries are very similar and one has the feeling that they had a great deal in common. Would the eight-year-old boy from Teshik-Tash fraternize with the children of much the same age from La Quina and Gibraltar?

Unlike the previous period, we can draw quite a lot of social information from the Mousterian burials. They are much more than fragments scattered on living floors, having been safeguarded by burial in caves which were themselves protected from the elements. Apart from general information gleaned from the inclusion of grave goods, these interments provide more personal details. From Mount Carmel we have the first clear evidence of man's violence to man: one of the more complete skeletons from Skhul had a deep wound in the pelvis, passing into the head of the femur. A cast taken of the cavity shows that it was made by a pointed wooden stake, probably not unlike the pointed stick from Clacton-on-Sea. As the edges of the exposed bone show no signs of

healing, the victim probably died from loss of blood or septicemia.

Some of the inhabitants of Shanidar were crushed by a fall of the cave roof, the result of a local earthquake. One had an old arm injury which must have greatly decreased his use to the band, but they seemed to have found a place for him, crippled though he was. A further very human touch, also from Shanidar, is the finding of a grave with a very high pollen content in the soil. This pollen was from flowering plants, suggesting that the body was buried with a bunch of flowers.

In contrast to this evidence of consideration for the dead are suggestions of cannibalism. Human bones representing at least fourteen individuals were found among food debris in the cave of Krapina in Czechoslovakia. Some were burned and others showed signs of having been cut up. Were these part of disturbed burials or were they the remains of meals? The evidence from Krapina itself is insufficient to support the charge of cannibalism, but there are further clues.

In the cave of Monte Cerceo near Rome a skull was found lying by itself on the cave floor, surrounded by small stones. The base had been cut away suggesting the removal of the brain. The isolation of the skull points to ritual rather than economic cannibalism and raises Neanderthal Man's status rather than lowering it.

Another interesting feature, unconnected with burials, is an apparent interest in the skulls of animals. In a cave in Switzerland a collection of bear skulls was found which, according to the excavator, were enclosed within a container of stones. From a Mousterian site in the Channel Islands came a number of rhinoceros skulls. It is difficult to imagine what practical value the skulls could have

Sangoan picks from Zaire. These are direct descendants of the East African hand axes.

possessed after the flesh and brain had been removed.

On the basis of this evidence the existence of some form of skull fetish has been suggested, but like most abstract aspects of prehistory it is not supported by much direct evidence.

At present it is no more possible to put one's finger on the origin of any of the Mousterian variants than it is to identify the men who made them. As far as Europe is concerned we know that the prepared core technique was an Acheulian invention as it was in Africa, and that many of the Mousterian tools (particularly some of the scrapers) were already in use in the Middle Acheulian during the Riss Glaciation. There is a good case for claiming that at least part of the Mousterian is derived from this source – certainly there is little doubt that the Levalloiso-Mousterian of the Middle East is of late Acheulian origin.

The immediate ancestry of the Charentian variant is not so easy to determine. Technically it has much in common with the Clactonian of the Mindel/Riss Interglacial, though there is no evidence that the Clactonian continued beyond this date. In Europe there are rather rough industries dated to the end of the Last Interglacial, and there is also some evidence of Charentian Mousterian being already extant at this date in Germany. Some variants, such as the Denticulated Mousterian, may well have developed in response to a particular activity and be derived as variants from one of the other groups. What is difficult to understand is the disappearance of the hand ax when the larger animals, for which it seems to have been designed, were still being butchered.

The Dordogne river, one of the best known areas in France for the study of prehistoric remains.

Modern man: the Upper Paleolithic in Europe. The modern classification of the hominids has closed the physical gap between Neanderthal and Modern Man, their differences being now only on a sub-specific level, with a possible common ancestor in Swanscombe and Steinheim Man.

At present our chronological information does not show whether the two groups were contemporary in any one area. Certainly we have no evidence of Modern Man being found stratified below a Neanderthal, but there is little doubt that the less specialized forms from eastern Europe and the Middle East were contemporary with the more extreme types from western Europe.

In the cave sequences of western Europe the archaeological succession seemed clear. The Mousterian industry of Neanderthal Man was abruptly replaced, not only by industries based on a blade technology and the use of bone tools, but by what was clearly a Homo sapiens, or what one would now call Homo sapiens sapiens.

This replacement of one hominid by another presented the early prehistorians with something of a dilemma. The original idea that one evolved into the other had to be ruled out as the time available for this process was quite insufficient. Alternatively the Neanderthals could have died out after failing to adapt to changing climatic conditions; however we now know that they lived in France through two major cold periods with great efficiency. A third possibility was that the two peoples interbred and, as the more advanced traits were dominant, the features we identify as Neanderthal slowly disappeared. A further suggestion was that the simple Neanderthals were overpowered by the vigorous and better-equipped Homo sapiens – a sort of prehistoric final solution!

By the beginning of the present century the French cave sequence as we know it was established, at least in outline. The succession of Mousterian flake industries by the blade industries of the Upper Paleolithic has been demonstrated in many caves in France, northern Spain, Germany, Belgium and Britain – in fact all the areas providing good cave sequences.

In 1912 Abbé Breuil, father of modern prehistorical studies, published his famous paper on subdivisions of the Upper Paleolithic, introducing a terminology that was to remain current for the next quarter of a century and be applied to regions far beyond western Europe.

Breuil's three main stages of the Upper Paleolithic (Aurignacian, Solutrean and Magdalenian) had several features in common – all, apparently even the earliest, were the product of Modern Man; the stone technology was based on blades rather than flakes and all made use of bone and antler for producing a wide variety of tools. Further, the majority (at least in western Europe) practiced some form of art, in the embellishment of personal objects or cave walls.

The first of Breuil's three stages, the Aurignacian, was

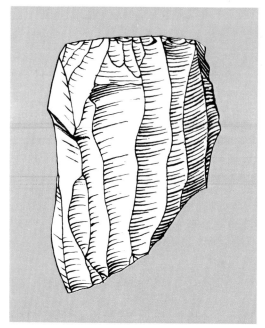

Above, left to right: a flint core used for the production of blades; heavy-duty Aurignacian blades, probably used for woodworking.

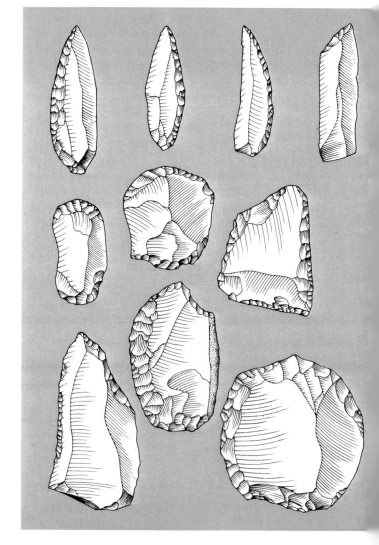

Below, left to right: Early Perigordian implements; Late Perigordian points, blades and scrapers.

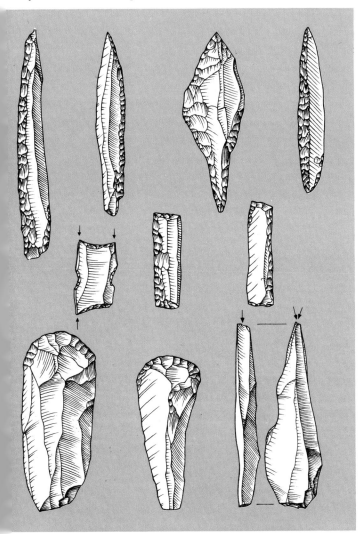

named after the cave of Aurignac, excavated by Lartet in 1860. Even as early as 1912 it was apparent that it was made up of clearly recognized stages of which Breuil distinguished three, Lower, Middle and Upper, which seemingly formed a developing sequence.

In many respects the Lower Aurignacian had much in common with the Mousterian which it supplanted. Many of the tools were made on flakes, some indistinguishable from the earlier material, but the greater part were made on blades. Many of the tools, such as the backed blades, the more sophisticated burins and the end-scrapers link this stage to the rest of the Upper Paleolithic. Moreover there was clear evidence of the use of bone and antler for points and awls.

Even in the early part of this century it seemed possible that Breuil's Lower Aurignacian had sufficient similarities to the late Mousterian (particularly the Mousterian of Acheulian Tradition) to have been directly derived from it, an idea supported by Breuil and many of his French colleagues. While there might be typological grounds to support this view, it was upset by the finding of a Homo sapiens burial in the cave of Combe Capelle. This remains the only hominid so far found in a Lower Aurignacian context, and certainly bears no physical resemblance to the French Neanderthals.

The second stage of Breuil's Aurignacian, the Middle, differs from the Lower from which it is supposed to be derived in a number of respects. First the Middle Aurignacian deposits are more frequent and thicker, suggesting a much larger population. Second, it is a richer industry with a typology bearing little resemblance to the earlier stage. The backed blades are absent, their place being taken by heavy blades with flat retouching, many with end-scrapers on one end; but what gives this stage its real character is the high proportion of steep-scrapers – scrapers made on thick chunks of flint. In addition there are special flat bone points, some with a split base for hafting. At least five stages of the Middle Aurignacian have been recognized in France.

The last of the Aurignacians, Breuil's Upper has, oddly enough, more affinities with the Lower than with the Middle from which it is supposed to have been derived. Like the Lower there are backed blades (but rather better made), an abundance of end-scrapers, numerous burins and bone points with beveled bases.

Logically the Lower and Upper Aurignacian make a very convincing development, while the Middle Aurignacian, which bears little resemblance to either, seems to be intrusive.

This situation led to the renaming of Breuil's three stages, the first and third being given the name Perigordian, after the region of Périgord, and the middle stage retaining the original name Aurignacian.

For a long time it was difficult to see the connecting links between the two stages of the Perigordian, since the stratigraphical sequence of Lower Perigordian, Auri-

A cast of a Solutrean "laurel leaf" spear point, over 13in long. These beautiful implements were prepared by delicate flaking across the surface.

An Australian aborigine holding in his left hand a spear thrower with which he increases his throwing power.

gnacian and Upper Perigordian was remarkably consistent. Recently more refined excavation techniques have not only brought intermediate Perigordian stages to light, but have shown that the Perigordian and Aurignacian are in fact largely contemporary, with the two traditions interdigitating in some of the cave sequences.

The hominids associated with both the Aurignacian and the later Perigordian are grouped under the name Cro-Magnon, from the small shelter in the village of Les Eyzies, excavated by Lartet in 1860. The Cro-Magnons were a tall people with stout limbs and broad faces. This type, with possible exceptions, seems to have been responsible for much of the Upper Paleolithic complex, at least in western Europe and possibly parts of North Africa. The man from Combe Capelle does not conform to this type, being much closer to the narrow-faced peoples who were responsible for the Upper Paleolithic of Eastern Europe.

Following the last of the Perigordian levels (of which at least eight stages have been recognized) is a short episode – the Solutrean. Stratigraphically this industry follows the late Perigordian and shares some tool types with it.

The difference between the two is that in its early stages the Solutrean adopts the technique of flaking across the surface of small, leaf-shaped flakes. Initially only the tips

and butts were treated in this way, but the retouching was gradually extended, first over the whole of one face and later over both. This type of retouching resembles the work of the terminal Mousterian, particularly in Germany and Czechoslovakia, but the Solutrean tools are generally thinner and better made.

By the middle stages these bifacial flakes became beautiful, leaf-shaped blades or points – some (the willow leaves) narrow, and some (the laurel leaves) broad, the latter reaching up to 35 centimeters in length. The best of the implements are made of good quality chert (a very tough variant of flint) and, in the case of the large specimens, are core tools flaked from thin blocks of tabular chert.

Three stages are recognized – the Lower Solutrean, with the tools retouched on one face only; the Middle, with the retouching reaching its height and characterized by magnificent laurel leaves; and the Upper, in which narrow willow leaves predominate with the addition of small, single-shouldered points, the tangs frequently made by delicate pressure flaking (a technique not to be seen again until predynastic Egypt). Apart from its distinctive flaking technique, the Solutrean does not differ greatly from the Perigordian which precedes it, except that the

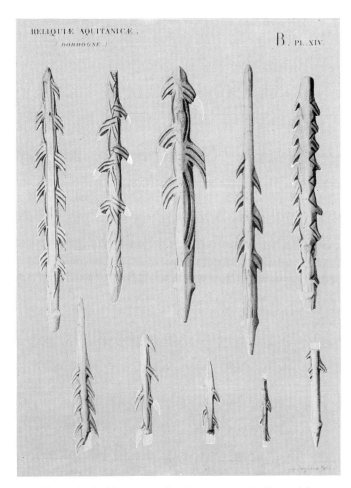

Magdalenian barbed harpoons of various types, probably used for fishing. This tool was first developed in the Magdalenian.

tools they have in common occur in different proportions.

The Magdalenian, the last of the French Upper Paleolithic industries, is probably the best known, and epitomizes one's idea of the prehistoric cave dweller. Its flint industry is not very impressive, and many of the earlier (particularly Perigordian) tools are still in use. The bone and antler industry gives the Magdalenian its special character, much of it beautifully decorated by engraving and sculpture.

The origin of the Magdalenian is still not very clear. Certainly there appears to be no connection with the underlying Solutrean and it seems more probable that it is the descendant of some form of late Perigordian. Six stages have been recognized, based largely on changes in the bone and antler industries. Two new tools made in these materials are spear throwers (a tool used by Australian Aborigines and the Eskimo) and barbed harpoon and spear heads. There are also finely made bone needles, an object first developed in the late Solutrean, though then rare.

The French Upper Paleolithic is of short duration if one considers the total timespan of human activity, covering only about 25,000 years, from about 35,000 to 10,000 (the end of the Last Glaciation).

In terms of environment there do not appear to have been major differences between that of the Mousterian and the succeeding Upper Paleolithic (the first covering the early stages of the glaciation and the latter the last two), each group having been subjected to two cold peaks. Both groups were hunters but the Upper Paleolithic peoples seem to have concentrated more on the herd animals – wild ox, horse, bison and reindeer rather than the elephants and rhinoceros, though this was not the case in Eastern Europe. We also have evidence of fishing in the Upper Paleolithic, with clues provided partly by tools (particularly barbed points) but also by depictions in art and the finding of fishbones in the occupational deposits (sometimes forming parts of necklaces). As with the Mousterian, there is evidence of open air camps being used through the short summers, and it is also possible that tents were erected inside some of the caves to provide extra protection.

The burials, of which we have far more than before, have provided information not only on burial customs but also on clothing and jewelry (of which the graves have produced a great deal). One feature of many burials of this period is the covering of the body in red ocher or the spreading of powdered ocher inside the grave. The positioning of the corpses varies – some lie on their backs and others are bent almost double as though they had been bound, as in some Peruvian burials. One body lying on its back had the thighbones reversed, suggesting that the bones were buried after the flesh had decayed, and it was probably at this point that the red ocher was applied. Jewelry was in the form of beads made from animal teeth, fish vertebrae and carved bone, and a variety of pendants, mostly bone. In a cave near Menton in the south of France a woman and a youth were found buried. Adhering to the boy's skull were four rows of shells, which had probably been sewn onto a cap. His companion had two bracelets made from the same shells. In an adjoining cave the body of an adult male was found with an elaborate necklace of deer's canine teeth, fish vertebrae and bone pendants. Further evidence for clothing comes from graves at Sungir near Moscow. One burial was that of an adult, which bore traces of fur upper garments and trousers onto which appear to have been sewn beads and teeth of arctic fox. The grave of two boys from the same site produced similar evidence as well as ivory fastenings for their collars, and alongside each boy was a long lance made of mammoth tusk.

Further evidence for clothing comes from home and cave art. A small figure from Siberia shows clearly that trousers and tunics with hoods were worn – garments not unlike the Eskimo parka, and a small painted figure from a Magdalenian deposit in France wears a fur coat, with a deep collar of a different fur indicated by a darker color. Also from a French Magdalenian site came engravings of rather bizarre figures of men and women wearing clothes and caps.

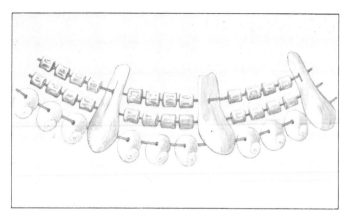

Above: reconstruction of a necklace made of shells, fish vertebrae and bone spacer beads, found in a burial in a cave on the French Riviera.

Left: an Aurignacian woman and a youth from the French Riviera burial. On her head are the four rows of beads from her cap, and on his arm the remains of a bracelet.

Right: an Upper Paleolithic burial in Russia, showing a mass of beads which would have been sewn onto skin shirt and cap.

Below right: three views of a small bone figure from Siberia, showing a skin parka similar to that worn by Eskimos today.

This outline of the French Upper Paleolithic has given little idea of its origin nor of post-Mousterian industries in the rest of Europe. The pattern for western Europe which we have just described applies, with small regional differences, to the greater part of the area, and comparable trends are visible in adjoining regions. Nevertheless it is possible to see Europe divided into two quite distinct provinces – eastern and western.

Outside France the early Perigordian is absent and the Aurignacian well represented, for example in Germany, Austria and Czechoslovakia, but it does not appear further east, and was not very typical in the Balkans if it existed there at all. The distribution of later stages of the Perigordian is more restricted than the Aurignacian. It is present in Belgium, Germany and parts of Spain, and was probably the origin of the rather localized industries of Italy which seem to remain in isolation up to the end of the Last Glaciation.

The distribution of the succeeding Solutrean is even more restricted. While its origin is still not very clear it has two possible sources – southwest France in the Charente or Dordogne region, and eastern France in the lower part of the Rhône Valley. With the exception of movement of late variants into southern Spain and traces in Belgium and Britain, the Solutrean episode seems to have taken place within the modern boundaries of France.

The Magdalenian also seems to have been of French origin and its movements outside France to have begun only in later stages. Late Magdalenian has come from Spain, Britain, Germany, Austria, Czechoslovakia, and possibly Poland. It is present in Switzerland, mainly on the Swiss-German border, but not in Italy, which has neither Solutrean nor Magdalenian.

The eastern zone, centered on the south Russian plains with westward extensions into Czechoslovakia, had a pattern of development differing from that of the west, and its Upper Paleolithic industries seem to be based on a different background and clearly independent of much of the later development in the west, such as the Solutrean and early Magdalenian.

In both east and west the so-called Upper Paleolithic industries are preceded by some form of Mousterian. In the eastern zone, where the local Mousterian appears to be mainly of Charentian type, there is a tendency for later stages to develop bifacial leaf-shaped implements, in some respects coarser versions of Solutrean points. These bifacial Mousterian industries, named Szeletian after a site in Hungary, develop into industries of mixed character with bifacial implements of the terminal Mousterian and tools of Upper Paleolithic appearance – for example backed blades of Perigordian type and elements similar to the Aurignacian. While it is still not clear whether these mixed industries are the origin of the Eastern European Upper Paleolithic, a good case can be made out for this claim.

Typologically the Eastern Upper Paleolithic has much in common with that of the west, in particular the Perigordian. This similarity is underlined by the use of the

term Eastern Gravettian, borrowed from the site of La Gravette in France, the type site of the early Upper Perigordian. Common to both are backed blades, end-scrapers and several burin variants, but there are differences in the tool proportions and each has tools not present in the other.

In spite of this strong similarity in equipment there is a marked difference in living conditions and economy. The eastern plains are lacking in caves so that the sites in this area are all open stations, mainly on the banks of rivers. Clearly during much of the Last Glaciation wood was scarce and pieces of usable size must have been hard to obtain. This shortage of house material was overcome to some extent by man's use of the by-products of his main source of food, the mammoth.

Mammoths roamed across the open plains, apparently in vast numbers, and migrated over great distances. Their meat was the major food supply for the local hunters, who killed them in large numbers. Their bones and tusks provided the framework for houses. A typical structure is made from the larger bones – skulls, long bones and shoulder blades formed the walls and the long curved tusks the roof; this bone frame was probably covered with turfs or skins. Although such huts are generally associated with the Upper Paleolithic, they were first

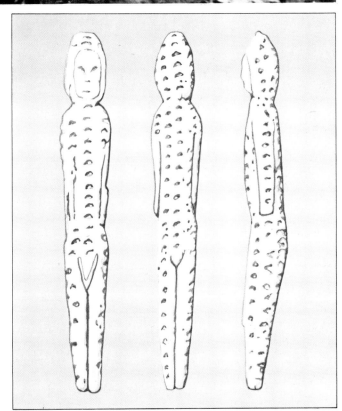

Reconstruction of a south Russian prehistoric hut made of mammoth bones and tusks.

used in the period of the Mousterian in much the same form.

In some areas wood seems to have been available and lighter structures, possibly summer tents, have been found. These were presumably made of skins stretched over a simple frame. Many of the huts, both bone and wood, have several hearths and some are divided into more than one compartment.

The Eastern Gravettian industries seem to have continued without much change in typology or economy throughout the latter part of the Last Glaciation, its place being taken in the west by the Solutrean and Magdalenian.

In the early stages of the Eastern Gravettian the human type is narrow-faced and narrow-headed, much closer to the hominid from Combe Capelle than the later Cromagnons. This narrow-headed form or Brun race seems to be well-defined in the early stages of the Eastern Upper Paleolithic, but the distinction between Brun and Cromagnon becomes rather blurred later.

The Upper Paleolithic outside Europe. In Europe there seem to have been two distinct traditions of Upper Paleolithic which, though both derived from Mousterian variants, to some extent went their own ways with perhaps only slight contact with each other on the edges of their territories. A similar area of independent Upper Paleolithic development is the Middle East, which has produced a mass of material over the last forty years.

Work on Middle East caves, particularly those of Mount Carmel, has thrown much light on the development of the early post-Mousterian industries, and may help to show more clearly the processes by which the change from Mousterian to full Upper Paleolithic took place in Europe.

At Tabun, the Mount Carmel cave containing the oldest material, the late Acheulian was well represented, with examples of the prepared core technique as well as typical hand axes. In Tabun and other caves in the area the Acheulian and its contemporary the Jabrudian were followed by various stages of the Levalloiso-Mousterian. The third cave in the group, el Wad, appeared to continue the sequence into the Upper Paleolithic, but its main industries bore little resemblance to the earlier Levalloiso-Mousterian and no case could be made out for a direct succession from one to the other. Subsequent excavation in other sites showed that there were in fact thick deposits between the Levalloiso-Mousterian and what is referred to as the Levantine Aurignacian. These intermediate deposits are particularly well represented in the rock shelter of Ksar 'Akil near Beirut, with over 60 feet of archaeological deposit, of which 15 feet lay between the Mousterian and the Levantine Aurignacian.

Technically, these intermediate industries are mixed,

with flakes made on prepared cores but with Upper Paleolithic tool types, mainly end-scrapers and burins. Towards the top of the level these mixed industries become more Upper Paleolithic in character with the flake technology receding. Unfortunately there are two breaks in the archaeological sequence – one between the Levalloiso-Mousterian and the mixed or "Transitional" industries, and a corresponding break between the Transitional and the Levantine Aurignacian. While it is not clear whether the Transitional developed into the Levantine Aurignacian industries or whether the latter came in fully developed from elsewhere, there is little doubt that the Levalloiso-Mousterian developed into the Transitional.

Evidence from eastern and western Europe as well as the Middle East suggests that, allowing for local variations, the Terminal Mousterian industries developed into what we call Upper Paleolithic, and by the end of the second stage of the Last Glaciation the latter were associated with Homo sapiens sapiens.

Unfortunately the picture emerging from archaeological evidence is not as simple as the above remarks suggest. The seeds of the Upper Paleolithic typology are rooted not only in the preceding Mousterian but in industries contemporary with the late Acheulian, at least in the Middle East and North Africa.

From Tabun and at least two other sites in the Middle East come "Blade and Burin" industries which, though rather rough, come within the typological range of the early stages of the Perigordian and include backed blades. These typologically Upper Paleolithic or Pre-Aurignacian industries as they have been called, have been found contemporary with late Acheulian levels and, if one considers dates for the local Levalloiso-Mousterian to be between 52,000 and 42,000 years, they are as early as much of the French Mousterian.

The problem of the transition from Middle to Upper Paleolithic is much the same as the change from Neanderthal to Modern Man, and prehistorians have tended to complicate the issue by oversimplification: we are looking for too little rather than too much. There is no single transition from one stage to another. The seeds of the Upper Paleolithic go back beyond the Mousterian, and the techniques and typologies to which it gave expression had long been in the repertoire of competent stoneworkers, to be brought into use when occasion demanded, irrespective of time or human type. This can be seen in parts of Africa and the Far East, where in many cases Modern Man remained content with industries which, in European terms, would be classed as archaic.

In Africa north of the Sahara the Mousterian tradition continues inland apparently contemporary with the development of industries of Upper Paleolithic type on the coast. This inland Mousterian derivative, the Aterian, is based on a flake and prepared core technology but develops bifacial tools similar to those of the late Mousterian in Eastern Europe and special tanged points. Dates of between 30,000 and 27,000 have been obtained for this industry – a timerange during which the early French Upper Paleolithic was well established, and the Levantine Aurignacian at Ksar 'Akil (with a date of 28,000) was in an advanced form.

On the coast of Cyrenaica, from the cave of Haua Fteah, came a sequence of Levalloiso-Mousterian succeeded by an industry of Upper Paleolithic type – the Dabban. This included examples of backed blades, end-scrapers and burins, and was followed by industries belonging to the early stages of the North African postglacial.

Such a sequence represents a familiar pattern – Mousterian–Upper Paleolithic–Mesolithic but, like some of the sites in the Levant, there is another element in the Haua Fteah sequence. At the base of the deposit, underlying the Mousterian, was an industry with the same basic elements as the "Pre-Aurignacian" from the cave of Tabun. There is so far no evidence to show whether these proto-Upper Paleolithic industries from the Levant and North Africa are connected, but they show that such traits were already extant at a very early period.

With the exception of late excursions into Upper Paleolithic tool types which are mostly post-Pleistocene in date, Africa south of the Sahara tends to develop regional industries based on earlier flake traditions or, in the case of the Sangoan of the Congo, from the terminal hand ax industries.

Along the East African coast down to the Cape there are many examples of industries which, though far removed from the original flake industries, are nevertheless clearly derived from them.

This tendency to continue with older traditions can also be seen in India and the Far East, where the highly developed blade technologies and tools that go with them are absent. Like much of Africa, India seems to pass from Late Mousterian type industries into post-Pleistocene

Aterian implements from North Africa.

groups based, like those of Europe, Africa and the Levant at that time, on small geometric tools.

A similar pattern occurs in China. In the Upper Cave at Choukoutien two proto-Mongoloid skulls were found, associated with an industry with Middle Paleolithic elements still strong.

The unity of Modern Man. The post-Mousterian industries reviewed here fall within a time range of 34,000 to 10,000 BC. The earliest carbon 14 dates for the French Upper Paleolithic are between 34,000 and 29,000, covering the first stage of the Perigordian and the early Aurignacian. In Eastern Europe slightly earlier dates of c. 38,000 have been obtained for the transitional stage, and c. 31,000 to c. 30,000 for the early Aurignacian of Hungary. There are dates of around 27,000 to 25,000 for some stages of the later Perigordian in France and the Eastern Gravettian in Czechoslovakia, and 18,000 for the Solutrean. The late Magdalenian continues to the end of the Last Glaciation – about 11,000 BC.

Like all carbon dates, these are not precise enough to give more than an indication of age and are certainly not accurate enough to establish priorities of invention or development. What these dates do show however is that in spite of the fact that at roughly the same time and over a wide area there was a transition from the Mousterian to the Upper Paleolithic in at least three centers, the presence of Homo sapiens sapiens as the only hominid does not result in uniformity of culture.

Our present rather limited information indicates that there are three possible centers of the Blade and Burin development – Western Europe, Eastern Europe and the Levant and along the coast of North Africa. The early prehistorians would have seen this distribution in terms of diffusion from a common center, either by the passage of ideas or by the movement of peoples. There seems a good case for at least three centers, which could well have been largely independent of each other, but if this is the case how are we to account for the strong similarities of their industries? The environments of the Perigordian and the Eastern Gravettian appear to have been very different and the economies based on different animals, but even so there must have been many common activities. Though wood was short in the east, woodworking tools were probably used on ivory, and both areas had bone and antler; in addition the processing of skins must have been universal, with backed blades most likely the principal implements used for this purpose.

The extraordinary similarity between the European and Middle East Aurignacian is harder to explain. The environments of the two regions are very different, and there is no evidence of migration. One suggestion is that they are both woodworking kits, for which heavy blades and steep-scrapers would be very suitable.

While much archaeological evidence is based on changes in tool traditions, taking the sum of evidence drawn from all the supporting sciences it is possible to reconstruct something of prehistoric man's life, particularly in the later periods.

The French Perigordians, though living in a generally cold climate, were certainly not struggling with tundra conditions. The valleys of southwest France in which many of the caves occur must have provided shelter, and pollen from a number of sites shows that there were always some trees, principally pine, to provide fuel and raw material. Game was obviously plentiful, particularly reindeer in the Late Perigordian and Magdalenian eras.

This environment seems to be in marked contrast to that of southern Russia, where steppe conditions prevailed throughout much of the Late Pleistocene. Tree cover was scarce and there were probably biting winds for the greater part of the year. In spite of these very bleak conditions prehistoric man seems to have been resourceful enough to survive. Judging by his art, which was probably a leisure pursuit, his struggle for survival could not have been too arduous. Houses and skin clothing must have kept him reasonably warm, even if he had to depend on bones for much of his fuel.

Stepping back and looking at the Old World as a whole over the period from about 35,000 BC to the end of the Pleistocene around 10,000 BC, we see the danger of a serious misconception. In the cultures of the Blade and Burin areas we have vigorous peoples with highly developed equipment – tough, resourceful and obviously of considerable mental stature – the supermen of the Old Stone Age. By contrast the inhabitants of Africa south of the Sahara and the Far East seem to have remained in something of a cultural backwater, continuing in old ways apparently without the urge to develop.

This suggestion of first and second class citizens brings us back to the comparison of Eskimo and Pygmy which we made earlier – artifacts are a reflection of the conditions not the man. Without their highly developed technology, the prehistoric inhabitants would not have survived at all in Europe during the greater part of the Last Glaciation. Those fortunate enough to have lived in more congenial southern climates had only the problem of the quest for food to contend with, but in this hunting was less important than food collecting, and thus a much simpler toolkit was required.

The Art of Early Man

One of the most appealing of early man's activities is his art. While the motives underlying this form of self-expression remain obscure, we can appreciate the technical skills involved and attention paid to detail. This last is of particular interest in the rendering of extinct animals such as mammoth and rhinoceros, and in the case of the mammoth enough remains have been found in the frozen ground of Siberia to show how true-to-life early man's drawings were. We will probably never know when art had its beginnings – certainly no examples have been preserved dating from before the advent of modern man (Homo sapiens sapiens), but traces of earth pigments used for cave paintings have been found in Neanderthal sites in France and earlier sites in Africa. This early use of pigments was probably for body paint or for the decoration of objects which have not survived. Examples of art which have survived in Europe, cave paintings in particular, must represent only a tiny part of the total output. Stretching eastwards from southwest France and northern Spain as far as the Russian Urals, paintings have been found preserved in deep caves, but were probably also executed on rocky outcrops in the manner of more

recent African paintings. During the 20,000-odd years which make up the lifespan of art in Western Europe, the development of various techniques and styles can be clearly seen, though it is not always obvious whether differences in style are regional or chronological. An enormous help in assessing the development of styles and attributing them to the correct chronological spread is the presence of art specimens in various archaeological deposits whose styles can be compared with paintings found on cave walls for which there is no direct dating evidence. One is also intrigued by the artist's understanding of his material, particularly in carving, and while there is clearly a serious purpose behind much of the art, there is no doubt that an impish sense of humor can also be detected.

The archaeologist Henri Edouard Prosper Breuil (1877–1961) became an authority on prehistoric art, a study which he took up shortly after being ordained in 1897. His copies of paintings, one of which is shown below, capture the essence of the artists' style, and in many cases provide valuable evidence of the appearance of works which have since deteriorated.

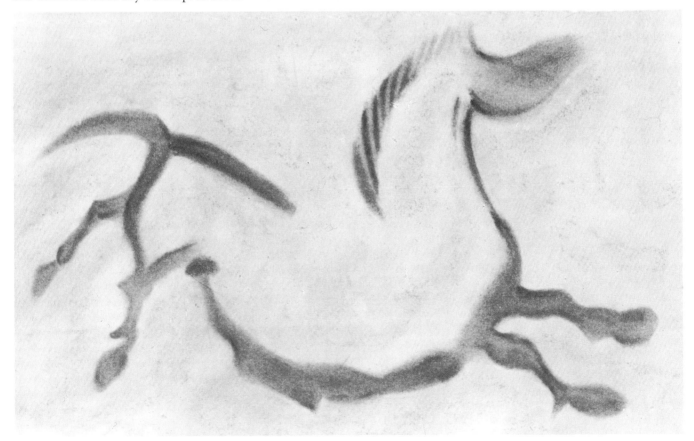

Left: Magdalenian horse head carved in bone – one of the most beautiful examples of prehistoric carving. Found in a cave excavation, its date is fixed to about 12000 BC. The structure of the bone did not allow for carving in the round, and the reverse side is flat.

Left below: entrance to the cave of La Vache in France. Even the small caves were probably decorated, but paintings located in full daylight by the entrance are not likely to have survived. In cases such as Angles sur l'Anglin, a shallow rock shelter, decoration has survived in the form of carving on the walls, protected from the weather by the rock overhang.

Below: painting of a mammoth in black, from Pech Merle in southwest France. An attempt has been made to indicate the beast's characteristic long heavy coat, and the domed head is clearly shown. Though not drawn as accurately as some other examples (for instance that shown on p 122), there is no question that this is a mammoth, dating probably from the Solutrean or Early Magdalenian. The original is about $31\frac{1}{2}$ in long.

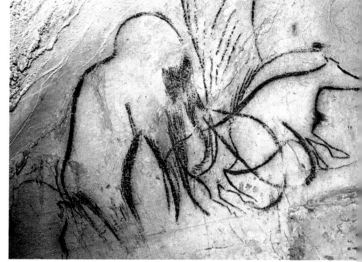

Above: part of a painted panel from the cave of Lascaux in France. This is one of several composite scenes using both outline (for the oxen) and flat wash (for the horses and deer). The central ox overlaid by a horse is a good example of superposition, while the horns and hooves of the oxen and the antlers of the small deer illustrate the use of twisted perspective. The identity of the strange spotted beast on the extreme left is uncertain. Probably Solutrean or Early Magdalenian.

Right: a woolly rhinoceros painted in red, from the cave of Font de Gaume in the Dordogne, France. The hair is clearly indicated, as in the case of the mammoth from Pech Merle (shown on the opposite page). Evidence of modeling can be seen under the chin, the belly and the hind legs. A completely preserved woolly rhinoceros from Rumania confirms the accuracy with which the artist has shown the way the animal's head hangs. The painting is of uncertain date, but the technique suggests possibly the Magdalenian. Length 27 in.

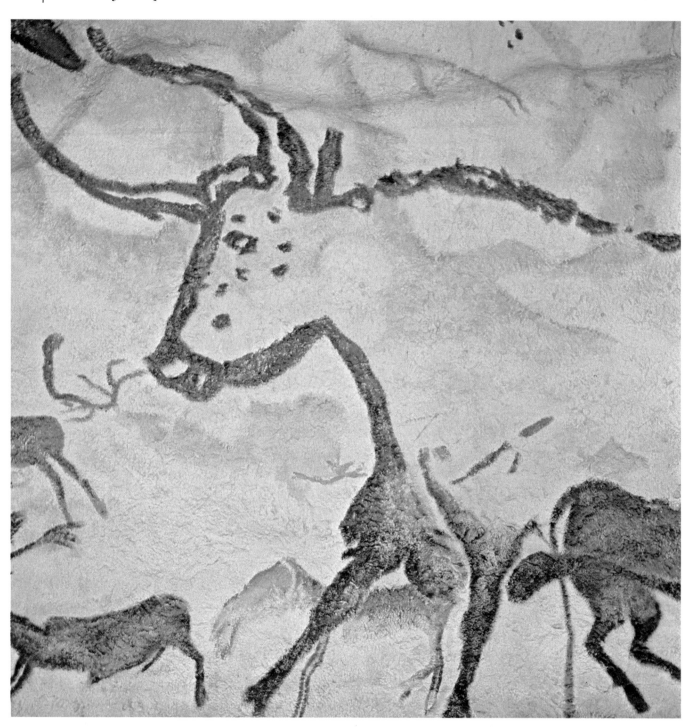

Detail of ox from Lascaux (see p 119), showing clearly the artist's treatment of his subject, and making possible a comparison with the other ox depicted in the center of the panel. The beast is drawn in black outline, the pigments used being probably manganese or charcoal laid on with some kind of brush, the simplest form being the chewed end of a stick. One's immediate impression is that the paint was very liquid and easy to apply. The painter's confidence is quite apparent – there is hardly any sign of hesitation or uncertainty. The animal has been drawn many times and is based on a lifetime of familiarity. The only area of uncertainty (see p 119) is in the hindquarters, where the junction of the left hind leg and the trunk is a little odd, but the rock surface may well have been a causal factor here. The drawing of the horns in twisted perspective is probably a matter of convention rather than a result of the artist's inability to draw in true perspective. Unlike the other ox on the panel there are very few spots on the animal's face, and their muzzles are slightly different. When the artist began this painting the small deer and horse were already drawn. Were they painted over because no longer required? The companion ox suffered similarly, being painted over by another artist's horse.

Above: bison from Altamira. Unlike the other bison on this page, which is a copy of the original made by the Abbé Breuil, this one a short distance away has been photographed direct from the cave wall. The use of black and red and the treatment of the tail are very similar.

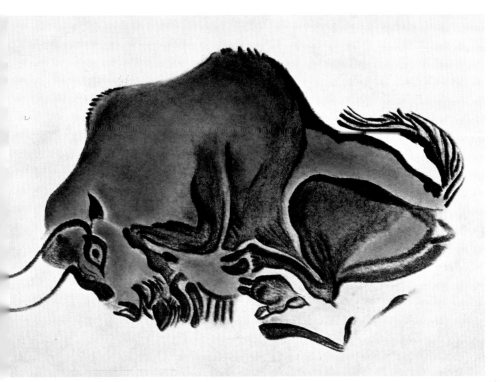

Below: red deer and salmon engraved on bone. The original is executed on a cylindrical piece of bone but is here drawn out flat. The deer turning its head is unusual as the majority are drawn in full profile. The jaw of the left-hand fish is particularly fine. Magdalenian.

Above: one of the many bison from the ceiling of the famous cave of Altamira in Spain. Paintings in similar style occur in Font de Gaume in France, though the strong black/red contrast is confined to Altamira. The Altamira bison are shown in various attitudes, and the unusual position adopted by the animal shown here suggests that it is dead. The black pigment is used not only to depict mane, tail and hooves, but also as a means of modeling.

Top: a small horse painted in black from the cave of Niaux in the French Pyrenees. The shaggy coat and short upright mane are clearly seen. The horse is similar in type to the Mongolian wild pony. Of Magdalenian date, it measures 27 in.

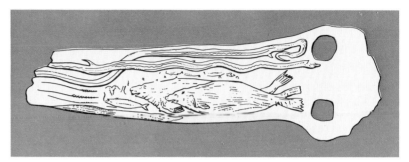

Above: a beautiful engraving of a mammoth from a cave wall. The long hair is clearly shown and the problem of depicting the feet is neatly overcome by detaching them from the body. This is one of several engraved mammoths executed in a more true-to-life style than the elongated examples from Pech Merle.

Right: this engraving of a bison on a small limestone slab makes an interesting comparison with the engraving shown below. Both entail the problem of cutting a deep line, but here the artist has retained a high standard of drawing. Magdalenian.

Below: head of a horse deeply incised in the cave wall at Lascaux. The effort involved has lost the work its sense of freedom.

Left: seals and eels engraved on a bone. There is no doubt as to the identification of the eels, as the fins are clearly shown. It has been claimed that the creature below the seal's face is a whale. Although there is no direct evidence of the Magdalenians having a coastal economy similar to the Eskimo, they must have frequented the seashore and estuaries.

Below: a female figure made of a mixture of clay and powdered bone, from Dolni Vistonice in Czechoslovakia. Like many such figures, it tends to taper towards the feet. Eastern Gravettian, about $4\frac{1}{2}$ in high.

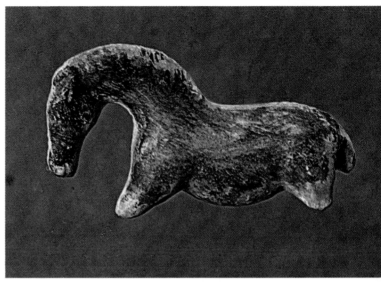

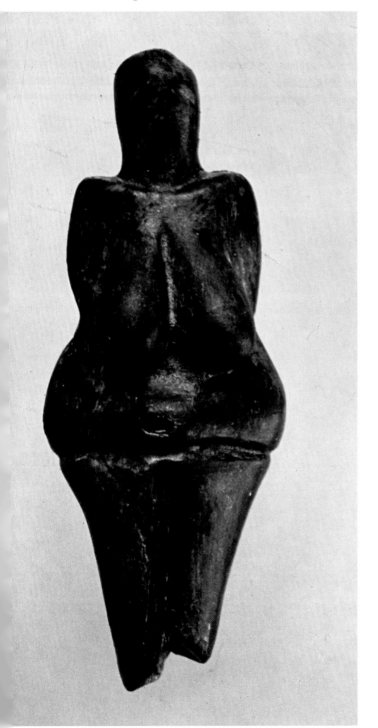

Above: small ivory carving of a horse from an Aurignacian deposit in Germany. These little animals occur fairly frequently in Eastern Europe, sometimes in bone or ivory and sometimes, as in a site in Czechoslovakia, in baked clay.

Below: head of a bison drawn with the fingers on the clay floor at Niaux, French Pyrenees. It lies over half a mile from the cave entrance. Dating from the Magdalenian period, it measures 24 in in length.

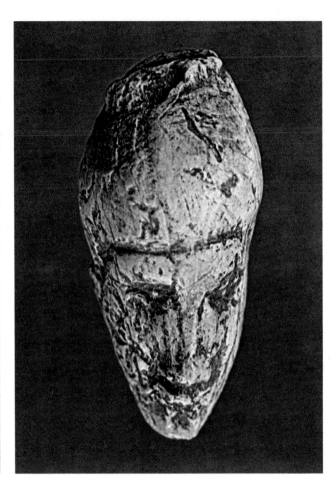

Above left: the Venus of Willendorf – a female statue made of stone, from a Gravettian site in Austria. Traces of paint suggest that it was covered with red ocher. The precise depiction of the hair contrasts with the absence of a face. Female figures carved in the round have been found from France as far east as southern Russia, and stylized forms as far as Siberia. It has been suggested that they represent mother goddesses, but they are more likely to have been house goddesses like those of some Siberian tribes.

Above center: a strange object carved in ivory from Dolni Vistonice, Czechoslovakia, generally recognized as a highly stylized female figure.

Above: small ivory head from Dolni Vistonice. Unlike the majority of the Venuses the facial features are clearly defined. This example may be a portrait, since the face is not symmetrical. A burial uncovered in the same settlement included a skull whose face was deformed in a similar manner through paralysis of the facial nerves, and the site also yielded up a smaller and cruder ivory head exhibiting the same deformity.

Left: a human figure crudely carved from a mammoth footbone and found in Czechoslovakia. About 12 in high, it does not appear to belong to the same group as the smaller Venuses and may therefore have been a doll, fashioned from the hundreds of mammoth bones scattered around the camp. It is possible that prehistorians do not make sufficient allowance for the presence of children, and this figure and some of the carved animals may well have been toys similar to those made by the Eskimo for their children.

To the non-specialist prehistoric art is by far the most intriguing aspect of early man's activities. The appeal is two-fold: first, one has a feeling of being on common ground with the artists – their skills, insight and, in some cases, their sense of humor bring them to life more than any other aspect of their behavior; second, the layman feels that he can make critical assessments of their work as art without the need for a profound study of prehistoric archaeology as a whole.

Previous page: head of a young girl carved in ivory, 1½ in high, from Brassempouy in France. Probably Perigordian.

Right: two animals painted in red ocher on the walls of a Magdalenian cave in France.

Below: Australian aborigines painting each other for a religious ceremony. In the period prior to cave paintings, natural pigments were probably used for this purpose.

Forms of prehistoric art. Prehistoric art can be divided into home or mobile art and cave or parietal art. This distinction is extremely important as the dating and consequently the authenticity of cave art depends largely on the former. Since by far the greater part of both home and cave art finds come from France and northern Spain, the descriptions which follow are based on material from these areas.

Home art consists of decorated pieces of personal equipment, of which only bone, antler and ivory objects have survived. Under this heading are also included engravings and paintings on small limestone plaques, and carvings of humans or animals – in short, anything portable. By contrast, cave art consists of paintings, engravings and sculpture on the walls of caves and shelters.

The importance of these two divisions is that cave art is not generally found in direct association with datable archaeological material. Apart from the resultant difficulties in assigning particular aspects to their correct date, in early studies of the subject this led to grave doubts as to the genuineness of much cave art. With home art the dating position is much more secure – small objects are found sealed in dated archaeological deposits and are as authentic as the other objects with which they occur.

The date of the birth of prehistoric art is impossible to determine. Coloring matter in the form of earth pigments seems to have been collected from early times – red ocher from the early Acheulian in Africa and manganese black from the French Mousterian. The original use of these pigments was probably as body paint (a practice still very widespread) and its purpose more likely ritual than cosmetic. It is also likely that perishable material such as wood or leather was painted. However the first actual evidence for any form of art is not available before the

The main caves sites of France and northern Spain.

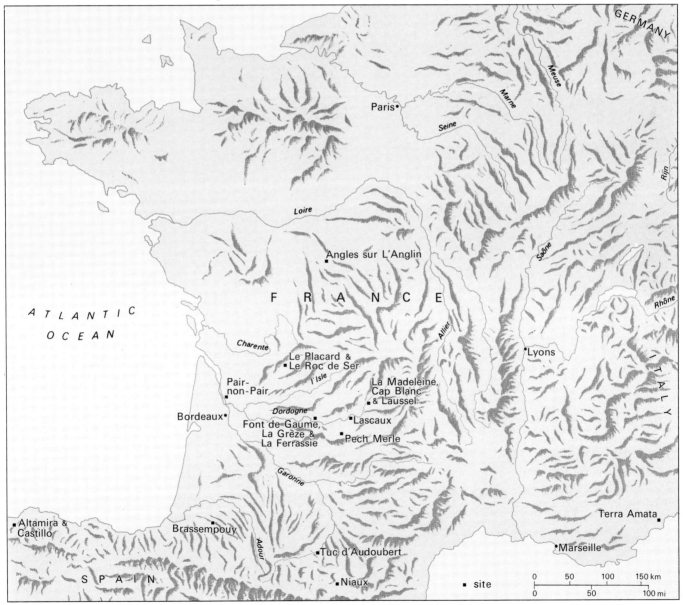

Upper Paleolithic and is so far linked to Homo sapiens sapiens alone.

Home art. The earliest examples of home art have been found in Aurignacian levels. The little we have from this period is mainly from La Ferrassie in the Dordogne and is associated with Aurignacian Stages III and IV. It consists of simple engravings and outline paintings of animals, some so schematic that it is not easy to identify them and others, like the rhinoceros, easily recognizable. There are also vague lines and what appear to be, by comparison with later examples, female sex symbols.

It is from the following stage, the later Perigordian, that the well-known Venuses came. These are small female figurines of stone, bone or ivory carved in the round or (like the famous Venus of Laussel) in relief. This particular example was carved on a large slab of limestone which, though now loose and included under home art, was probably originally attached to the shelter wall.

The Venuses generally have two characteristics in common – obesity and an absence of facial features, one exception being the small ivory head of a girl from Brassempouy. These very attractive figures also occur in eastern Europe in the Eastern Gravettian, though here they become more abstract, sometimes to such an extent that it is difficult to recognize them as human figures.

Little apart from these figures has been attributed to the late Perigordian, the exception being engraved pebbles from a site in eastern France. These show very overdrawn animals, among which are a deer and a rhinoceros with what appear to be arrows stuck in them – the first indication of such a weapon.

Similar engravings on limestone slabs are known in the French Solutrean, also with a tendency to overdraw, so that the subject matter is often obscured.

In southern Spain the late Solutrean site of Parpallo has produced many painted and engraved stone plaques in a style very similar to those from the north. No decorated tools have so far come from either the Aurignacian or Perigordian, and it is not certain whether the marks cut on some Solutrean tools are decorative or purely utilitarian – ie to facilitate gripping.

The home art of the early part of the French Upper Paleolithic is very simple and rare. It is not until the Magdalenian, in particular its middle stages, that it really blossoms. So strong is the urge to decorate their possessions at this time that these early men seem to have affinities with the makers of cuckoo clocks!

Of the six recognized stages into which the Magdalenian is divided, home art is at its best in Stages IV and V, where the main emphasis is on sculpture. In the early stages of the Magdalenian the decoration consists mainly of abstract designs on bone tools, such as points. These

Left: sculpture of a female figure or "Venus", from the rock shelter of Laussel, southern France. Her face is not defined. She is holding a bison horn.

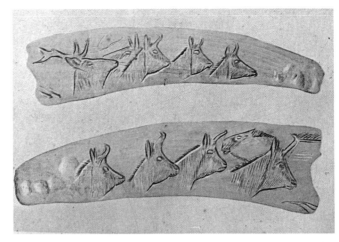

Red deer and ibex heads. Examples of Magdalenian decoration on bone tools.

give way to simple engravings of animals, with the drawing not yet very secure, together with early attempts at sculpture on larger tools such as spear-throwers.

One would without hesitation claim that in Stage IV home art reached its peak. Within the limitations imposed by the material used these carvings have rarely been surpassed, and the artists' technical skill and understanding of their material is a clear indication of their mental stature. Belonging to this phase and illustrating the standards reached are two carved spear-throwers, their distinctive motif suggesting the work of one man though they were found in sites over 60 miles apart.

Towards the end of the Magdalenian there is a return to abstract design and stylization and the standard of both engraving and sculpture seems to decline. Carving almost disappears and the accurately depicted animals give way to drawing with heavy lines and lose their sense of spontaneity, the gay colts becoming attenuated cab horses. As with the Solutrean and earlier Perigordian, engraved slabs are plentiful in the later stages of the Magdalenian – one site's unusually large number of examples show a wide range of skill as though the site were an academy of art.

A late Magdalenian engraving, suggesting a broken-down cab horse.

Magdalenian sculpture of an animal on the back wall of a rock shelter in Angles sur l'Anglin, France.

Taking the sequence of home art as a whole there seems to be a clear development in competence from its beginnings in the Aurignacian to its peak in the second half of the Magdalenian. The major differences in the cultures involved suggest that this is not a continuous process but is somewhat uneven. The standard of carving shown by the Perigordian female figures is not reached again until the middle of the Magdalenian. Even within the Magdalenian there seem to have been styles confined to particular stages, the geometric designs of Magdalenian III being an example. These internal differences apart, the succession through the six stages of the Magdalenian (for example Stages IV, V and VI from the type site of La Madeleine in the Dordogne and the first three stages from La Placard in the Department of Charente) shows a general progression to a peak followed by a decline.

As one would expect, home art in western Europe follows the distribution of industries, and this applies particularly to the late Magdalenian, whose typical art is found in Spain, Germany, Switzerland and Czechoslovakia. Proceeding further east we come into the area which, on cultural grounds, has been designated the eastern zone. In this area not only is there a divergence from the west in stone and bone tools, but the home art also suggests traditions independent of the west.

As we have seen earlier the division between east and west does not follow a clear geographical line. For example Czechoslovakia contains material of typical Eastern Gravettian, Aurignacian and late Magdalenian types. In such border areas one would expect some exchange not only of technical ideas but of art motifs, but if this was the case it is difficult to prove. The similarities in the two areas seem to be the result of direct migration, as with the late Magdalenian, rather than culture contact.

There is one possible example of common art motifs, and that is the female figurine. These have been found over an area stretching from southwest France across eastern Europe into Siberia. Like those of the west the eastern figures are characterized by obesity and facelessness, but the further east one goes the more stylized they become. The well-covered lady from the Austrian site of Willendorf has much in common with the Venus from Laussel in concept, and there are many similarities between the stone industries from the two sites. However, figures from the south Russian sites of Gargarino and Kostenki may belong to a separate group, those from the Siberian site of Mal'ta are probably very late and may be either in the French or the Russian tradition.

An attractive group of objects so far not found in any quantity in France are the small animals carved in bone from the Aurignacian site of Vogelherd in Germany. Similar small animals have come from Vistonice in Czechoslovakia and some Russian sites but here, like the Venus from the same site, they are made from a mixture of clay and powdered bone hardened in fire.

Cave art. Painting and engraving have been mentioned in connection with home art, as well as sculpture and carving in relief. Turning to cave art, we find that the cave walls provide larger working areas resulting in more impressive works.

As with home art, the pigments used for painting are derived from natural sources – red and yellow from ochers, black from manganese or (more probably) charcoal, and white, almost unknown in Europe, from China clay. These pigments can be used either direct in the form of a crayon, examples of which are known from archaeological deposits, or mixed with a liquid, water or possibly animal fat. As some of the pigments are water-repellent these "oil based" paints are most likely those used in works involving washes. In addition to the red ocher crayons hollow bones were used as containers, and limestone slabs have been found on which pigments were ground. It has been assumed that the burin was the tool employed for engraving, support for this idea coming from the finding of a burin on a ledge below a large wall engraving. However it seems that this tool was also used for many other purposes.

As well as painting and engraving, cave sculpture was carried out on a grander scale than was possible in home art. The Venus of Laussel, which is usually discussed as home art since it was found as a detached piece of work, was undoubtedly one of the many reliefs carved on the walls of caves and shelters. Some of these reliefs are of considerable size. The group of horses on the wall of the shelter at Cap Blanc, dated to early Magdalenian, includes one animal nearly seven feet long. Many of these works are in high relief, necessitating the removal of a great deal of hard rock. Much of this work was probably done by hammering and thus crushing the rock crystals. Some of these reliefs are very attractive, revealing a great sense of freedom, a good example being the small chamois head from the middle Magdalenian site at Angles sur l'Anglin.

A rare aspect of cave art is modeling in clay, a medium which would have a poor chance of survival. The only complete example known is the pair of bison in relief from the Pyrenean cave of Tuc d'Audoubert. There is also a freestanding bear from the same region. Rolls of clay have been found on the floors of some caves, suggesting that modeling may have played a large part in prehistoric art.

As with home art, the subject matter of cave art is predominantly the animals whose remains are found in occupation levels. Particularly appealing to us today are drawings of now extinct animals, the mammoth and woolly rhinoceros, whose appearance has been handed down with great accuracy by their artistic contemporaries.

By the very nature of its physical location, cave art is almost always out of archaeological context. This made it difficult for early prehistorians to accept cave art as the work of prehistoric man, and the final establishment of its true age was the result of a number of factors. By the end of the 19th century the work of Lartet and Christy in the Dordogne and Edouard Piette in the Pyrenees, primarily in Magdalenian deposits, had produced a mass of art

material whose authenticity was not in question. It seemed a reasonable argument that if prehistoric man were capable of producing home art there was no reason to doubt his ability to execute cave paintings, particularly as the two seemed to complement each other.

Some hesitation in accepting all prehistoric art was excusable, since nothing like the bison from Altamira or the polychrome reindeer from Font de Gaume had been found in cave deposits. However, many of the engravings from stratified occupational deposits were identical in style to those found on cave walls. An oft-quoted example is the head of a hind engraved in a rather unusual style on a shoulder blade and found in an early Magdalenian deposit in Altamira, Spain. A hind's head in exactly the same style was found on the wall of the cave of Castillo nearby.

Further evidence came from Laussel in France, where the Venus was found in a level originally described as Aurignacian, sealed by two undisturbed Solutrean levels. As there is little doubt that it was originally part of the shelter wall, its obvious date lends support to dates attributed to the reliefs from Cap Blanc which are very close in technique.

Some of the best evidence for the age of cave paintings comes from examples found in recesses whose entrance was blocked by later archaeological debris, or cases where late levels were found to be covering paintings or engravings on the wall. An accumulation of such evidence meant that by the beginning of this century most doubts about the authenticity of cave art had disappeared, though suggestions of forgery are still made from time to time.

Above: head of a hind engraved on a shoulder blade. *Below:* a head in identical technique engraved on a cave wall. Both from Spain.

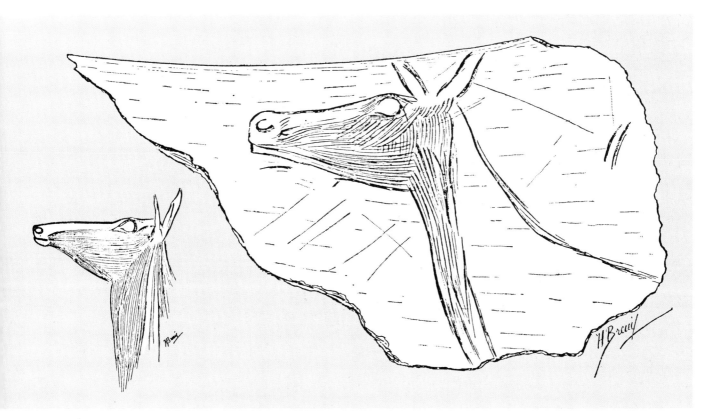

Having established authenticity, the next problem was that of marshaling a mass of apparently unrelated material, executed in a wide variety of styles and techniques, into correct chronological order. Some cave art could be attributed quite easily to the late Magdalenian on the grounds of dated styles in the home art, but there was a mass of material executed in simpler styles which appeared to be a great deal earlier and had no home art equivalent.

Since home art began in the Aurignacian, it was assumed that cave art was at least as old. Confirmation came from the cave of Pair-non-Pair in Gironde, where simple engravings were covered by undisturbed Perigordian deposits and must thus have been of an earlier date, and a finely engraved bison found in La Grèze and covered by Solutrean deposits. Such evidence, together with a knowledge of the sequence of styles of home art, formed a basis on which a framework could be constructed. More detailed information on the development of cave art styles came from the study of superposition. Fortunately the early cave artists had little regard for the work of their predecessors and very commonly engraved or painted on top of earlier work. Sometimes superposition was several layers thick.

By establishing the order in which various works were executed it was possible to see a number of clearly defined styles. Breuil, who studied European cave art for over fifty years, postulated four stages of development, but there is some doubt as to whether this number can be substantiated and the tendency now is to accept two as a working hypothesis – one covering the Aurignacian–Perigordian and the other the Solutrean–Magdalenian. One must bear in mind however that this twofold division is basically for the sake of convenience and may not be significant.

As with home art, early attempts at cave art are simple, and the first drawings were done with fingers dipped in clay. Some of these have survived in the soft surfaces of cave walls, hardened by a fine stalagmite film. Many are no more than parallel lines made by two or more fingers drawn across the rock surface. Others, for example some from northern Spain, depict recognizable animals drawn with one finger.

The most authentic of the early engravings are those from Pair-non-Pair already mentioned, which are simple outlines of animals in full profile. Probably contemporary with these are paintings, sometimes in outline and sometimes in flat wash. Examples of both techniques are known also from home art in Aurignacian levels.

A distinctive feature of much of this early work is what is known as twisted perspective. The animal is drawn in full profile except for certain aspects such as horns and hooves which are portrayed as though they were seen full face; for example both horns might be shown on an animal drawn in profile whereas in reality only one would be visible.

Quite often engraving and painting are combined in the same piece of work, the outline possibly being scratched as a draft before being filled in with paint. It is also possible that later painters filled in old engravings.

Towards the end of the first cycle of cave art, principles of shading were beginning to be mastered. Sometimes hair was shown in such a way that it served to give depth to the drawing, or the same result was achieved by using another color, generally black, to accentuate shadows.

Usually the animals are drawn as naturally as the competence of the early artists allowed, but sometimes distortions (presumably deliberate) are introduced. This is

Successive Magdalenian paintings, one on top of another, from the cave of Niaux in the French Pyrenees.

particularly noticeable with some of the early horses whose heads are very small and apparently badly drawn compared with the body.

Drawings of hands apparently belong to the Aurignacian, since one was found in an Aurignacian deposit. These appear either in negative, where the hand is laid flat against the wall and painted around or, conversely, in positive, where the hand is covered with paint and pressed onto the wall. It has been remarked that most examples of negative hands are left hands and most positive ones, right. Hands of either type are rare, occurring only in a few caves in France and northern Spain.

The beginning of the second cycle of cave art is hard to establish. No cave art can be assigned with certainty to any stage of the Solutrean, the only substantial piece of work clearly belonging to this period being the frieze of limestone blocks from Le Roc de Ser, which in fact more properly belong to home art, since they are portable though very large.

The cave of Pech Merle contains examples of strange elongated mammoths, a magnificent spotted horse and negative hands. There are no archaeological deposits in the cave, but nearby is a Solutrean site whose inhabitants may well have been responsible for at least part of the cave decoration. It has also been suggested that part of the material at Lascaux may be Solutrean.

Cave art as well as home art reaches its peak in the middle Magdalenian, and it is to this period that most of the impressive works belong.

The decline seen in home art towards the end of the Magdalenian cannot be isolated in cave art, but it is extremely unlikely that the best of cave painting occurred at the very end of the period.

Problems and interpretations. The extent to which one can use the word composition in connection with prehistoric art is open to question. The apparently haphazard placing of many works makes it difficult to understand the artist's intentions, particularly when he has chosen a previously used area to work on. Certainly there is no attempt to portray any of the subjects in natural settings – trees, rivers and hills are not featured. In general groups of animals are as far as composition goes, and even here it is not always clear whether the animals in such a group were all painted at the same time. As far as subjects are concerned, almost the whole range of the known fauna is represented, including seals, birds, snakes and even a pair of eels. Humans play a very subordinate part in cave art. The faithful rendering accorded the animals is not extended to the artist's own kind, who are invariably reduced to caricatures. Sometimes they are shown wearing animal skins complete with horns or antlers, as though disguised, possibly for stalking. Occasionally they appear in groups, one of the best examples being the "bison feast." Even more scarce than humans are plants, of which none can be identified with certainty in cave art, though there are

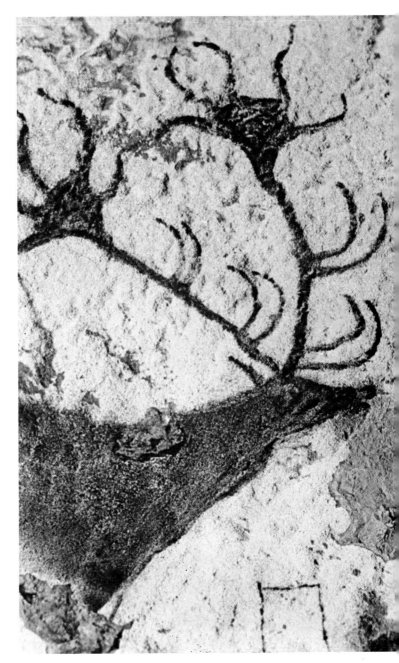

Head of a red deer showing the use of twisted perspective.

possible examples in home art as decoration on bone objects.

By far the most enigmatic aspect of prehistoric art, particularly in the realm of cave art, are the signs or symbols. These have fascinated the prehistorian since they were first recognized, since their purpose is not apparent and is open to a wide range of interpretation. Some are tent-shaped, some look like clubs or throwing sticks, others resemble shields, a further group arrows or spears, and others traps.

The mass of material we have discussed so far covers the concrete side of prehistoric art which is visible and can be handled, photographed and argued about. However, with

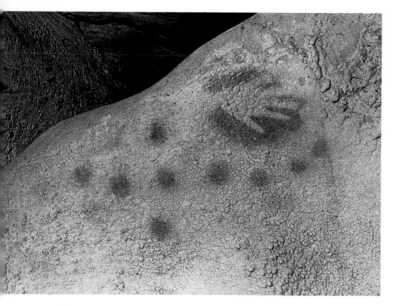

A human hand placed against the wall and surrounded by red ocher, from Pech Merle, France.

the question of motive we move into the realm of the abstract. Opinions expressed about the motives underlying early man's activities have caused more contention than discussion of the activities themselves, since they do not have to be based on anything as sordid as evidence.

It was natural that prehistorians should turn to anthropological data to explain the purpose of early art. The obvious explanation "art for art's sake," while being a possible motive for much of the decoration of personal possessions, certainly cannot be stretched to cover the greater part of cave art (though one is tempted to see doodling as the explanation for finger drawings in the clay). Only a small part of prehistoric man's artistic output survives, but one may reasonably assume that the majority of permanent homes were decorated, although only the sculptured examples have survived the weathering of the last 12,000 years. While we cannot deny a decorative motive for much of the art in occupied parts of caves and shelters, it does not explain the greater part of surviving art, found in almost inaccessible regions of the caves which must have been without natural light.

Anthropology provided two possible explanations for art preserved in deep recesses of the caves, which must have been executed with great difficulty and was probably intended to be seen by very few people. The first possible motive lay in the ideas surrounding totemism. To simplify what is rather a complicated subject, one can say that bands or clans (or in some cases individuals) associate themselves with a particular object, generally animal or vegetable, with which they claim a special relationship. Some clans, like some of the Australians, practice elaborate ceremonies in honor of their totem in which only initiated members can participate. It has been claimed that this could account for at least some of the animals depicted on cave walls, each being drawn as part of a totem ritual.

The second possible motive, which seemed to fit the facts better, was that of sympathetic magic, whereby the hunter obtains power over an animal by drawing it prior to setting out on a hunt; moreover by reproducing its image he can make the species itself increase. This idea of hunting magic was strengthened by the number of cases where animals are shown with wounds or spears sticking into their flanks.

Examples of both totemism and sympathetic magic can be found among modern hunting peoples, and these two theories seemed to provide adequate explanations for even the most inaccessible paintings. It required little imagination to conjure up visions of ceremonies in the dark recesses of the cave, with only simple lamps throwing weird shadows, while tribal elders practiced magic rites or initiated terrified youngsters into manhood.

Recently attempts have been made to put these ideas aside and look for other motives for cave art. An analysis of a large number of animals portrayed shows that particular species tend to be placed in particular parts of the cave – bison, horse, ox and mammoth are most frequently found in a central position in the main chambers, bear and lion towards the back and deer in a side position. This arrangement is not completely consistent and probably only applies to later periods where enough material is available for such an analysis. As far as interpretation is concerned, this information does not get us much further.

Matters are complicated by new attempts to interpret the signs and symbols found in cave art. The distinguished French prehistorian André Leroi-Gourhan sees the majority of these as sex symbols, with wide forms representing the female element and narrow the male. While there are certainly obvious examples of female sex symbols such as those from Angles sur l'Anglin, it is difficult to see some of the more abstract signs filling this role. So far no convincing phallic symbols have been found to represent the male element, and the narrow signs are open to a variety of interpretations. This idea has been extended to include the sexing of animals irrespective of the sex the artist gave them. Narrow signs which would appear to be spears are now considered as indicating the sex of the animal with which they are associated, thus horse, ibex

"Bison feast" – a group of diners around a dismembered bison.

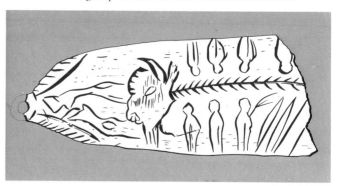

Above: this painting by George Catlin, with its masterful use of color, shows a group of North American Indians dressed in bison skins carrying out a ritual hunting dance. This suggests a possible explanation for the "sorcerer" shown right.

Right: "the sorcerer" – a human figure in a reindeer skin. It has been suggested that this is part of some hunting ritual.

and deer would be male and bison, cattle and mammoth female. These ideas at present get us no further than we were before, but at least they show that any interpretation must be preceded by a much more systematic analysis of the art than was attempted by earlier prehistorians.

Before accepting or rejecting any of these theories or, for that matter, any new ones, two things must be borne in mind – first, the art whose motives we are trying to establish extends over 20,000 years, time enough for any number of ideas to have been developed and discarded; second, we are treating the art as though it were part of an unbroken cultural sequence, whereas in reality at least four cultural stages were involved – Aurignacian, Perigordian, Solutrean and Magdalenian, with very little evidence of any direct connection between them.

In this field of archaeology we will always be short of answers, and for this reason art will remain one of the most attractive aspects of prehistory.

Epilogue

It may seem strange to write an epilogue for so early a chapter in the history of Man, but in the story of human development we have reached the end of Man the Hunter.

Between the close of the Ice Age in Europe and the invention of farming was a gap of some 4,000–5,000 years. Climatic changes, though slow, led to modifications in living patterns not only in Europe but over much of the Old World.

By the end of the Last Glaciation the inhabitants of both western and eastern Europe had reached the peak of their efficiency as hunter-gatherers. Their life-style, though differing in west and east, enabled them to flourish in extremely difficult climatic conditions. The Victorians' admiration for the noble hunter was not without justification. The main factors which made occupation of such inhospitable regions possible were the same for early man in Europe as for the Eskimo in the Arctic: abundant supplies of meat and suitable conditions for preserving it over long periods. Like the Eskimos' exploitation of the reindeer and marine mammals, the western European Magdalenians depended on the herds of reindeer, horse, bison and wild ox, and the eastern Gravettians on the mammoth not only to make survival possible but to allow a standard of living which was not to be enjoyed by the postglacial hunter-gatherers.

The passing of the rigorous conditions of the Last Glaciation around 10,000 BC had a profound effect on cultural patterns. Environmental changes resulting from the retreat of the ice and its final disappearance from Scandinavia occurred in two main stages, the conifers and birch trees of dry and cool conditions later replaced by deciduous forests as the climate became wetter and warmer.

One would expect that the lifting of so many environmental pressures as the climate improved in postglacial Europe would have led to an improvement in living standards, but this does not seem to have been the case. Following the Magdalenian in western Europe, the fine bone and antler work and magnificent paintings disappear. The Magdalenians' immediate successors could rise no higher than clumsy harpoons and limestone pebbles painted with abstract designs.

At the same time, changes took place whose significance is far from clear. In Europe the period between the end of the Last Glaciation and the advent of farming (the Mesolithic) is characterized by a curious change in tool typology, a change which occurs at much the same time and stems from much the same cultural levels over most of the Old World.

In France the Mesolithic industries following the last of the Magdalenian are based on the production of very small tools, often geometric in shape – triangles, crescents and trapezoids. Many of these microliths are less than an inch in length, and though accompanied by larger tools they predominate in assemblages. The trend towards small tools follows the local Upper Paleolithic equivalents throughout Africa, the Middle East, India and the Far East.

So far there is no adequate explanation for this phenomenon. One suggestion is that the small tools are components of composite tools, such as the barbs of harpoons. At least one Mesolithic group in Europe has both antler harpoons and microliths, so this does not appear to be the whole answer, nor does it explain why this change of emphasis was so widespread. Neither can it be seen as a response to climatic change, since in Europe the climate moved from cold to temperate but in the Middle East and Africa from damp to very dry.

As one would expect, the improvement in climate in Europe led to the greater use of open campsites. Such sites are of course known from the Mousterian and throughout the Upper Paleolithic as summer camps, but they now became alternatives to the caves, which show signs of much less occupation.

There is no evidence to show that changes in environment made any difference to the hunting and gathering economy, but certainly the hunters would have had to make considerable adaptations to new conditions, the most significant being the dispersal of herd animals due to the spread of forests. Game drives such as that indicated at one site in France, where the remains of over 20,000 horses were found at the base of a slope, were no longer possible, and communal hunting on the plains probably gave way to more individual hunting and trapping in the forests.

Some communities, such as the Maglemosians of North Germany, Denmark and Britain, have left well-preserved summer camps dating from the early part of the post-Glacial. These are situated on the banks of rivers and lakes, where damp conditions have preserved much organic material including bows, canoe paddles and fish traps. Although fishing and fowling contributed largely to the food supply, the hunting of game, mainly red deer, was still of major importance. We know that the French Upper Paleolithic peoples fished, as this is revealed in their art and their use of fishbones for beads but, as with the inland Eskimo, this was probably only a summer occupation when meat was scarce.

Other Mesolithic groups lived on dry heathland, but their bone and wood artifacts are not sufficiently well preserved to give any idea of their way of life, though there is evidence that they lived in shallow pits.

In the Middle East similar Mesolithic groups such as the Natufians augmented their food supply by reaping wild cereals with sickles made of bone with flint insets, but did not reduce their hunting activities.

From communities such as these in areas bordering the southern Mediterranean the early farmers gradually spread across Europe. In this way the tradition of the great hunters was eventually replaced by the farmers' more self-sufficient way of life, and the foundations of what we call civilization were laid.

Further Reading

Bordaz, Jacques, *Tools of the Old and New Stone Age* (New York, 1959).

Bordes, François, *The Old Stone Age* (London, 1968).

Breuil, Henri, *Four Hundred Centuries of Cave Art* (Montignac, 1952).

Clark, Grahame, *The Stone Age Hunters* (London, 1967).

Coles, J. M. and **Higgs, E. S.,** *The Archaeology of Early Man* (London, 1969).

Cornwell, I. W., *The World of Ancient Man* (London, 1964).

Day, Michael H., *Fossil Man* (London, 1969).

Howells, W. W. *Mankind in the Making* (London, 1959).

Le Gros Clark, W. E., *History of the Primates* (London, 1949).

Oakley, Kenneth P., *Man the Tool-maker* (London, 1949).

Oakley, Kenneth P., *Frameworks for Dating Fossil Man* (London, 1964).

Pilbeam, David, *The Ascent of Man* (London, 1972).

Simons, Elwyn L., *Primate Evolution* (New York, 1972).

Tattersall, Ian, *Man's Ancestors* (London, 1970).

Ucko, Peter J. and **Rosenfeld, A.,** *Palaeolithic Cave Art* (London, 1967).

Readings from "Scientific American," *Biology and Culture in Modern Perspective* (New York, 1972).

Acknowledgments

Unless otherwise stated, all the illustrations on a given page are credited to the same source.

Aerofilms Ltd 27 (bottom), 29 (top)
Alan Hutchison, London 38, 58, 95 (top)
Helmut Albrecht/Bruce Coleman Inc., 47 (top)
The American Museum of Natural History, New York 52
Animal Photography 47 (bottom)
Australian News and Information Bureau 99 (top), 110 (right)
Dick Barnard, London 89 (top right), 112 (right), 113 (bottom)
Barnaby's Picture Library, London 94, 97 (bottom left), 98 (bottom and top right), 126 (bottom)
L'Abbé Breuil, by permission of the copyright holder Arnold Fawcus, Paris 117, 119 (bottom), 121 (center), 131, 134 (bottom), 135 (bottom)
The British Museum (Natural History), London 16, 18, 19, 49 (bottom), 53, 59 (bottom left), 61 (bottom), 89 (top left)
Canadian High Commission, London 39
G. Catlin, *North American Portfolio* (1844) 43, 135 (top)
David Collison/Alex Hooper 100, 118 (bottom left), 130
Crown Copyright: Institute of Geological Sciences photograph; reproduced by permission of the Controller of Her Majesty's Stationery Office 68 (bottom)
Michael Daniell/Robert Harding Associates, London 57 (bottom)
Professor Michael Day 51, 59 (top), 62
Elsevier, Amsterdam 21, 26, 45 (top)
Mary Evans Picture Library, London 15 (center)
Alain Fournier, Blois, France 118 (bottom right), 121 (top left), 132, 134 (top)
John R. Freeman, London Frontispiece, 13 (top)
Professor P. V. Glob 41 (bottom right)
Roger Gorringe, London 64, 69 (lower right), 76 (top) (after Mary Leakey), 77 (bottom right) (after Mary Leakey), 122 (top right)
Sir W. E. Le Gros Clark and American Philosophical Society 20
Haddon Collection, University Museum of Archaeology and Ethnology, Cambridge 44, 96 (bottom left and top right)
Michael Holford Library, London 121 (top right)
Alan Hughes, by permission of Professor P. V. Tobias, University of Witwatersrand, South Africa 49 (top)
J. Hürzeler 56 (top)
G. Kinns/Associated Freelance Artists Ltd., London 72 (top right)
Peter Kolb, *Vollstandige Beschreibung des Afrikanischen Vorgebürges der Guten Hofnung*, Nuremberg (1719) 96 (bottom right)
E. Lartet and H. Christy, *Reliquiae Aquitanicae* (1875) 14 (top), 41 (bottom left), 42 (left), 63, 111
John Launois/Black Star 95 (bottom), 96 (top left), 97 (bottom right)
Andrew Lawson/Dr. J. Waechter 60, 68 (top), 71 (top right), 72 (bottom left), 73, 74, 75 (top), 79, 84, 86, 87, 88, 89 (bottom), 91 (bottom right), 102 (center), 106 (left), 107 (top), 109 (top), 110 (left), 115, 118 (top left), 123 (left and top right), 124 (top right and bottom left), 125, 129 (top)
Lovell Johns, Oxford 10, 27 (top), 48, 75 (bottom), 91 (top), 105, 127
Michael Lyster, London 45 (bottom)
Malcolm McGregor 13 (bottom)
Hazel Martingell 40, 78, 83, 90, 91 (bottom left), 102 (top and bottom), 106 (right), 108, 109 (bottom)
Moravski Museum, Brno 124 (top center)
Musée des Antiquités Nationales, St Germain-en-Laye 123 (bottom right), 128
Musée du Périgord, Périgueux 119 (top)
Museo Archeologico Nazionale, Naples 24 (left)
National Geographic Society, London 57 (top), 77 (top), 82
Naturhistorisches Museum, Vienna 124 (top left)
A. van den Nieuwenhuizen 46
Novosti Press Agency 32 (top), 113 (top)
Dr. Kenneth Oakley, Oxford 85
Oxford Illustrators 35, 92, 139–149
Picturepoint Limited, London 28, 36, 76 (bottom), 93, 97 (top), 98 (top left), 99 (bottom), 107 (bottom), 122 (bottom), 133
E. Piette, *L'Art pendant l'Age du Renne* (1907) 32 (bottom), 121 (bottom right)
Punch Magazine, London 24 (right)
Radio Times Hulton Picture Library 14 (bottom)
Servizio Editoriale Fotographico, Turin 77 (bottom left), 120
Shell International 34
The Society of Antiquaries, London 11 (right)
Spectrum Colour Library, London 126 (right)
Staatliches Museum für Naturkunde, Stuttgart 61 (top)
William Stukeley, *Stonehenge* (1740) 11 (top left and bottom left)
The Tate Gallery, London 9, 12
Vanity Fair 15 (left), 15 (right)
R. Verneau, *Les Grottes des Grimaldi*, Monaco (1906) 112 (left)
Dr. J. Waechter, London 17, 25, 29 (bottom), 30, 37, 66, 67, 68 (center), 69 (left and top right), 70, 71 (bottom), 72 (top left), 122 (center), 129 (bottom)
Werner Forman Archive, London 56 (bottom left)
Maurice Wilson 22–23, 54, 80–81, 104, 114
Maurice Wilson, by permission of the British Museum (Natural History), London 50, 56 (bottom right)
Christopher J. M. Wood 41 (top)

The Publishers have attempted to observe the legal requirements with respect to the rights of the suppliers of photographic materials. Nevertheless, persons who have claims are invited to apply to the Publishers.

Glossary

Note : asterisks indicate separate entries on words thus marked

Abbevillian An industry named after the town of Abbeville on the River Somme in France, the gravels of which were explored by Boucher de Perthes and produced many hand axes. The term is used for the early hand axes★ made with a hard hammer.

Absolute dating Dating usually by some method of atomic physics. Many different methods are used depending on the time range. Carbon 14★ for example is usable back to about 50,000 years, whereas potassium–argon dates are possible for several million years. Non-atomic dating methods include counting tree rings or the annual sediments in lakes.

Acheulian Named from Saint-Acheul, a suburb of the French town of Amiens on the river Somme. The term covers the more refined hand axes made with a soft hammer. The name is used to cover all of these hand axes wherever they are found.

Acid soils Soils with a marked acid content as opposed to calcareous★ soils. Acid soils are poor preservers of bone and shell, but are good preservers of pollen.

Anthropoid ape The four man-like apes: gibbon, orangutan, chimpanzee and gorilla. Anatomically these are the nearest relations to man. The gorilla and chimpanzee are confined to central and west Africa and the others to the Far East; all four are mainly forest dwellers, the gibbon and orangutan living almost exclusively in trees.

Anthropology Literally, the study of Man. The science is divided into several branches such as Social, Cultural and Physical. In the 19th century anthropology was principally thought of in terms of primitive peoples. The subject has been gradually extended and the study of any community could now come under the term. The purpose of archaeology is to study past societies and thus the two subjects are closely related.

Antler Antlers are confined to deer and are carried by the males with the exception of reindeer, where they are carried by both sexes. They are shed annually and a larger set grown in their place. During growth the antler starts as soft tissue with a blood supply which, as the material hardens, gets cut off. In composition very like bone, but easier to work, antler was used extensively by Upper Paleolithic man.

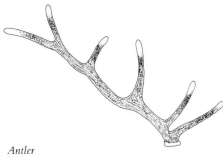

Antler

Anyathian A group of tools found on the terraces of the Irrawaddy river in Burma. The industry, which is rather simple, is partly made of fossil wood. The shape of the tools is governed to some extent by the shape of the raw material and consists mainly of simple scraping and chopping tools. Although not very securely dated, it seems to cover the period from the Mindel★ Glaciation to the early part of the Würm★ Glaciation.

Assemblage This term is used to describe the total archaeological content of a particular level. Some sites, such as caves, contain many different assemblages. Sometimes the term "faunal assemblage" is used to cover all the animal remains.

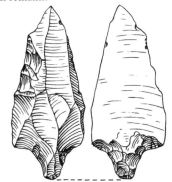

Two views of an Aterian point

Aterian A stone industry from North Africa. A development of the North African Mousterian, it is characterized by tanged points made on flakes and, in its later stages, by bifacial points. It stretches across North Africa from the Nile Valley to the Atlantic. The type site is Bir el Ater in Tunisia and is dated to about 30,000–27,000 BC.

Atlanthropus A generic name given to the jaws from Ternifine in North Africa found associated with Acheulian hand axes. These jaws are now grouped with Telanthropus and Homo 9 from Olduvai as African variants of Homo erectus.

Aurignacian One of the stages of the European Upper Paleolithic. The type site is the cave of Aurignac in southwest France, excavated by Lartet in 1860. The name Aurignacian was originally given to the first three stages of the French Upper Paleolithic, but is now restricted to the middle, the other two being called Perigordian★. Characterized by thick scrapers, heavy blades★ and flat bone points★, it occurs throughout France and into Germany. It is absent in peninsular Italy and southern Spain, but occurs in Hungary and Austria. Similar material from the Levant has been called Aurignacian. The origin is uncertain. Western European dates: 34,000 to 27,000 BC. (*See also* **Perigordian**).

Australopithecus The southern ape, name given by Raymond Dart to the Taungs★ skull; it is now used as a generic name for three African groups. These are Australopithecus africanus, the thin variant which includes the Taungs child and the material from Sterkfontein; Australopithecus robustus from Swartkrans in South Africa and Zinjanthropus★ from Bed I at Olduvai. Comparable material has been found in Lake Rudolf in Northern Kenya, the Omo river in Ethiopia and other sites in East Africa. Of the three members of this group, Australopithecus robustus appears to have continued later than the other two, possibly overlapping in parts with Homo erectus. In terms of human evolution the Australopithecines are considered as being parallel to a Homo stem rather than ancestral to it. It has been suggested that a rather primitive jaw from Java may be a variant of the same group, thus widening its distribution.

Awl A small finely-pointed tool made of either bone or stone, presumably used for

Awls

punching holes in skin and possibly also beads. Some of the Magdalenian★ flint examples have more than one point. The bone varieties, which differ from needles by having part of the articulation as a handle, occur in most of the Upper Paleolithic industries and continue into the Neolithic★ and later.

Bifacial Tools retouched over both faces. Examples are hand axes and the leaf-shaped tools from the Solutrean★. Some of the finest examples of such flaking are the Predynastic blades from Egypt and the modern glass spearheads from Australia.

Bipolar This technique of flake production consists of placing the core on an anvil; when struck there is a force at each end of the flake, one from the hammer and the other from the rebound of the anvil. Flakes struck off by this method have a bulb of percussion at each end. Cores worked from both ends are sometimes referred to as bipolar.

Bison The European Bison, similar to but larger than the American equivalent, is now nearly extinct, a few herds remaining in the Bialowieza forest on the Polish-Russian border. During the Upper Pleistocene they were abundant over most of northern Europe and are frequently represented in French and Spanish cave art.

Blades A term applied to flakes whose length is greater than their width. Most of the silica rocks such as flint produce flakes sharp enough for cutting without modification, and many blades were used this way. They are also made into other tools such as end scrapers and burins, and are characteristic of the Upper Paleolithic industries.

Two views of a blade

"Blade & Burin" A very inaccurate term describing Upper Paleolithic industries in various parts of the world based on the frequency of these tools. As both blades and burins occur in earlier industries, the term is meaningless.

Blank A flake or blade struck from a core but not yet modified into a formal tool.

Bolas A hunting implement used principally on the pampas of South America. It consists of one, two or three balls wrapped in hide and joined by leather thongs. Thrown at a running animal it wraps itself around the legs. The South American version has stones about the size of an orange. The Eskimo use a similar version with small ivory balls, principally for birds. Several examples of stone balls have been found, particularly with the hand ax industries of Africa, suggesting that bolas may have been in use for a very long period.

Bolas

Boulder clay A geological term covering tough clays made up of material transported by an advancing ice sheet or glacier. Characteristically they are structureless and frequently contain rocks carried from a considerable distance. These erratics, as they are called, often give an indication of the direction from which the ice came. There are extensive sheets of boulder clay in Britain, North America and Europe.

Browridge The bony arch above the eye socket. In modern man the two arches are separate, but in primitive man they are joined as a bony ridge above the nose. Though present in gorillas and Homo erectus and to a lesser extent in Neanderthal man, they do not necessarily represent a primitive trait as they are almost absent in Skull 1470★.

Brun race Named after the town of Brno in Czechoslovakia. A narrow-headed group of Upper Paleolithic peoples to which the skull from Combe Capelle in France appears to belong. This skull is early Perigordian★.

Bulb of percussion The swelling on the surface of a flake where it was attached to the core. This swelling occurs just below the point of impact and corresponds to a depression or negative bulb on the core. The silica rocks such as flint show well-marked bulbs, but they are less easy to see on the coarser rocks.

Burin A chisel-like tool. Though occurring earlier, it is characteristic of Upper Paleolithic industries in many parts of the world. The chisel-like edge is obtained by removing a sliver from the edge of a flake or blade. It was originally thought that only the narrow end was used, but it seems possible that the whole length of the edge was used as well. Tools of this type have proved very satisfactory in the working of bone and antler.

Calcareous A term applied to soils with a high calcium content, the opposite of acid soils★. These are easily determined in the field by fizzing in contact with hydrochloric acid. These soils are good preservers of bone but generally not of pollen. Where the calcium is dissolved out by percolating water, the soil is said to be weathered or decalcified.

Cannibalism The eating of human flesh. Generally practiced for ritual purposes, eg the acquiring of attributes of an admired enemy; more rarely as food, though generally only in emergencies. There are hints of possible cannibalism in the Mousterian★ of eastern Europe and also in the Mesolithic★ in Denmark.

Carbon 14 A method of absolute dating by calculating the known rate of decay of the carbon 14 isotope. Modern techniques have made it possible to obtain dates as far back as 50,000 BC with the margin of error increasing as the dates become older. The dates are expressed either as BC or BP – this last means before present. The "present" date being used is 1950.

Carbonized Anything which has been burned. Burned material such as wood or stone is very suitable for carbon 14 dating.

Charentian Named after the French department of Charente. A form of Mousterian★ with a high percentage of scrapers★ and a very low percentage of prepared core★ techniques. The type site of this form of Mousterian is La Quina in the same department, and from this site came two classic Neanderthals★ including a young child.

Chellian Originally used to describe the early hand axes. The name is derived from Chelles-sur-Marne near Paris. As the site does not in fact contain early hand axes, the term has been replaced by Abbevillian★. The older term Chellian is sometimes used in Africa: hence Chellian Man.

Chellian Man Homo 9 from the upper part of Bed II at Olduvai. Although not directly associated with archaeological material, it came from the same horizon as hand axes in other parts of the gorge, hence the name. Clearly

Burin

more developed than Homo habilis★, it is classed as Homo erectus.

Chopper A term used by prehistorians for cutting tools★ made on pebbles. Where the flaking is from both sides they are distinguished by the term chopping tool.

Clactonian An industry based on choppers★ and large blades. Type site: Clacton-on-Sea, England, represented by a few sites in England and North France, one of the best of which is Swanscombe.

Cleaver

Cleaver Unlike the ordinary hand ax, the cleaver has a straight edge at the end. Sometimes cleavers are made in exactly the same way as hand axes with the ends squared. But many of the African examples are made on large flakes with the natural edge of the flake forming the cutting edge, and the retouching★ only to facilitate holding in the hand.

Core tool Tools made from a block of raw material by chipping off flakes. These range from the very early pebble tools★ to Neolithic axes. The best-known examples are hand axes, though some of these are made on flakes in the later stages. Throughout the stone ages these core tools were the heavy-duty equipment.

Core tool

Cro-Magnon Early form of modern man from France, named from the cave of Cro-Magnon in the village of Les Eyzies, excavated by Lartet and Christy. The "old man of Cro-Magnon" skull is the type specimen of the Cro-Magnon race. They were tall and broad-faced and were responsible for most of the Upper Paleolithic cultures of Western Europe. Possible relations have been claimed from North Africa and China.

Culture A word borrowed by prehistorians from anthropology★, where it means the total achievements of a particular people – material culture, religion, social practice, art, etc. In prehistory the term is much more restricted and is used very loosely to cover such groups as "the hand ax cultures," "the Mousterian cultures," etc.

Dabban An Upper Paleolithic industry from North Africa. The type site, in Cyrenaica, is characterized by small backed blades and end scrapers. Deep deposits of this industry occur in the cave of Haua Fteah, also in Cyrenaica, with carbon 14★ dates ranging from 34,000 to 14,000 BC.

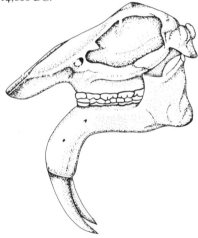

A deinotherium jawbone

Deinotherium An early form of elephant with tusks curving downwards and simple molar teeth. It dates from the early Pleistocene★ and was hunted by early man at Olduvai.

Dendrochronology A method of absolute dating★ by which the annual growth rings revealed in cross-sections of trees are counted. Patterns caused by small variations of local climate allow rings of various ages to be matched up and the wood dated over very long periods. Burned wood, which has been dated by its tree rings, is now being used as a cross-check for carbon 14 dating.

Denticulated Literally "with teeth." Flakes or blades with a serrated or saw-like edge obtained by making small notches at regular intervals. These notches may be large as in some of the Mousterian industries or small as in the late Magdalenian. In the Middle East many of the early sickle blades are denticulated.

Denticulated Mousterian A variant of Mousterian with a high percentage of denticulated tools, sometimes as high as 80% of the toolkit. So far there is no known reason for this form of specialization.

Derived Material not found in its original position. Many finds from river gravels, for example, have been washed into the stream and though probably not carried very far are no longer in their original context.

Digging stick

Digging stick Pointed stick, usually about 3 ft long, used in many parts of the world for digging up roots and for planting. The Bushmen examples are fitted into a stone with a hole bored through it, which gives extra weight. Generally used by women.

Eoanthropus dawsoni "Dawn Man." The scientific name given to the Piltdown skull. The specific name dawsoni commemorates its finder, Charles Dawson. Now known to have been a forgery, the name is no longer used.

Eocene The first subdivision of the Tertiary. Beginning about 70 million years ago, it is a period of great expansion of the early mammals including early forms of primate★.

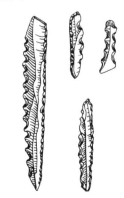

Denticulated flakes

Eoliths "Dawnstones." Objects claimed to have been made by man. The collector Benjamin Harrison amassed a vast number from the hills around Maidstone in Kent, consisting of flakes out of Tertiary gravels. They have been subjected to an enormous amount of natural battery and are no longer accepted as being man-made implements.

Eolith

Eustatic change The rise and fall of sea level due to the increase or decrease of permanent ice. During glacial★ periods a large amount of water is locked up in the form of ice, thus reducing the level of the sea. During warmer conditions, the ice melts and the sea level rises.

Fauresmith A late form of Acheulian from southern Africa. The hand axes are small, heart-shaped and rather rough. This industry, dated in Zambia to about 58,000, is associated with Saldanha man★ and probably represents the final stages of the hand axes in this part of Africa.

Femur The thighbone. In humans the curvature of the bone and the angle of attachment to the pelvis can give some idea of the individual's posture. The Java Man★ was called erectus, or upright, on the basis of the thighbone found associated with the skull bone.

Fissures Large cracks in rock. In many limestone caves these fissures reach the surface with the result that the caves contain material which has fallen in through the fissures in the roof and does not belong with the occupational deposit.

Flake tool Tool made on the piece detached from a block of stone, ie the flake. Many tools are made of flakes, such as the Mousterian scrapers, late hand axes★ and the very large tools from China. In technical terms flakes and blades are the same, distinguished only by their length/breadth ratio.

Two views of a flake tool

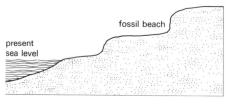

Fossil beach

Fossil beach A term applied to the remains of a shoreline above present sea level, although equally applicable to those below present sea level. A number of such beaches have been found, the earliest about 600 ft above the sea. They indicate high sea levels occurring in warm interglacials★ and are often recognizable by actual beach deposits or wave-cut notches.

Fossil wood Wood whose vegetable structure has been replaced by a mineral, generally silica. When thus transformed it has the characteristics of the other silica rocks, such as flint, and is suitable for making stone tools. Used extensively in Burma and in the Egyptian desert, where complete fossilized tree trunks are found lying on the sand.

Free stone A stone which is homogeneous and will thus cleave equally well in any direction. Laminated rocks such as slate will only split in the direction of the plates and not across them.

Frontal bone The bone of the skull forming the forehead. During human evolution the angle of the forehead gradually becomes more vertical.

Genus Plural *genera*. The last but one of the zoological classifications, combining members of a group who belong closely together – ie horses and zebra belong to the same genus, Equus. The genus Homo includes all races of modern man and several fossil forms such as Homo erectus.

Glaciation A period of intense cold characterized by ice sheets over Scandinavia and radiating from the high mountain ranges in Europe. Similar conditions occurred in North America. Four major glaciations are recognized in Europe and America, separated by three warm interglacials★.

Glaciers Rivers of ice running down the valleys of a mountain range. During periods of intense cold they extend out onto the plain, forming local ice sheets.

Gravettian Name taken from the cave of La Gravette in southwest France. It is the type site of the Upper Aurignacian★, now referred to as Upper Perigordian or Gravettian. The term Eastern Gravettian is used for some of the eastern European Upper Paleolithic which bears some resemblance to the French Gravettian.

Gunz Named after a small river in southern Germany. The first of the main European glaciations★. Few physical traces remain of this period, since the more extensive following glaciation has obliterated most of them. The maximum dates given are from around 1,000,000 years BC.

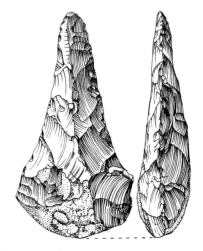

Two views of a hand ax

Hand ax Large bifacial stone implement, generally made on a core. It takes various shapes such as pear-shape or oval. There is no evidence that these tools were hafted. Averaging about 6 to 8 inches long, they were well adapted for use in the hand, and were probably used for grubbing up roots and butchering large animals. They were the characteristic implement of the Abbevillian and Acheulian. Ranging from Africa and Western Europe into India, they cover a period of some 500,000 years.

Harpoon In modern use a harpoon is the detachable head of the fishing or whaling spear with a line attached. Used by prehistorians, the term means any spearhead with barbs, whether detachable or not. Many examples have been found dating from the late Magdalenian of Europe and in the succeeding Mesolithic★ period.

Harpoons

Hominidae The zoological family in which man belongs. Included under this heading are the near men such as Australopithecine and more primitive forms such as Ramapithecus. The living great apes, the nearest creatures to man, belong to a separate family, Pongidae★.

Homo habilis Handyman. A hominid with a brain capacity of between 670cc and 680cc, found in Bed I at Olduvai. Slightly older than Zinjanthropus★ and apparently more developed, it has been assumed that he rather than Zinjanthropus was responsible for the tools found on the living floor. How Habilis stands in relation to the older, more developed, 1470 from Lake Rudolf is not clear.

Horn From cattle, antelope, sheep and goats. Grown as a sheath on a bony core attached to the skull, and not shed annually. Less useful to prehistoric man than antler★, horns of small antelope mounted on a stick nevertheless make a very efficient weapon. Horn does not generally survive in archaeological deposits, as it is made of the same material as hooves.

Interglacial Temperate interval between two glacials★. In the Pleistocene there are three interglacials separating the four main glacials. These are of varying duration. We are probably in an interglacial at present.

Interpluvial Drier period between two wet phases or pluvials★. Pluvials and interpluvials take the place of glacial and interglacial in the temperate and tropical areas, though the two do not necessarily coincide.

Interstadial Short, less cold periods occurring during glacials★. Four are recognized in the last glaciation.

Isostatic change Rise of land in relation to the sea due to movement of the earth's crust. At the end of the last glaciation parts of Northern Europe began to rise owing to the removal of the weight of ice. As one area rises others tend to sink, on a see-saw principle.

Jabrudian From sites at Jabrud in the Syrian desert. An industry of scrapers similar to some aspects of Mousterian, sometimes found with rough hand axes. The Jabrudian is contemporary with the late Acheulian★ in Israel, Lebanon and Syria.

Java man A name given to a collection of human material from the Trinil beds in Java, found by Eugène Dubois in 1894. Originally named Pithecanthropus erectus, it is now grouped with Peking man★ as Homo erectus. In addition to this material the area produced finds of later hominids known jointly as Solo man, who appears to be nearer the Neanderthals of Europe.

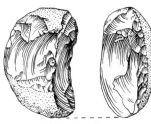
Two views of a Kafuan "tool"

Kafuan A supposed industry of quartz pebbles from the Kafue River in East Africa, now regarded as being of natural origin.

Kenyapithecus A small creature found in Kenya and dated from the late Miocene★, closely related to Ramapithecus and similarly put at the base of the human stem, immediately following the divergence from the anthropoid stem.

Knuckle-walking A common method of walking by chimpanzees and gorillas. This involves walking on hands and feet, the weight on the hands being supported on the knuckles rather than on the palms.

Laminated Rocks such as slate made up of thin plates, generally derived from mud forming in still water. Slate splits along its bedding plane and is thus generally an unsuitable material for making stone tools, though the Eskimos make scrapers★ out of it.

Lantien A middle Pleistocene site in the Shensi province of China which has produced a human jaw akin to the Peking Java group, Homo erectus. Associated with it were a few rough tools resembling a pebble industry. Geologically this material has been dated as slightly earlier than Peking man★ and possibly earlier than Java.

Levallois From Levallois-Perret near Paris. A flake industry made principally on a prepared core★ technique. At one time the Levallois was considered as a separate industry, but now only as a technique within the Late Acheulian and Mousterian. Flakes and cores made from a prepared core technique are often referred to as Levallois.

Levallois-Mousterian A term used for some Mousterian industries in the Middle East indicating tools of Mousterian★ type made on Levallois flakes. This term is no longer generally used.

Living floor A surface on which a group lived and worked. Usually recognized by discarded tools★ – the by-product of the group's manufacture – and animal bones, in the later period there are often indications of fires and some form of dwelling.

Loess Fine yellow dirt blown out from the edge of an ice sheet. Carried on the wind, it banks up against hills and fills hollows. Widespread over parts of Europe during the Pleistocene, it indicates glacial conditions. Four separate loesses are recognized as belonging to the last glaciation and three to the Riss★ glaciation. The Yellow Earth of China is composed of loess.

Magdalenian From the cave of La Madeleine in southwest France. Excavated by Lartet and Christy in 1863, it is the type site★ of the Magdalenian. This, the last of the Upper Paleolithic industries of Western Europe, is dated roughly from 15,000 to 10,000. Very rich in bone and antler tools, it occurs in France, Spain, Belgium, Germany, Switzerland, Austria, Czechoslovakia and Britain.

Mesolithic A term used for the period between the end of the last glaciation★ in Europe and the advent of farming communities. Used worldwide, the term is no longer very precise in its application.

Micro-fauna Small creatures, such as rodents, from an excavation. Sometimes these small creatures form more reliable climatic indicators than the larger animals. There is, however, a risk in using many of them as they tend to burrow through several archaeological levels and can thus be unreliable.

Middle Stone Age A term used in East and South Africa and India for the flake industries following the hand ax★ complexes. These correspond to the Mousterian industries of Europe, North Africa and the Middle East, but appear to have continued much later.

Mindel The second of the Pleistocene glaciations and in Europe the most extensive. It is divided into two phases separated by an interstadial★. Dated to about 600,000.

Miocene The third stage of the Tertiary★, beginning roughly 35 million years ago. The human and ape stems appear to have separated during this period.

Mousterian From the cave of Le Moustier, excavated by Lartet and Christy. Type site of the Mousterians. The site comprises two caves, one above the other, containing several levels of Mousterian and the burial of a youth aged about 16. The term Mousterian is used to cover a wide range of flake industries generally associated with Neanderthal★ man. Dates in France of about 70,000–40,000 years.

Mousterian of Acheulian tradition Mousterian industries with hand ax. Industries of this type occur in France, Britain, Germany, North Africa and the Middle East. The last of the French Mousterian industries are of this type.

Neanderthal A group of hominids named after the site of Neanderthal near Düsseldorf in Germany. This group, dating from the early stages of the last glaciation, is widely distributed, occurring in Europe, North Africa and the Levant. The heavy facial features of the western European group, or classical Neanderthals, are less pronounced in those from eastern Europe and the Levant, but this is probably a regional rather than an evolutionary difference. Originally considered as an ancestor to modern man, and separated from him by being classed as a different genus★, Neanderthal man is now considered as only a subspecies of Homo sapiens. Similar individuals have come from South Africa, Rhodesia and Java, apparently of roughly the same age. The last recognizable Neanderthal seems to have died out in Europe between 40,000 and 45,000.

Needle Throughout most of the Stone Age skin garments were probably joined by making holes with stone or flint awls. During the end of the French Solutrean★ slim bone needles with an eye were introduced, continuing throughout the Magdalenian. Sinew was most likely the thread used, being readily obtainable from larger game animals.

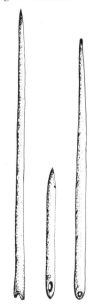

Needles

Neolithic The New Stone Age. The period which saw the introduction of agriculture and stockbreeding. These changes of economy appear to have started in the Levant and slowly penetrated northwards into Europe, although it is possible that there were centers of this development elsewhere, such as India and China. The introduction of these new economies seems to have taken place about 6,000 BC or later.

Obsidian Volcanic glass. This has all the properties of ordinary glass, and although

rather brittle produces superb cutting edges. Obsidian from Kenya was used as far back as the Acheulian★ period. In the Mediterranean, where the main supply came from Anatolia and the island of Melos, little use was made of it before the Neolithic, when it was traded over long distances. Colors range from black to near transparent; there are also green and brown variants. The material was also used extensively in Mexico.

Occipital bone The bone at the back of the skull containing the attachments of the spine and the main supporting muscles of the neck. The forward ends join to the right and left parietal bones★. The original skull fragment from Swanscombe was an occipital, as was the bone from Vertesszöllös in Hungary.

Olduwan The pebble industry from the lower beds at Olduvai. Two stages are recognized, the early Olduwan from Bed I and the lower part of Bed II and the developed Olduwan from the upper part of Bed II. The later stage is richer in flake tools and has primitive hand axes possibly borrowed from the contemporary Acheulian. Pebble tools★ similar to those from Olduvai have been found in other parts of East Africa dating back to about 2.5 million years.

Order A larger zoological group than Family. The order primates★, to which man belongs, contains two suborders and eleven families, ranging from tree shrews to man.

Organic Living matter. Most organic material does not preserve well, exceptions being some of its most durable by-products such as bone and ivory. Nevertheless, some organic material has survived under special conditions. Apart from pollen, which is almost indestructable, wood has been found in several sites, such as the yew-wood spear from Clacton-on-Sea and the wooden clubs from Kalambo Falls in East Africa, the first dating from about 250,000 and the second from about 60,000. The preservation of soft tissue is rare. Good examples are the almost complete mammoth from frozen deposits in Siberia and the complete rhinoceros from Poland. From later periods there are a number of bodies from the Scandinavian bogs, with bodies and clothing perfectly preserved, including the contents of the stomach.

Ostracod Minute crustaceans resembling shrimps. These creatures frequently occur in river and marine deposits, for example at Swanscombe in Kent. They can give some indication of water temperature and salinity. This type of evidence, as well as that from other animals and plants, goes towards reconstructing a picture of local conditions at a particular time. Small creatures such as ostracods and snails are often more sensitive climatic indicators than larger animals.

Paleolithic The Old Stone Age. Term used originally to distinguish between the Neolithic★ or New Stone Age with agriculture, and the earlier periods. The Paleolithic was subsequently divided into the Low to include the hand ax industries, the Middle covering the Mousterian, and the Upper covering the remaining part of the cave period to the end of the last glaciation. While still being useful in the areas where it was originally used (ie Western Europe), it is less precise in other parts of the world and has no chronological meaning.

Parietal bone The two bones forming the sides of a skull. One end joins the occipital bones★ at the back and the other is the frontal bone.

Patjitanian The name given to a group of stone tools from central Java. It is largely a flake industry made from limestone and fossil wood★. In addition there are pebble choppers and rough blades. So far the industry has only been found in the upper Trinil beds and is thus later than the Homo erectus material.

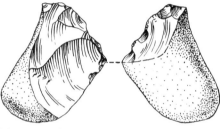

Two views of a pebble tool

Pebble tool Chopping tool produced with the minimum amount of work. In its simplest form it is merely a water-worn pebble, generally oval with one flake taken from one end. The flake surface forms the striking platform for further flakes. Sometimes the flaking is down one side instead of across the end. These tools are the earliest recognized human artifacts, dated in East Africa about 2.5 million years; but such tools also occur in small numbers in most Stone Age assemblages★.

Peking man Found in the limestone quarries of Choukoutien, near Peking. The first specimen was discovered in 1921. Originally called Sinanthropus pekinensis, it is now included with Java man★ as a member of the Homo erectus group. This group is generally

Ostracod

considered as being on man's ancestral stem. The original material was lost during World War II, but several casts are available and much new material has come to light since.

Pelvis The girdle of bone at the base of the trunk. The angle of the pubic bones and their shape is a useful indication of a creature's mode of locomotion. The pelvis of the Australopethecines★ shows that they walked upright.

Perigordian A name taken from the district of Périgord in southwestern France and given to what was originally called Lower and Upper Aurignacian★. At least seven stages are recognized in France.

Phallic symbols Signs depicting human reproductive organs, frequently associated with fertility cults. Male organs are rarely reproduced in prehistoric art but female symbols are more frequent, often occurring isolated from the rest of the body.

Picks Long narrow core implements claimed to have served the purpose of hand picks. The best known examples are the Neolithic picks, which were probably hafted. Rough examples come from the Sangoan★ of central Africa dating from about 40,000.

Pliocene The fourth and last subdivision of the Tertiary★, beginning about 14 million years ago. During this period the human and ape stems were separated.

Pluvial Periods of increased rainfall in tropical and subtropical regions. The wet phases, the pluvials, are separated by the drier phases, the interpluvials★, much as are the glacial and interglacial periods. The relationship between glacials and pluvials is not clear.

Points Tools assumed to have been used for some form of spear or projectile, such as arrows. They range from the triangular Mousterian★ point to the tanged point of the Perigordians. Some of the bifacial pieces such as the thicker Solutrean and Stillbay points from Africa probably served the same purpose. Bone points such as the Aurignacian and Perigordian examples were probably hafted in the same way as the Magdalenian harpoons.

Pongidae The family containing the four great apes – gibbon, orangutan, chimpanzee and gorilla. Ancestors of this group appear to have separated from the human stem some time during the Miocene★. From then on the two families went their two ways, developing along different lines in response to different needs.

Pontian A Mousterian industry from Italy, made on very small pebbles, mostly by prepared core★ techniques.

Postcranial The bones of the body other than the skull, or cranium.

Power grip Holding an object in the whole hand as one would a hammer or stick. Many of the simple tools could have been made with a power grip alone, but it is clear that throughout man's toolmaking activities he also had precision grip.

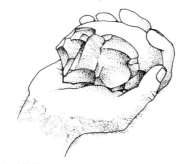
Tool held in a power grip

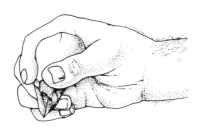
Tool held in a precision grip

Pre-Aurignacian A name given to an industry with backed blades and end scrapers contemporary with the Late Acheulian★ in the Middle East, occurring in Mt Carmel, Israel, Jabrud in Syria and on the Lebanese coast. Recently the name Amudian has been substituted.

Precision grip The ability to hold an object between finger and thumb, for example holding a pencil or using a knife. The change to a prehensile forelimb is a very important

Bone points

feature of man's development, without which the manufacture of tools would be impossible.

Pre-Crag The name given to a group of stone objects claimed to be human implements. These were found over a number of years in the base of Shelly Crag deposits in East Anglia in Britain, hence the name. Although now known not to be as old as originally claimed, they are in fact Pleistocene★ and are now generally considered as natural.

Prepared core While all cores require some preparation if reasonably sized flakes are to be obtained, the term prepared core is applied to the method of setting up a core to obtain flakes of predetermined size and shape. If further predetermined flakes were required the core needed to be reprepared. Preparation of cores plays a large part in some of the Mousterian complexes, but seems to have been invented in the late Acheulian★.

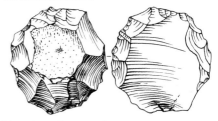
Two views of a prepared core

Presapiens A term used for the skulls such as Swanscombe, Steinheim and Fontéchevade, all earlier than the typical Neanderthals★. Some anatomists saw these skulls as being ancestral to modern man independent of the Neanderthals, which they placed on a side branch. The present trend is to group all these under the same head, Homo sapiens, only making differences at specific levels.

Primary flake A flake struck from a core★ and not subjected to modifications. Many flakes were used for cutting in their primary condition and were then discarded.

Primary flake

Primate The zoological order which includes lemurs, bushbabies and their relations, the Old and New World monkeys, apes and man. The primates are recognized as a definite order as far back as 70 million years ago at the beginning of the Tertiary★.

Prosimians A suborder within the order★ Primates, it includes the tree shrews, lemurs, aye-ayes, bushbabies and tarsiers. This group is the first of the Primates to be recognized, dating from about 70 million years ago.

Quaternary An alternative name for the Pleistocene★, being the fourth major geological stage following the Tertiary.

Radiometric dating Methods of absolute dating by calculating known rates of decay of radioactive isotopes. Carbon 14★ is an example of this.

Relative dating Two sites or industries associated with the same geological or climatic event are said to be of the same relative age. The short intervals of some periods, such as the climatic phases established by pollen for the early postglacial, make the possible time differences comparatively small, but if they are only dated in relation to a major geological period, such as the Middle Pleistocene, then the comparative dating falls within the duration of the geological episode.

Retouch This is the modification of a primary flake to convert it into a formal tool; for example flakes or blades are converted into scrapers★ or points by chipping or retouching.

Retouched blade

Rhodesian man Homo sapiens rhodesiensis from Broken Hill in Zambia. The skull was found during mining for lead and zinc. It is almost complete, the left side being in perfect condition, but the jaw is missing. An arm and leg bone and part of a pelvis were also found. The associated archaeological material is Middle Stone Age, which has been dated between 40,000 and 35,000 by finds further south. This figure corresponds to the very end of the European Neanderthal★ range.

Riss The third of the main Pleistocene glaciations★ in Europe. Divided into three parts, it appears to have ended about 150,000 years ago.

River terraces Remains of old river banks left on the sides of valleys as the river cuts down its bed. Some are due to the rise of sea level into which the rivers flow and others to material dumped into the river bed by erosion

during glacial conditions. The former are referred to as Eustatic terraces and belong to an interglacial★, and the latter as Climatic terraces belonging to a glacial.

Rock shelter A rock overhang sufficiently deep to provide shelter for prehistoric man. Many of the occupied sites in France are shelters rather than caves, and similar sites occur in parts of Africa. A few rock shelters in France have traces of carving on the walls and they have also been painted.

Rock shelter

Saldanha man A skull cap from South Africa associated with a late form of Acheulian called Fauresmith★. The Saldanha skull closely resembles the Rhodesian skull from Broken Hill in Zambia. While there is no date for the Saldanha skull, comparable archaeological material from Kalambo Falls in Zambia was given a date of 58,000. This is within the time range of the Neanderthals of Europe and the Middle East.

Sangoan An industry★ from the Congo or Zaire and parts of East Africa consisting of large flakes and particularly large picks. Similar material has been found as far south as South Africa, north to the northern Sudan, and west to West Africa. At Kalambo Falls on the southern end of Lake Tanganyika the Sangoan follows a late Acheulian, from which it is probably derived, and has a carbon date of 40,000. In central Africa the Sangoan developed with smaller and better-made tools throughout the remainder of the Pleistocene.

Scraper A flake or blade★ tool assumed to have been used either for cleaning skins (the side scraper) or for woodworking (the steep scraper and end scraper). Australian aborigines mount a tool similar to an end scraper onto the end of a thick stick and use it for woodworking.

Secondary flaking Generally this term means the same as retouching★. In the case of hand axes the roughing out is sometimes referred to as primary flaking, and the finer flaking as secondary.

Silica Silicon dioxide. The principal component of many rocks used by prehistoric man for making stone tools, including flint, volcanic glass, quartz and many others.

Skull 1470 A skull found near Lake Rudolf by Richard Leakey. Though broken into many pieces it is almost complete. With a brain size of some 800 cc, it is much more developed than either Australopithecus★ or Homo habilis, and with a date of 2.6 million years it is much older than one would have expected from so developed a skull. From horizons of the same age have come tools similar to those from the base of Olduvai.

Skull cap Generally the four bones of the skull – the occipital★, the two parietals and the frontal – minus the facial area and the base. In a skull subjected to erosion the face and base are generally the parts which are lost, which is why so many skulls are represented only by these four bones.

Soan An industry from northern India, originally found in the vicinity of the Soan river. The early stages contain pebble choppers and flakes. In its later stages it develops flakes made with the prepared core★ technique. The dating of any of the Soan stages is uncertain. The early phases are said to occur during the second Himalayan interglacial, but whether these local glacials correspond to those of Europe is also not clear. If there was a correlation, then the early Soan would be contemporary with the Clactonian of Europe.

Solar radiation The amount of radiation emanating from the sun. Variations in the amount of solar radiation have been suggested as a possible cause for the Ice Ages.

Solifluction Strictly speaking, a soil which has slipped down a slope and thus has become an unsorted mass. In the geology of the Pleistocene★ the term is generally applied to soils sliding over permanently frozen subsoil during the summer thaws in glaciated and periglacial areas. These solifluctions thus indicate extreme cold conditions.

Solutrean The type site is Solutré in eastern France. The industry lies between the Perigordian/Aurignacian and the Magdalenian★ in the French cave sequence, and is characterized by beautifully-made thin bifacial tools. It is divided into three stages, each apparently developing into the next. Rather restrictive in distribution, occurring in France, Spain, Britain and Belgium. Its origin is uncertain but dates from 19,000 to 18,000.

Spear thrower An implement used by Australian aborigines, Eskimo and some South Americans to increase the distance a spear can be thrown. Basically it is a stick, usually with a

Spear thrower with spear in position

flattened side and a hook at one end. The butt of the spear is engaged in the hook with the spear shaft resting on the flat surface of the spear thrower. By holding the two together, and using the length of the spear thrower as an extension of his arm, the thrower can obtain greater leverage and thus greater range.

Species The last but one of the zoological groupings. Homo is the generic name and sapiens the specific. Homo erectus and Homo sapiens are separated at specific levels. Neanderthal★ and modern man are separated on a subspecific level – Homo sapiens neanderthalensis and Homo sapiens sapiens respectively.

Stadial The peaks of cold during a glacial, being separated by slightly warmer conditions, the interstadials★. The last glaciation shows a curve of four cold peaks separated by three interstadials, all of varying length. The Riss glaciation is thought to have three such peaks and the Mindel and Gunz two each.

Stegodon An early form of elephant, occurring in the Far East during the Early Middle Pleistocene.

Stegodon

Stratification A succession of geological or archaeological deposits superimposed one on another and in their correct order of deposition. An example is the sequence of many cave deposits. Archaeological material is said to be unstratified if not found in its original geological or archaeological context, or if found in isolation.

Subspecies The lowest grouping of the zoological classifications. (*See* **Species**).

Superposition In prehistoric art the term means one engraving or painting executed on top of another. In many cases superposition has made it possible to put different styles in their order of execution. Why prehistoric artists should obliterate their predecessors' work and to some extent spoil their own is not clear.

Sympathetic magic The idea that drawing an animal or person gives the drawer some power over that animal or person. This concept has been evoked to explain some aspects of prehistoric art. Among modern peoples hunting magic has long been

recognized, such as drawing animals in the sand and sticking spears into them as part of the ritual before hunting.

Szeletian An industry from Hungary and Czechoslovakia with rough bifacial points. Originally thought to have been the parent of the French Solutrean, it is now known to be derived from a late form of eastern Mousterian dated to between 40,000 and 35,000. It may have continued in a modified form somewhat later.

Taungs A site in South Africa which produced the first Australopithecine★, found in 1924 and described by Raymond Dart. It was the original specimen of Australopithecus africanus.

Technology The method by which tools are made. This differs from typology, which is concerned with the classification of tools. Hand axes★, for example, can be made either on cores or large flakes, and there are instances of industries with a very similar tool kit, but one using blades as blanks and the other flakes. Some Mousterian industries use prepared cores for the production of flakes and others disk cores.

Telanthropus A name given to human remains from Swartkrans in South Africa, clearly more advanced than the Australopithecus★ robustus material from this site. It is now considered as belonging to Homo erectus.

Tertiary The third of the four major geological subdivisions. It is itself divided into four – Eocene, Oligocene, Miocene and Pliocene – and ranges from about 70 million to 14 million years. It is followed by the fourth major subdivision, the Quaternary★ or Pleistocene.

Tool Strictly speaking an object, either natural or manufactured, used for a particular purpose. Egyptian vultures pick up stones to break open eggs and chimpanzees use grass stems to extract termites from their nest. Man in his earliest stage of development must have used these ad hoc tools. But they have either not survived or have not been recognized as such. The earliest recognized tools are the pebble choppers★ from East Africa dating from over 2.5 million years. In classifying later industries, retouched pieces are separated from primary flakes, and the more formal objects are classified as tools in contrast to the wastage of manufacture.

Totemism The adoption by an individual or group of some natural object such as a plant or animal, considered special to themselves. There are frequently strong taboos relating to totems. For example, one cannot kill or eat one's own totem in some societies, though this

rule may not apply in others. Sometimes elaborate ritual is associated with totems and they are sometimes included in modern cave paintings, for example in Australia. It has been suggested that totemism may be one of the motives for some of the animal drawings in prehistoric art.

Trihedral Three-sided. Some early hand axes★, for example from North Africa and Israel, are triangular rather than two-sided in section. Similar sections occur in some of the later picks.

Tundra The barren ground in the region of the arctic circle, examples of which occur in northern Canada and parts of Alaska. Vegetation is sparse and the subsoil is permanently frozen. Such regions, though inhospitable, can support human life such as the Eskimo, who depend for their existence on seals or inland on the migrating caribou. Provided there is sufficient game to be stored during the winter, occupation of such regions is possible though difficult. Some peoples such as the northern Red Indian tribes, who are not so well adapted to such conditions, only penetrate the tundra during the short summers.

An example of twisted perspective

Twisted perspective A convention in prehistoric art whereby certain aspects of an animal, such as antlers and hoofs, are shown full face when the rest of the animal is drawn in profile. This is generally considered to be an early trait, corrected in later periods. Good examples of twisted perspective can be seen in the bull paintings from Lascaux.

Type site The site at which an industry was first recognized, eg Mousterian from Le Moustier. Sometimes this rule is broken as in the case of the Solutrean★, which was originally found at Laugerie Haute near Les Eyzies. As the material was found with several other industries, the site of Solutré where it was better represented was chosen to provide the type name.

Typology Classifying prehistoric assemblages★ into tool types: scrapers, points, blades, etc. Tool types and their proportions can show up differences between various assemblages.

Varve Annual deposits of sediments laid down in still water. In Scandinavia seasonal melt water forms a characteristic deposit at the bottom of lakes. Cutting through such deposits makes it possible to count years, a technique similar to counting the annual rings of trees. Some of these varve series can be matched over long distances and go back as far as 10,000 years. They have provided the dates for various stages of the retreat of the Scandinavian ice sheet.

Vault The main part of the skull, containing the brain. During the course of human development the vault becomes higher as the brain increases in size.

Villafranchian A geological term used to cover the early part of the Pleistocene★. Deposits of this age are recognized in Europe, Africa and the Far East, and probably extend from 4 million to about 1 million years.

Wave notch A notch or undercut in a cliff, worn away by waves continually pounding against it. With softer rocks such as chalk, the rapidly developing notches lead to cliff falls,

and therefore do not survive for very long. With harder rocks these notches remain for very long periods and can often be seen as indications of old high sea levels, several hundred feet up.

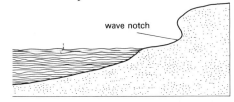

Wave notch

Weathering The change in the surface appearance of rocks due to the effects of wind and rain. In soils the soluble components are dissolved out of the upper part and carried down to lower levels. Extensive weathering of a deposit indicates long periods with the surface exposed to the elements. In the European loesses★ the various deposits are separated by horizons of weathering,

indicating periods when they were not deposited and warmer interstadial conditions prevailed.

Würm The fourth European glaciation★, named like the others after a small river in southern Germany. It is divided into four stages, the first two covered by the Mousterian and the last two by the Upper Paleolithic industries. The whole period dates from 70,000 to 10,000.

Zinjanthropus Christened Zinj or Nutcracker man. An almost complete skull from Bed I at Olduvai originally given the generic name of Zinjanthropus, it is now included with the other Australopithecines★ as Australopithecus boisei. The brain capacity of 530 cc is larger than Australopithecus africanus and about the same size as Australopithecus robustus. Dated to about 1.7 million years, it seems to have died out before some of the other Australopithecines such as Australopithecus robustus.

Index

Page numbers in italics refer to illustrations or
their captions.

Abbeville/Abbevillian 12, 82–83, *83*, 84, 86
aborigines, Australian *94, 96*, 97, *98, 99, 110,
    126*
Acheulian 82–84, 86, 87, 88, 89, 90, 92, 105,
    107, 114, 115, 127
aggradation 30–31
Altamira, cave of *121*, 131
Angles sur L'Anglin 134
animals 11, 12, 31, 43–44, 47, 52, 53, *70*, 78,
    86, 93, 106, 111, 136
    deer 43, 66, *70, 72*, 116
    elephant 31, 88
    in art *118, 119, 120, 121, 122, 123, 126, 129,
    129*, 130, 131, 132, 133, 134–135
    modern *46, 47*
    skins 44, 116, 133
    woolly rhinoceros *25*, 31, 33, 44, 66, 86,
    117, 119
    see mammoth; gorilla
anthropology 35, 42–44, 134
Anyathian industries 90, 105
Arambourg 53, 55
archaeology 10–13
    environmental 31
    methods 35–38
art of early man 40, 108, 111, *117–124*,
    126–135
    home 127–130, 132
    cave 127, 130–133
    see carving; ornaments, personal
Aterian 115, *115*
Atlanthropus mauritanicus 55, 83
Aurignacian 108–109, *108*, 110, 112, *112*, 114,
    115, 116, *123*, 129, 130, 131, 132, 133, 135
Australopithecus 48–51, *50*, 53, 55, 57, 78,
    79–82, 90

Black, Davidson 52
Bordes, François 101, 103
boulder clay 28, *28*, 29
Breuil, Abbé 108, 109, 121, 132
Bronze Age 36, 40
Broom, Robert 49, *49*, 50, 55
Brun 114
Buckland, William 12, 13, *13*
burial 40, 58, 59, 63, 103, 106, 111, 124
Bushmen, Kalahari *94*, 97, *98, 99*

cannibalism 106
Cap Blanc 86, 131
carbon 14 dating 26, 34, *34*, 116
carving *117, 118, 123, 124, 125*, 129, 130
Casablanca *48*, 62, 63, 83, 84
Catastrophic Theory 12, 13, 14
cave 36, 37–38, 44, 49, 58, 61, 62, 63, 86, *95*,

103, 105, 106, 109, 111, 114, 116, 136
    dwellers 43, *95*, 111
    paintings 40, 108, 111, 127, 130–133, 134
Charentian 103, 105, 107, 112
Chellian man 55, 57, 82–83
    see Abbeville/Abbevillian
China 29, 51, 52, 60, 90, 105, 116
Choukoutien 52, *52*, 53, 65, 90, 91, 116
Christy, Henri 13, 101, 131
Clactonian 87, 88, 107
    see flakes, flint
climatic change 28, *34*, 136
clothing 111–112
Combe Capelle, cave of 109, 110, 114
Combe Grenal, cave of 103
Conyers 11, 82
Crag deposits 75
Cro-Magnon *42, 63*, 110, 114

Dabban 115
Dart, Raymond 48, 49
Darwin, Charles 14–16, *14, 15, 24*
dating, methods of 19, 26, 33–35
    radiometric 33
    relative 29, 30, 31
Dawson, Charles 18–19
de Perthes, Boucher 12, 13, *13*, 16, 82
Djeble Irhoud, cave of 105
Dolni Vistonice *123, 124*, 130
Dordogne *107*, 129
Druids 11, *11*
Dryopithecus 48, 52, 55
Dubois, Eugène 52

Eastern Gravettian 113, 114, 116, 129, 130,
    136
el Wad, cave at *63*, 114
Eoanthropus *see* Piltdown
errors and forgeries 16–19
Eskimos *39*, 43, 44, *94, 96*, 97, 123, 136
eustatic change 30
excavation 10, 36, *39*–42, 78
    methods of *67*–71

fire, use of 53, 85, 88, 92, *96*
fishing 111, *111*, 136
flakes, flint 40, 66, *70, 71*, 78, 84, 86, 87, 90,
    101, 105, 110, 115
Flint Jack 17, *17*
Font de Gaume *121*, 131
Fontéchevade 62, 65
food collecting 92, *97*, 116
forgeries *see* errors and forgeries
Fort Ternan 48
Frere, John 11, 13, 82, 87

Galley Hill skeleton 16–17
Gargarino 130

geology 10, 13, 26–31
Gibraltar 16, *16*, 37, 38, 58, 59, 106
Glacials 28–31, 34, 69
glacier *27*, 28, 29
Gorham *37*
gorilla *20, 21*, 45
Gunz glaciation 35, 60, 86

Haeckel, Ernst 52
hand ax 67, *68*, 79, *79*, 82, 83, 88, 101–103, *102*,
    105, 107, 115
    early 82–84, *83*
    late 84–88
    see tools
Harrison, Benjamin 74, 75
Haua Fteah, cave of 115
Heidelberg man 60
Homo erectus 51, 52, 53, 55, 57, 58, 60, *60*, 62,
    63, 79, 83, 84, 88
Homo habilis 57, 58, 77, 78, 79, 82
Homo neanderthalensis *see* Neanderthals
Homo sapiens 21, 61, 65, 108–116, 129
Hottentots *96*
Hoxne *see* Frere, John
hunting 36, 38, 44, 53, 78, 93, 111, 116, 136
    today 44, *93–99*, 134
huts, early 36, *77*, 77–78, 85, 88, *100*, 114
    primitive *95*
Huxley, Thomas 15–16, *15*

Ice ages *see* Glacials
ice cap 30
India 90, 116
Interglacials 27, 28, 29, 34, 60, 61, 62, 65, 86,
    88
Interpluvials 31
Interstadials 27, 33, 88
Iron Age 36, 40, 85
isostatic change 30
Israel 89, *89*, 105

Jabrud, cave of 105
Jabrudian 105, 106, *106*, 114
Java man 16, 18, 19, *21*, 51, 52, 55, 60, 74, 90

Kalambo Falls *48*, 84–85, *85*, 88, 105
Kenyapithecus 48, 58
Kostenki 130
Krapina, cave of 106
Kromdraai 50
Ksar 'Akil 114, 115
Kurten, Finnish paleontologist 35

La Chapelle aux Saints 59, *59*, 103, 106
La Ferrassie 59–60, 103, 129
La Gravette *see* Eastern Gravettian
La Grèze 132
Lake Rudolf 21, *48*, 57, *58, 80*, 85, 92

La Madeleine, cave of 13, *14*, 130
La Micoque 38
Lantien 90
La Placard 130
La Quina 59, 103, 106
Lartet, Edouard 13, 101, 109, 110, 131
Lascaux, cave of *119, 120, 122*, 133
Last Glaciation 29, 33, 36, 43, 60, 62, 92, 93, 107, 111, 115, 116, 136
La Vache, cave of *118*
Leakey, Louis 48, 53, 55, 57, 77, *82*
Leakey, Richard 57, *57*, 82
Le Moustier 59, 101, 103
    see Mousterian
Le Roc de Ser 133
Leroi-Gourhan, André 134
Les Eyzies 110
Levallois technique 101, 103
Levalloiso-Mousterian 105, 106, 107, 114, 115
loess 29, 105

Magdalenian 43, 108, 111, 112, 114, 116, *118*, 123, 129, 130, 131, 132, 135, 136
magic, sympathetic 134, *135*
Maglemosians 136
Makapansgat *48*, 49, 50
mammoth 12, 13, *14*, 31, *32*, 36, 44, 96, 111, 113–114, *114*, 117, *118, 122*, 124, 131, 133
Marston, G. 67, *68*
Mauer 18, 60, *60*, 86
Mesolithic Age 36, 38, 136
Milankovitch 33
Mindel glaciation 35, 53, 60, 75, 86, 87, 88, 90
Miocene 47–48
Modern man 108–116
Montmaurin cave 61–62
Morocco 62 *see* Casablanca
Moulin Quignon jaw 16
Mount Carmel 63, 89, 105, 106, 114
Mousterian 101–107, *102*, 109, 111, 112, 115, 127, 136
    Denticulated *102*, 103, 107
    see Le Moustier

Natufians 136
Neanderthals 16, 18, *21*, 58–65, *59*, 84, 101–107, *104*, 105, 106, 108
Neolithic Age 36
Niaux, cave of *121, 123, 132*
Nutcracker man *see* Zinj

occupation sites 31, 77–79, 84, 88, 92, 111
    see caves; sites
Olduvai *48*, 53, 55, *56*, 57, 60, *76, 77*, 75–82, 83, 84, 85, 92

Olduwan, Developed 78–79, 82, 83, 84
Oligocene 47, 48
Omo river *48, 57*, 82
ornament, personal 40, *42, 98, 112, 113*

Pair-non-Pair, cave of 132
Paleolithic Age 36, 38
    Upper 108–116, 129, 136
Parpallo 129
Patjitanian 105
Paviland, cave of 12, 13
Pech Merle *118*, 133, *134*
Peking man 52, 53, *53, 54*, 63, 90, 92
Perigordian *108*, 109–110, 111, 112, 113, 115, 116, 129, 130, 132, 135
    Piette, Edouard 131
pigments 40, 117, 120, 127, 130
Piltdown 18, 18–19, *19*, 74
Pithecanthropus 52
Pleistocene 25, 26–31, 33, 34, *35*, 51, 52, 63, 74
    Early 33, 35, 74, 75, 86
    Lower 34, 35
    Middle 34, 35, 82, 86, 89, 90, 101
    Upper 34, 65, 101
    Late 116
Pliocene 33, 58, 74
Pliopithecus 52
Pluvials 31
Praesapiens 62, 65,
Primate 20, 24, 45
Proconsul 52, 55
pygmy *38, 39*, 95

Quaternary geological division *see* Pleistocene

Ramapithecus 48, 52
Rhodesian man *62*, 65
Riss glaciation 35, 60, 62, 88, 107
Robinson, J. T. 49, 50, 55

Saldanha skull 65, 84
Sangoan industry 105, 107, 115
sea-level variations 29–31, *29, 30*, 86
Shanidar, cave of 63, 105, 106
sites, enclosed 36, 37
    open 36–37, 38, *113*, 136
    see caves; occupation sites
Skhul, cave at 63, 105, 106
Skull 1470 57–58, *57*, 82, 92
Smith, Woodward 19
Solo man 63
Solutrean 108, 110, *110*, 111, 112, 114, 116, *118*, 129, 131, 132, 133, 135
Somme gravels 12–13, 16, 82, 86, 87, 91
Spy, Belgium 59, 103

Steinheim 60–61, *61*, 62, 65, 87, 108
Sterkfontein *48*, 49, 50, *51*, 53, 82
Stonehenge 10, *11*
Stopes, H. 66
Sungir 111
Swanscombe 16, *25*, 38, 60, 61, *61*, 62, 65, *66*–72, 86, 87, 88, 92, 108
Swartkrans 50–51, *51*, 55, 57
Szeletian 112

Tabun, cave at 63, 105, 114, 115
Tasaday *95, 96, 97*
Taungs *48*, 48, 49, *49*, 50
Telanthropus 55, 57
Ternifine, Algeria *48*, 53, 55, 62, 83, 84, 88
Terra Amata 88, *89*, 92
terraces, climatic 31
    eustatic 31
Tertiary geological division 26, 45, 74
Teshik Tash *59*, 63, 105, 106
Tobias, Philip 55
Tollund man *41*
tools 11, 17, 39–40, *40, 41*, 43, 44, 53, 55, 60, *73, 74*, 75, 78, 84, *87*, 88–91, *90*, 91, 105, *105*, 112, 115, 136
    blade 108, *108*, 109, 115, 116
    bone 40, *41*, 78, 108, 109, 111
    Mousterian 101–103, 105, *106*, 107
    natural 74, *75*, 75
    pebble 75–82, *78*, 85, *86*, 86, 90
    spear throwers 110, 111, 129
    wooden 40, 85, 107
    see flakes, flint; hand ax
tool industry *41*, 55, 57, 62, 65, 66, *69*, 74, 79, 90–91, 112, 115
tree-ring analysis 34
trees 116, 136
Trinil beds 52–53

Ussher, Archbishop 10, 11

Vallonet, cave of 86, 90
varve analysis 34
"Venus" or female figurine *128*, 129, 130
Venus of Laussel 129, 130, 131
Venus of Willendorf *124*, 130
Vertesszöllös 60, *86*, 86, 88, 90
Von Koenigswald 55

Wilberforce, Samuel 15, *15*
Würm glaciation 35, 60, 88

Zinj 55, *56*, 57, 77, 78, 79, 82